A HISTORY OF THE ASIANS
IN EAST AFRICA

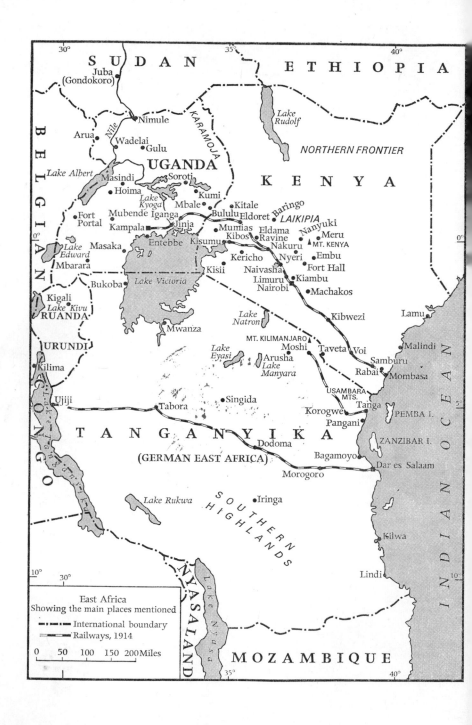

East Africa
Showing the main places mentioned

- - - International boundary
━━━ Railways, 1914

0   50   100   150   200 Miles

A HISTORY OF
THE ASIANS IN
EAST AFRICA

c. 1886 to 1945

BY

J. S. MANGAT

OXFORD
AT THE CLARENDON PRESS
1969

Oxford University Press, Ely House, London W. 1

GLASGOW NEW YORK TORONTO MELBOURNE WELLINGTON
CAPE TOWN SALISBURY IBADAN NAIROBI LUSAKA ADDIS ABABA
BOMBAY CALCUTTA MADRAS KARACHI LAHORE DACCA
KUALA LUMPUR SINGAPORE HONG KONG TOKYO

PRINTED IN GREAT BRITAIN

TO MY PARENTS

PREFACE

THE immigration and settlement of the Asians[1] in East Africa during the colonial period covered in this book has been the subject of hardly any major historical study. A number of published as well as unpublished works deal directly with the Asian community in East Africa, but none can be defined as a definitive study of the subject. This is true, for example, of George Delf's *Asians in East Africa* (1963) and D. Ghai (ed.), *Portrait of a Minority* (1965), both of which contain useful material on the social and economic conditions of the Asian community, but cannot be regarded as serious historical works on the subject. Similarly, L. W. Hollingsworth's *Asians of East Africa* (1960), which is the only serious attempt at a historical study of the Asians, suffers from being a general survey of the subject in outline form. The main weakness of these works, in fact, lies in the limited range of the primary sources of information consulted. More satisfactory in this respect are the studies of specific aspects of the subject. The recent social and economic characteristics of the Asian community have been frequently studied, and three unpublished theses merit particular attention.[2] Similarly, the Indian Question in Kenya has been dealt with in a number of works. But only a few of these can be listed as satisfactory,[3] since most of the studies relating to this topic tend to deal with the period immediately after the First World War and to assume that the Devonshire Declaration of 1923 effectively settled the political controversy between the Asian and European communities. The employment of indentured Asian labour

[1] The word 'Asian' is commonly used in East Africa to describe the people originating from India and Pakistan. But, for the period before the Partition of India in 1947, it is more appropriate to use the word 'Indian', as I have done in the text.

[2] These are: H. S. Morris, 'Immigrant Indian Communities in Uganda' (London Ph.D. thesis 1963); D. F. Pocock, 'Indians in East Africa, with special reference to their social and economic situation and relationship' (Oxford D.Phil. thesis 1955); and C. Sofer, 'Some Aspects of Race Relations in an East African Town' (London Ph.D. thesis 1953).

[3] Among the studies relating to the Indian Question, the following merit particular attention: W. K. Hancock, *Survey of British Commonwealth Affairs*, vol. i (London, 1937); M. R. Dilley, *British Policy in Kenya Colony* (New York, 1937); R. Oliver, *The Missionary Factor in East Africa* (London, 1952); G. Bennett, *Kenya; A Political History* (London, 1963) and W. M. Ross, *Kenya From Within* (London, 1927).

for the construction of the Uganda Railway, and of British Indian
troops for the 'pacification' of the East African territories, has also
been dealt with in the larger studies by M. F. Hill, *Permanent Way*
(1949), and H. Moyse-Bartlett, *The King's African Rifles* (1956),
respectively. Professor Oliver's *Sir Harry Johnston and the Scramble
for Africa* (1959) similarly provides valuable information about
certain aspects of the Asian association with the colonial occupation
of East Africa. Most of the larger studies of East African history or
of East Africa generally contain references to the Asians in the area—
but these are often as perfunctory as they are frequent. Notable
exceptions to this rule are the two volumes of the *History of East
Africa*.[1] Within the framework and the limitations inherent in a
larger study of East African history, these works have sought to
redress the imbalance that has existed in this respect.

The existing literature relating to the Asians in East Africa, however, leaves important gaps in the over-all assessment of the economic,
social, and political implications of their large-scale immigration into
East Africa during the colonial period. It is moreover almost entirely
unsatisfactory—if seen purely from an Asian point of view—in that
there is a wide divergence between the Asian tradition of their past
in East Africa and the views expressed about them in various
written accounts. The attempt in this book, therefore, has been to
deal with the subject in as detailed and balanced a fashion as possible,
and to provide fuller information about certain topics which,
although cursorily dealt with in existing works, feature prominently
in local Asian tradition. This is true, for example, of the nature and
extent of the Asian enterprise along the Coast on the eve of the
Partition, and its significance for the subsequent penetration of the
interior of East Africa by the old-established Asian traders. Similarly,
some of these traders who pioneered the commercial exploitation of
the interior during the 1880s and the 1890s have been little known
outside local Asian tradition.[2] The enterprise of these traders,
facilitated by the protection afforded by European rule, had far-
reaching importance for the spread of 'legitimate commerce' and for

[1] R. Oliver and G. Mathew (eds.), *History of East Africa*, vol. i (Oxford, 1963),
and V. Harlow and Mrs. E. M. Chilver (eds.), *History of East Africa*, vol. ii
(Oxford, 1965).
[2] With the exception of the more outstanding early Asian trader in the interior,
Allidina Visram. For an account of him, see *History of East Africa*, ii, ch. viii,
or C. Ehrlich, 'The Marketing of Cotton in Uganda 1900–1950' (London Ph.D.
thesis 1958), and K. Ingham, *The Making of Modern Uganda* (London, 1958),
pp. 98–9.

stimulating local production in various parts of East Africa. Moreover, the fresh trails of trade blazed by them paved the way for
increased immigration of their 'kith and kin' from western India.
Somewhat similar consequences followed the large-scale but short-
lived influx of indentured labour for the Uganda Railway and of
Indian troops. For, while important in itself, the officially sponsored
immigration of the Indians had a greater significance—which has not
received adequate attention in existing works—in initiating voluntary
emigration from parts of India, especially central Gujerat and Punjab,
that had had no previous contact with East Africa. The story of
much of the subsequent role of Asians in East Africa can, in fact, be
told in terms of the expansion of their activities on the twin foundations of commercial enterprise and subordinate employment laid
down during the early colonial period. Equally, the Indian Question
in East Africa merited a further study—especially in respect of the
pre-war background to the post-war controversies and the organization of Asian political activity in the territories generally, both before
and after 1923. In addition, it was hoped that a study of the inter-
war period would enable a comprehensive analysis of the political,
economic, and social development of the Asian community during
the colonial period to be undertaken.

Such a study of the Asians in East Africa can only be based on
extensive original research into the primary sources of information
available on the subject. But the paucity of written material—
especially of a non-political nature or as a record of the Asians
themselves—proved to be a major handicap. Evidently, the generally
illiterate petty Asian merchants, or the immigrant artisans and subordinate employees, were less interested in the concerns of history than
in the more immediate tasks of earning a livelihood. They have
therefore left hardly any written accounts. A few of the early immigrants are, however, still alive in East Africa and an attempt was
made to collect the personal reminiscences of some of them. Such
information, although highly subjective and localized, and frequently
coloured by subsequent events, helped to provide an insight into the
life and work of the early Asian immigrant. More important, the
local traditions of the various Asian communal and religious groups,
obtained generally from a number of the older immigrants,[1] proved

---

[1] The interviews for the collection of oral information were conducted in a
mixture of languages—but chiefly in English and Hindustani. The names of the
more important informants are given in the Bibliography.

valuable in presenting a picture of the Asian past in East Africa as seen by themselves. This was of crucial importance, for, by high-lighting certain events, policies, and the personalities who made the greatest impact on them, such oral information indicated aspects of the subject that required further research and verification from the primary sources. I am grateful to the University College, Nairobi, for research grants which enabled me to visit various centres of Asian settlement in East Africa, and also to the older immigrants who readily accepted the opportunity to talk about their past experiences.

Primary information about this subject has been derived from a wide range of archival sources and contemporary publications. Among the official archives, the single most important source of information was the India Office Records in London. The Pro-ceedings of the Emigration Department at the India Office contain comprehensive information relating to various aspects of Indian immigration and settlement in East Africa since 1895. Much of the original correspondence with the Government of India regarding the whole question of Indian immigration, as well as correspondence with the Foreign and Colonial Offices on the subject generally, is found in these records. The corresponding Proceedings of the Emigration Department of the Government of India in New Delhi virtually duplicate the material in the India Office, and are also open for consultation beyond 1922 up to 1935. In addition, the Proceedings of the Foreign Department of the Government of India contain important information about British Indian affairs in Zanzibar during the nineteenth century—especially for the period 1873–83, when the Government of India exercised direct jurisdiction over the Zanzibar Agency. They are also valuable for the period of the I.B.E.A. Company rule. Another important Indian source is the records of the former government of the Bombay Presidency. The Bombay Government exercised control over the Zanzibar Agency from the time of its establishment in 1841 until 1873, and it was also more immediately involved in the whole process of Indian emigration to East Africa during the early colonial period. Its records therefore —especially the Proceedings of its Political and General Departments —provide valuable details about the recruitment of Indian labour for the Uganda Railway, the emigration of the 'free' or 'passenger' Indians, and the position of the Indians in Zanzibar during the nineteenth century. I would like to express my grateful thanks to the Rockefeller Foundation, New York, for generous financial assistance which enabled me to make a research trip to Bombay and Delhi.

The records of the Foreign and Colonial Offices in the Public Record Office in London contain indispensable primary information. A few volumes, especially in the series F.O. 2, deal with specific aspects of the subject, such as the employment of Indian troops, coolie emigration for the Uganda Railway, and the Agency in India for the African Protectorates. But both the series F.O. 2 and F.O. 84 contain a number of dispatches dealing with the Indians—in the former for East Africa up to 1905 and in the latter for Zanzibar during the nineteenth century. The same is true of the Colonial Office series C.O. 533, which contains important references to the position of the Indians in Kenya after 1905. Frequently, however, the relevant material contained in the Foreign and Colonial Office records is reproduced in the India Office Emigration Proceedings.

Of comparable value to the records in London and India were the official archives in East Africa. These, however, presented greater difficulties in consultation because of their generally disorganized state and inconsistency in the application of the fifty years' rule during the period when this study was undertaken. The Kenya and Uganda archives were particularly valuable in providing detailed information about certain aspects of the subject which are not fully dealt with in the official dispatches to the Foreign or Colonial Offices. The story of the Asian commercial penetration of the interior of East Africa, during the early colonial period in particular, could be adequately told only by reference to the series of the District and Provincial Reports available in these records. The same is true of the Asian role as subordinate administrative employees. But these Reports, while invaluable for the early years, were rather disappointing for the inter-war period, when very few references to the Asians could be found in them. The Kenya and Uganda archives also provide valuable material relating to the careers of a few prominent early Asian merchants, and also contain files dealing with specific aspects of the subject, such as Indian education, representations by Indian Associations, and Indian immigration. The Zanzibar archives contain useful material relating to the Indians in East Africa during the nineteenth century, although much of this could be more readily obtained from the better-organized records of the Foreign and India Offices or of the Bombay Government.

In the case of mainland Tanzania (Tanganyika), only a few useful files could be traced for the period after 1919, while the lack of a knowledge of German proved a distinct disadvantage in consulting the records relating to the German period. For the same reason the German Colonial records in Leipzig could not be consulted. Information about the Asians in German East Africa has therefore been derived largely from other official sources—particularly the Foreign and India Office records, which contain substantial references to the Asians in that territory. I am also grateful to Dr. John Iliffe for permission to consult his thesis: 'The German Administration in Tanganyika 1906–1911' (Cambridge Ph.D. thesis, 1965), and for advice regarding the value of the German records for a study of the Asian community. From the information supplied by Dr. Iliffe, it appeared that the material available in the non-German sources would enable a reasonably adequate study of the Asians in German East Africa to be undertaken.

Among the unofficial records consulted for this study the most important were those of the East African Indian Congress.[1] These are deposited in the Congress's offices in Nairobi and consist of a series of files, miscellaneous papers, and valuable printed material ranging from the presidential addresses and resolutions of the various sessions to offprints of memoranda and a variety of pamphlets. While these records inevitably presented the Asian point of view of political controversies in East Africa, they were particularly valuable in tracing the history of Asian political activity in the territories— from the formation of the Congress in 1914 until the Second World War, when the Congress finally ceased to function as an East Africa-wide political organization. The corresponding records of the Central Council of Indian Associations in Uganda and of the Asian Associations in Dar es Salaam and Zanzibar are relatively meagre and contain material relating largely to the more recent period.

Another important unofficial source was the papers of Dr. J. H. Oldham deposited at the International Missionary Council, Edinburgh House, London. These contain indispensable information relating to the Indian Question in Kenya. Similarly, the papers of Sidney Webb (Lord Passfield) at the London School of Economics provide valuable information about the Asian representations before the

---

[1] Since 1952 the Congress has been known as the Kenya Indian Congress. I am grateful to Mr. S. G. Amin, president of the Congress on successive occasions, and Mr. A. J. Pandya, the present president, for permission to consult these records.

Joint Select Committee on Closer Union in East Africa. A limited amount of material, which is relevant to a study of Asian political activity in Kenya during the inter-war period, was also derived from the papers of Lord Francis Scott, deposited at the University College, Nairobi. For a study of Asian commercial enterprise in East Africa, the proceedings of the Federation of the Indian Chambers of Commerce and Industry in Eastern Africa, which are available in the Kenya archives or the Congress records, proved useful—especially in providing information about some of the leading Asian traders during the 1930s. Similarly, the minutes of the multi-racial Uganda Chamber of Commerce, which are deposited at the Makerere University College Library, contain useful references to the early Asian traders in Uganda for the decade after 1905.

A few archival sources, however, were not consulted for this study. These include the Mackinnon papers at the School of Oriental and African Studies, London. A study based on these papers has been undertaken by M. J. de Kiewiet, 'History of the Imperial British East Africa Company 1876–1895' (London Ph.D. thesis, 1955). It appeared after consulting this work, together with P. L. MacDermott's *British East Africa or IBEA* (1893), that the information available from other sources—chiefly the Foreign and India Office records—provided an adequate picture of the Asian position in East Africa during the brief period of Company rule. Similarly, in view of the substantial information available about the Indian Question in East Africa, some of the sources were not consulted. These included the records of the British Anti-Slavery Society[1] at the Rhodes House Library, Oxford, and of the Indian National Congress[2] in Delhi. In addition, no attempt was made to trace the papers of the Indians Overseas Association, London (or of its secretary, H. Y. S. Polak), the Imperial Indian Citizenship Association, Bombay, and Colonel J. C. Wedgwood—who were all closely involved in the political controversies in East Africa. Mention should perhaps also be made of the American records—especially those of the Salem merchants,[3]

---

[1] I am grateful to my colleague Mr. B. G. McIntosh for providing a microfilm of the relevant file in the papers of the Anti-Slavery Society, which deals with the Indian Question in the early 1920s.

[2] An official study based on these records has been undertaken by N. V. Rajkumar, *Indians Outside India* (New Delhi, 1951).

[3] These records are deposited at the Peabody Museum and Essex Institute in Salem, Mass. Some idea of their relative value for this subject is provided, among others, by the studies of Dr. N. R. Bennett of Boston University.

which were not consulted, but should prove useful for a study of Indian commerce in Zanzibar during the nineteenth century.

Among the wide range of contemporary official and unofficial publications relating to East Africa, of particular value for this study were some of the Parliamentary Papers, reports of various commissions, the accounts of a few explorers and officials, census returns, newspapers, and the proceedings of the Legislative Councils. The Proceedings of the Kenya Legislative Council contain indispensable information about this subject for the inter-war years—as also do, but to a lesser extent, the Proceedings of the Uganda and Zanzibar Legislative Councils. But those for Tanganyika are disappointing. Among the newspapers consulted for this study, greater reliance as primary sources of information was placed on the leading English language newspapers. The *East African Standard* and the *Leader of British East Africa* were particularly valuable for the early colonial period, but for the later years most of the newspapers contain little information about the Asian community.

Much of the published material relevant to this work could ideally be consulted only in London. The Colonial Office Library, especially, has a valuable collection of publications relating to East Africa—including official reports on the territories and a number of important contemporary pamphlets which contain a certain amount of primary evidence for this subject. I would like to express my gratitude for the permission granted to me to undertake research in the various archives and libraries mentioned in this Preface, and including the British Museum and the Institute of Commonwealth Studies, London.

In spite of the extensive search for material, much of the information available on this subject was predominantly of a political and polemical nature. And as befits interracial polemics, it tended frequently to be both repetitive as well as contradictory. This posed considerable difficulty in interpretation—especially in seeking a balance between the extreme views expressed about the Asian community in East Africa during this period. The result has been a study that is largely sympathetic towards the Asian community, but the origins of the prevalent anti-Asian feeling have not been ignored.

In selecting the period for this study, it was found that the history of the Asians in East Africa could not satisfactorily be confined within any well-defined limits of time. But the period from *c.* 1886 to 1945 represented adequately the crucial years of the historical process whereby the scattered Asian commercial population along the Coast was transformed into a major Asian settlement in the interior of East Africa. The Partition of East Africa in 1886 initiated a shift of emphasis from the Coast to the interior, and led, as a result, to a direct association of the British Indians with the Imperial effort in the interior. This formed the background to the unprecedented and increasing influx of Asian immigrants into East Africa during the colonial period—until the enforcement of identical immigration restrictions in the territories in 1944. Similarly, by the end of the Second World War, the character of the modern Asian settlement in East Africa had to a large extent been determined by the economic, social, and political developments of the preceding decades. Moreover, East Africa at the end of the war stood on the threshold of a new nationalist era, which provides a convenient watershed in the study of the history of the area and of its Asian population, which had by then emerged as an integral part of the local scene. It is hoped, therefore, that by focusing attention on the Asian community during the period of crucial importance for the evolution of modern East Africa this book will help to fill an important gap in the historical study of East Africa.

The word 'settlement' has been used to indicate no more than a progressive 'act of settling' on the part of the Asian immigrants. For, in the course of this period, the Asian immigrant became progressively less of a temporary visitor, attracted to East Africa by the prospects of economic improvement, and more of a settler with an increasing stake and commitment in the territories. In preferring the use of the word 'Indian' in the text, rather than 'Asian'—as is current practice in describing people originating from India and Pakistan—I was motivated only by historical considerations. At any rate, the two words 'Indian' and 'Asian' have been freely used in the book, especially for the period after 1947.

I am greatly indebted to Professor Roland Oliver, who very kindly agreed to supervise this study and gave valuable advice and guidance in the course of preparing the original thesis on which this book is based. I would also like to record my debt to the comments and criticism offered by Dame Margery Perham, Mr. George Bennett, and Dr. Cyril Ehrlich in respect of a draft chapter on the Asians in East Africa—which, although not specifically related to this study, have proved invaluable in its preparation. My thanks are also due to my colleagues, both past and present, at the University College,

Nairobi—especially Professors H. P. Gale, A. J. Hanna, K. O. Bjork, and B. A. Ogot and Drs. G. H. Mungeam and J. A. Kieran—for assistance at various points in the course of my research work; and to Miss S. Sharma and Miss S. Panesar for typing the final draft of the original thesis.

Material drawn from Crown-copyright records in the Public Record Office appears by permission of the Controller of H.M. Stationery Office.

J. S. MANGAT

University College
Nairobi
November 1967

CONTENTS

ABBREVIATIONS

B.E.A.	British East Africa
C.O.	Colonial Office
C.O.C.P.	Colonial Office Confidential Print
Comp.	Compilation (in Bombay records)
E.A.I.N.C.	East African Indian National Congress
E.A.S.	East African Standard (Nairobi)
E.A.P.	East Africa Protectorate
F.O.	Foreign Office
F.O.C.P.	Foreign Office Confidential Print
G.D.	General Department, Bombay Government
G.E.A.	German East Africa
I.B.E.A.	Imperial British East Africa (Company)
I.O.	India Office
P.D.	Political Department, Bombay Government
Pros.	Proceeding(s) in India Office and Indian Archives

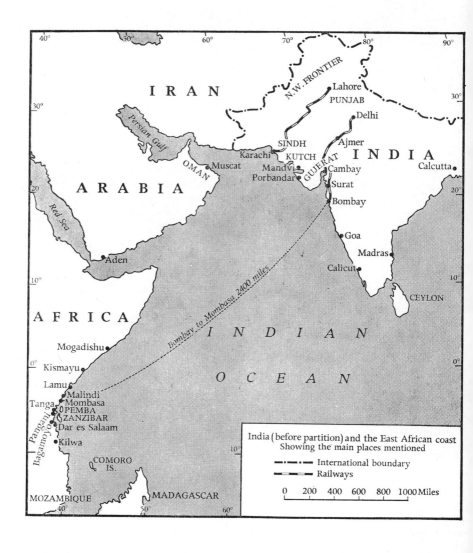

India (before partition) and the East African coast
Showing the main places mentioned
— ·· — International boundary
━━━━ Railways

0   200   400   600   800   1000 Miles

CHAPTER I

The Nineteenth-Century Origins

FROM the earliest times the east coast of Africa has been involved in the network of Indian Ocean trade; and merchant seamen from India, Persia, and Arabia have a long history of commercial intercourse with the East African Coast. The full extent of this historic Indian mercantile connection, however, is yet to be explored, for unlike the Arabs or Persians the Indians do not appear to have established any comparable or permanent settlements in this region.[1] But it is probable that from the earliest times they have played an active role in the commercial and financial life of the area—largely as an extension, aided by the geographical proximity and the trade winds, of the traditional pattern of trade along the western coast of India and in the Persian Gulf. Frequent, but perfunctory, references are found from the earliest times—beginning with the 'Periplus of the Erythrean Sea' in the second century A.D.—to the existence of a 'close-knit network of Indian Ocean trade' and the role of the Indian merchants along the east coast of Africa as the principal suppliers of cotton cloth, beads, and sundry manufactured articles and as importers of ivory, gold, iron, gum copal, ambergris, incense, and slaves—the last possibly following the expansion of Islam into the Indian sub-continent after the fourteenth century, when the occasional presence of African slaves at the courts of certain Muslim rulers is recorded. The excavations of Indian-made glass beads along the Coast and at Zimbabwe and Ingombe Ilede, the use of the Indian system of weights and measures and of Indian cowries as currency, the Indian origins of certain African plants—notably the coconut palms—and similar other information provide further evidence of early Indian contacts with East Africa. Portuguese records also speak of the important role of Indian traders in the flourishing

---

[1] The 'Wadebuli tradition' in Zanzibar, however, seems to suggest the settlement of immigrants from 'Dhabol'—variously identified as being in the south or west of India—during the pre-Portuguese period. See Sir John Gray, *History of Zanzibar* (London, 1962), pp. 25–8; G. S. P. Freeman-Grenville, *The Medieval History of the Coast of Tanganyika* (London, 1962), p. 204.

B

Afro-Asian settlements all along the east coast of Africa, and of the western Indian city of Cambay as the chief entrepôt of the ivory trade during the sixteenth and seventeenth centuries. As Freeman-Grenville explains: 'The contribution of India to the civilisation of the Swahili cannot easily be measured; but its presence is certain.'[1]

During the nineteenth century the traditional Indian commercial connection with the East African Coast entered a phase of revival after the prolonged vicissitudes of Portuguese rule and of recurrent hostilities in the Indian Ocean among seamen of rival Powers. Indian trade had also languished as a result of the Portuguese monopoly of trade at first and later of a similar monopoly enforced by the East India Company. The revival of Indian commercial enterprise was encouraged both by the recovery of their former influence in Zanzibar by the Imams of Muscat—a process completed during the reign of Seyyid Said (1806–56)—and by the establishment of British rule in India and the emergence of British naval supremacy in the Indian Ocean after the Napoleonic Wars. While the former led to the establishment of a Zanzibar sultanate committed in some respects to an enlightened commercial policy by Said, the latter ensured direct British political support for the Indian merchants now trading under the British flag.

The pattern of Seyyid Said's commercial policy in East Africa was provided by the existing economic framework in Muscat. Indian traders from Kutch, Porbundar, and Surat had been traditionally active in the Persian Gulf—operating largely from Muscat, where, helped by their particular aptitude for business, they had won the confidence of the Imams as financiers and customs collectors. Before Said moved his capital to Zanzibar in 1840, there were already more Indian merchants in Muscat than anywhere else in the Persian Gulf, and they constituted 'a body of the principal merchants of the place' enjoying freedom of enterprise and religious toleration.[2] These traders were thus to provide the nucleus for the expansion of Indian enterprise to the Imam's new dominions—a process

---

[1] Freeman-Grenville, op. cit., p. 204. For fuller information about early Indian contacts with East Africa see, inter alia, Gray, op. cit.; History of East Africa, i. Chs. IV and V; J. Strandes, Portuguese Period in East Africa, tr. Jean F. Wallwork (Nairobi, 1961), pp. 18–19, 28–30, 92–4; R. Coupland, East Africa and Its Invaders (Oxford, 1938); and R. Oliver (ed.), Dawn of African History (London, 1961), pp. 45–53.

[2] Salil ibn Razik, History of the Imams and Seyyids of Oman, tr. G. P. Badger, (London, 1871), p. 81 n.

accelerated by the appointment in 1833 of one of their number, the firm of Wat Bhima,[1] to the prestigious post of customs collectors for Zanzibar. The precedent for this was not to be found in Muscat alone, for Indian traders appear to have earlier occupied similar positions of trust elsewhere—notably at Zanzibar and Mombasa.[2]

British interest in the affairs of the Indian merchants in Zanzibar and along the Coast began as part of a wider web of diplomacy aimed at controlling the sea-routes to India and abolishing the slave trade in the western Indian Ocean.[3] Beginning early in the century, with Captain Smee's visit to Zanzibar in 1811, and later during the short-lived protectorate over Mombasa, 1824–6, a policy of political support for Indian merchants trading under the British flag and engaged in 'legitimate commerce' was initiated.[4] The opening of a British consulate in Zanzibar in 1841 helped to reinforce this policy, and successive British Consuls sought to strengthen the link that had been forged with the British Indian subjects in the sultanate. The British Consul was in fact appointed and paid by the Bombay Government and, while corresponding with the Foreign Office, he acted mainly as the political agent of the Bombay Government in the territories of the Imam of Muscat, and was subject to over-all direction from Bombay. As Robinson and Gallagher point out: 'Much of the correspondence about the east Coast went to Bombay, since Zanzibar was regarded merely as an outpost of India.'[5]

In the circumstances, the influence of the Bombay Government on the policies of the Sultans of Zanzibar steadily increased—although the presence of Indian traders did not initially prove conducive to the

---

[1] Bombay Archives, P.D. vol. 280 of 1874, Comp. 1963, Kirk to Govt. of India, 12 Sept. 1874; Gray, op. cit., p. 143; and F.O.C.P. no. 1936, pp. 17–18, Kirk's report on Zanzibar 1870–1.

[2] ADM. 52/3940, Lt. James Emery's Journal 1825–6 makes frequent mention of the Indian customs master at Mombasa. See also Gray, *The British at Mombasa* (London, 1957), p. 60 and Gray, op. cit., p. 94.

[3] For a fuller discussion of British policy, see R. E. Robinson, J. Gallagher and A. Denny, *Africa and the Victorians* (London, 1961), pp. 14–15, 42.

[4] *History of East Africa*, i. 157–8, and Gray, *The British at Mombasa*, pp. 60, 84–5, 130–1, 139–40, give details of such British support in respect of a series of complaints by Indian traders regarding ill treatment under Arab rule. Similar Indian complaints relating to extortion of money or goods by compulsion were later made to the British Consul; see Zanzibar Archives, Serial E. 24 of 1856, *passim*.

[5] Bombay Archives, P.D. vol. 43 of 1842, Comp. 350, and vol. Muscat, 1842, Comp. 145; and Robinson and Gallagher, op. cit., p. 14.

achievement of British diplomatic objectives. In fact one of the first tasks of the British Consul, Captain Hamerton, was to counteract what he described as 'bad feeling on the part of the Imam's authorities towards English merchants'; and to induce the Imam to break up a monopoly of trade enjoyed by the American Consul-cum-trader, R. P. Waters, and the leading Indian firm of Jairam Sewji, which farmed the customs at Zanzibar. Hamerton's attempts in this respect were opposed by 'all the people of influence at Zanzibar' and the resulting friction led to a brief attempt by some Indian traders to repudiate the jurisdiction of the Consul and to seek Zanzibar citizenship.[1] However, after this initial distrust, British jurisdiction over the Indian merchants was steadily exerted after 1845[2]—until under Hamerton's successor, General Rigby, there was a brief repetition of this earlier movement of protest. Between 1862 and 1869 a number of Indian traders once again disputed British jurisdiction over them and sought the Sultan's protection—following Rigby's high-handed methods of forcing emancipation without compensation of domestic slaves held by them.[3] The situation was complicated by the fact that most of the Indian merchants originated from the British protected state of Kutch and were not liable to direct British jurisdiction. Eventually in 1869 the Rao (ruler) of Kutch was persuaded by the Bombay Government to issue a proclamation whereby his subjects residing in Zanzibar were brought under the jurisdiction of the Consul—a process finally completed by another proclamation

[1] F.O. 84/425, Hamerton to Aberdeen, 21 May 1842, and Bombay Archives, P.D. vol. 316 of 1841/2, Comp. 101.

[2] Bombay Archives, P.D. vol. 280 of 1874, Comp. 1963, Kirk to Govt. of India, 12 Sept. 1874, points out that: 'a very large number of Hindoo [sic] and Mohamedan traders from Kutch and elsewhere in India were settled in Zanzibar many years before the English acquired any interest, commercial or political, in the place. The head of the principal Bhatia house here, that of Wad Bhima [sic], is fifth in descent from the founder of the Zanzibar firm; and several Khojas can show a still longer ancestry. These Indians were under the undisputed rule of Muscat authorities until, apparently, the year 1845, . . . when they began to claim British protection.' See also N. R. Bennett, 'Americans in Zanzibar 1845-65', Tanganyika Notes and Records (Sept. 1961), p. 124.

[3] C. E. B. Russell, General Rigby, Zanzibar and Slave Trade (London, 1935), pp. 141-2; Bombay Archives, P.D. vol. 135 of 1868, Comp. 478, Churchill to Bombay Govt., 22 Dec. 1867, shows that the Indians held about 1,200 slaves; F.O. 84/1391, Frere to Granville, 7 May 1873, enclosed 'Memorandum on the Position and Authority of the Sultan of Zanzibar', dated 17 Apr. 1873, pp. 31-3, refers to the initial renunciation and subsequent acceptance of British jurisdiction by the Indians; and Bombay Archives, P.D. vol. 280 of 1874, Comp. 1963, Kirk to Govt. of India, 12 Sept. 1874, mentions that of the 350 Indians under the Sultan's protection in 1869, 76 held slaves.

of 1873; while the Bombay High Court acquired appellate jurisdiction over British Indian subjects in Zanzibar.[1]

Meanwhile the influence of the Indian Government in the affairs of Zanzibar had greatly increased following the succession crisis of 1859. A commission of inquiry into the dispute between Seyyid Thuwein and Seyyid Majid was appointed by the Bombay Government[2] and its report formed the basis for the Canning Award of 1861. Subsequently, when Majid refused to continue payment of the subsidy to Muscat after Thuwein's death in 1866, the Bombay Treasury undertook to make the payment on behalf of Zanzibar.[3] Eventually the control of political relations with Zanzibar and of consular appointments there was transferred from the Bombay Government to the Government of India in 1873.[4] At the same time the Government of India took the responsibility for the payment of the Muscat subsidy as well as the expenses of Sir Bartle Frere's mission to Zanzibar.[5] The Bombay Government at first and later the Government of India were thus to spearhead the growth of British diplomatic influence in Zanzibar; and their increasing involvement in East Africa reflected in part the importance of the Indian merchants in the area. In fact during most of the nineteenth century the growth of British influence and of the activities of the Indian traders were quite closely interrelated. Sir John Kirk, in his evidence to the Sanderson Committee, defined one aspect of this interrelationship: ' It was entirely through the Indian merchants that we were enabled to build up the influence that resulted in our position' in East Africa.[6] Similarly the activities of the Indian traders were greatly stimulated by the political support extended to them by British officials—and

---

[1] F.O.C.P. no. 2314, 'Slave-dealing and Slave-holding by Kutchees in Zanzibar 1819–70', pp. 41, 52; India Archives, Foreign Dept.—July 1873, Pros. 23, Sec. 'Publication of the proclamation by the Rao of Kutch'; and Dec. 1874, Pros. 61–4, Pol. A, 'Status of Indians at Zanzibar'.

[2] Bombay Archives, P.D. vol. 33 of 1861, Comp. 15, Brig. Coghlan i/c Muscat–Zanzibar Commission to Bombay Govt., 4 Dec. 1860.

[3] F.O. 84/1391, Frere to Granville, 2 May 1873, enclosed memo. on the subject of the Muscat subsidy.

[4] India Archives, Foreign Dept.—1870, Pros. 214, S.I. 'Control of Zanzibar Agency by Govt. of India', and Jan. 1873, Pros. 226–31, Sec. 'Political relations with Zanzibar transferred from Bombay Govt. to Govt. of India'.

[5] India Archives, Foreign Dept.—July 1873, Pros. 235–6, Pol. A, and Feb. 1873, Pros. 119–21, Sec. See also Bombay Archives, P.D. vol. 280 of 1874, Comp. 52.

[6] Report of the Committee on Emigration from India to the Crown Colonies and Protectorates, Part I, Cd. 5192 (1910), p. 92.

particularly so after the British Consul came to exercise increased influence in Zanzibar following the 1859-61 succession crisis.[1] Equally important was the improvement in communications which resulted from the establishment of a regular steamer service between Bombay and Zanzibar by the British India Steam Navigation Company in 1872, and of a British Indian Post Office at Zanzibar.

The growth of Indian commercial enterprise in Zanzibar during the nineteenth century was perhaps best explained by Sir Bartle Frere in 1873 in a memorandum that drew heavily on oral information at a time when such information could be usefully employed for the purpose:

The Indian traders seem never to have quite foresaken the East African trade; when it was at its lowest, which was probably in the latter part of the last and earlier years of the present century, a few ships made an annual voyage [from Mandaive [in Kutch, and from Surat, Bombay and occasionally from other ports of the Kattywar [sic] and Malabar Coasts, bringing ivory and other African produce in exchange for Cloth, Metals and beads; but their return from what was then a most hazardous voyage was a great event at all the ports to which they belonged. . . . While Surat and Guzerat [sic] had a large manufacture of blue cotton cloth as late as fifty years ago, East Africa was the chief market for it. I have met during my present visit to this Coast few Indian houses which boast an antiquity of more than forty years. Some have told me that the usual system of trade in former days was for a super cargo to deal from the ship, though there were always a few Indian residents at each port where there was sufficient of a settled government to make their property secure. In Madagascar and elsewhere the Indians assured me that though their oldest house was not of more than sixty years standing, their Caste had traded on the Coast for ages previous.

During the past forty years, . . . Indian immigration to this Coast has gone on at a constantly increasing rate which bids fair to restore the Indian trade with East Africa to more than its old proportions. Many causes have contributed to this end—the general peace in Europe, the final suppression of Arab piracy, the establishment of the Muscat Arabs at Zanzibar and on the Coast, the appearance at Zanzibar and elsewhere of English, French, German and American houses, and probably, above all, the great impulse given to Indian trade by the extinction of the East India Company's monopoly. . . .[2]

The activities of the Indian merchants, coupled as they later were with the enterprise of European and American traders, contributed

---

[1] Robinson and Gallagher, *Africa and the Victorians*, p. 46. See also p. 3, n. 4.
[2] F.O. 84/1391, Frere to Granville, 7 May 1873, enclosed 'Memorandum regarding Banians or natives of India in East Africa'.

to the rise of Zanzibar as a major entrepôt of East African trade—especially by the 1850s, when it was described as 'rapidly becoming the Emporium of the trade of all the East Coast' and as 'the chief market in the world for the supply of ivory, gum copal and cloves'.[1] At about the same time, the British Consul also reported: 'The trade of this port with India is becoming very important.'[2] This in effect reflected on the important role Indian traders had come to play in the commercial and financial life of the Zanzibar sultanate. Their population had increased from about 1,000 in the early 1840s to between 5,000 and 6,000 by 1860; their activities spread into every conceivable business undertaking and were of crucial importance to the economic progress of Zanzibar. The position was best explained by General Rigby in his report on Zanzibar in 1860, which referred to the extensive trade with Bombay, Kutch, and Arabia carried almost entirely in dhows and to the vital role played by the Indian traders:

> There are about 5,000 British Indian subjects residing in the Zanzibar dominions, and nearly the whole of the foreign trade passes through their hands. The Ivory is consigned to them from the interior, the Gum Copal is purchased from the diggers by Indian Banians residing on the Coast, and the entire Cargoes of American and Hamburg vessels are purchased by them. All the shopkeepers and artisans at Zanzibar are natives of India.

Rigby further pointed out that 'Rich Copper mines are known to exist some distance in the interior of Africa, and the Copper is sometimes brought to the Coast and exported to Kutch.' The Indian traders meanwhile had spread all along the East African Coast and to some extent had begun to settle down. As General Rigby explained:

> They have settlements at all the towns on the East Coast of Africa, at the Comoro Isles, and on the West Coast of Madagascar. The number of settlers from India has greatly increased during the last few years, and they have obtained possession from the Arabs, by purchase or mortgage, of considerable number of landed estates in Zanzibar. . . .[3]

Import and export figures available for Zanzibar in the latter part of the nineteenth century similarly reveal Indian predominance in the

---

[1] Zanzibar Archives, Serial E. 26, Outward letter no. 46 of 1859, and Serial E. 28, Outward letter no. 3 of 1860, Rigby to Bombay.
[2] Zanzibar Archives, Serial E. 26, Outward letter no. 23 of 1858, Rigby to Bombay.
[3] Zanzibar Archives, Serial E. 28, Outward letter no. 3 of 1860, and C. P. Rigby, *Report on the Zanzibar Dominions* (Bombay, 1861). See also R. F. Burton, *Zanzibar: City, Island and Coast* (London, 1872), vol. i. 316–17, 332.

total volume of trade carried on with Zanzibar.[1] It was a trade based largely on the traditional pattern of exchange of Indian goods: cloth, metal ware, grain, and beads, etc., for African produce: ivory, cloves, gum copal, hides, horns, and copra, etc.[2] In addition it appears that much of the trade carried on by the European or American firms was conducted through the agency of Indian merchants—a precedent set in nineteenth-century Zanzibar that was later frequently adopted by European firms in East Africa during the colonial period. The Indian traders were supplied with trade goods by the European firms on credit terms extending up to six months— and the entire process of distribution was conducted by the Indian firms in Zanzibar and along the Coast. Much of the local produce was similarly collected by the Indian merchants in exchange for imported trade goods, both European and Indian, and the export trade was thus also channelled through them. Sir John Kirk in his evidence to the Sanderson Committee recalled that when he first arrived in Zanzibar in 1866, much of the import and export trade passed through the Indian traders, who bought all the goods from the

---

[1] For import and export figures relating to Zanzibar trade in 1859–60, 1864–5, 1882–3, and 1892 respectively, see Rigby, op. cit.; Bombay Archives, P.D. vol. 73 of 1866, p. 10, Seward to Bombay no. 65 of 1866, enclosing Administration Report on Zanzibar for the year ending 30 Apr. 1866; India Archives, Foreign Dept.—Apr. 1884, Pros. 26–8, B. Genl E., and *Zanzibar Gazette*, 27 Apr. 1892. The Zanzibar–India trade, which exceeded the European and American trade, accounted for £157,478 worth of imports and £173,552 of exports in 1859–60; while in 1892 imports from India stood at Rs. 604,560 and those from Europe at Rs. 363,774.

[2] Elton, for example, referred to 'a very great deal' of cloves, gum copal, hides, ivory, india-rubber, etc., being shipped in dhows from Zanzibar to Kutch, see *Travels and Researches among the Lakes and Mountains of East and Central Africa* (London, 1879), p. 34. For earlier information relating to the nineteenth-century pattern of Indian trade with East Africa, see ADM. 52/3940, Lt. James Emery's Journal 1825–6. Lt. Emery, who was in charge during the brief British Protectorate over Mombasa, speaks frequently of dhows arriving from Kutch and Surat, bearing imports of cloth and sundry other articles, and of the regular arrival in Mombasa of the 'Whanikas', who were the principal diggers of gum copal and supplied ivory and gum copal to the Banyans: 'Whanikas daily arriving with gum and ivory', see entries in the Journal, 28 Apr., 3 and 17 May, 21 and 25 June 1826. An earlier entry of 15 Sept. 1825 shows 'The inhabitants busily employed shipping their ivory aboard the dhows from Bombay. Several Whanikas still in town. These last three or four days the town has worn a different aspect. It is now all noise and bustle. What with their singing and beating of drums. . . . This rejoicing while shipping their goods is an old custom.' Similarly an entry of 20 Sept. 1825 in the Journal gives details of the cargo carried by a dhow bound from Mombasa to Bombay: 556½ *frasilas* of ivory; 337 *frasilas* of gum copal, 4½ *frasilas* of rhinoceros horn. See also Gray, *The British at Mombasa*, pp. 59–60, and R. F. Burton, *Zanzibar: City, Island and Coast*, i. 316–17, ii. 413–14.

French, German, and American traders on six months' credit; and also had agents all along the Coast to receive these goods and exchange them for copal, ivory, etc.—part of which was used to repay the European commercial houses.[1] In 1873, Sir Bartle Frere further explained this relationship between the European and Indian traders, pointing out that 'wherever there is any foreign trade, it passes through the hands of some Indian trader, no produce can be collected but through him; no imports can be distributed to the natives of the country but through his agency'—so that: 'The European merchant buys and sells with the aid and advice of a "Banian", who sometimes stands to the Foreign Firm in a relation more like that of a partner than a mere broker, agent or go-between.'[2] The Indian merchant acquired this position, as General Rigby remarked, by his reputation for 'punctuality of payment and probity'.[3]

As the volume of trade steadily increased, a growing number of Indian merchants settled along the East African Coast—especially at Kilwa, Bagamoyo, Pangani, Tanga, Mombasa, and Malindi. A majority of them, according to Holmwood, were 'merely agents for the houses having their headquarters in Zanzibar'; and Sir Bartle Frere thought that they did little wholesale business at the various coastal outposts, except in making advances of import goods to the caravans going inland—in return for repayment in up-country produce. In addition, they acted largely as retailers—bartering imported wares for local produce, which, in turn, they exchanged wholesale with the principal firms in Zanzibar for imported goods.[4] Hardly any of them ventured into the interior; as Frere pointed out in 1873: 'The Banians generally keep to the Ports, or within a short journey of the Coast or navigable parts of large rivers. The trade with the far interior is almost exclusively in the hands of Arabs, or Arab half casts, and Swahili. . . .'[5] There were, however, a few exceptions

---

[1] *Report of the Committee on Emigration from India to the Crown Colonies and Protectorates*, Part II, Cd. 5193 (1910), p. 238. See also Rigby, *Report on the Zanzibar Dominions*.

[2] F.O. 84/1391, Frere to Granville, op. cit., memo on Banyans.

[3] C. P. Rigby, 'Report on the Dominions of H.H. the Sultan of Zanzibar . . .' (1859), in Zanzibar Archives, Serial E. 26 of 1859.

[4] F.O. 84/1391, Frere to Granville, op. cit., and report on Zanzibar by Frederic Holmwood, Jan. 1875 in I.O. Political Dept., Letters from Zanzibar, 1875–Aug. 1883, vol. i, no. 2 of 1875 enclosure 48, p. 73.

[5] F.O. 84/1391, Frere to Granville, op. cit. See also J. H. Speke, *Journal of the Discovery of the Source of the Nile* (London, 1863), p. 86 and R. F. Burton, op. cit., i. 328, 339. Burton contradicts himself in stating, at first, that the Indians

—the most notable being Musa Mzuri, who was reputed to be a pioneer trader in 'Unyanyembe' (Tabora area).

If the population statistics available for Zanzibar, however, are to be believed, it would appear that the Indian population actually declined after Rigby's report in 1860! Sir John Kirk estimated the Indian population at 3,688 in 1871,[1] while Frederic Holmwood reported it at 4,257 in 1875.[2] It would appear that either Rigby's figures are unreliable, or that, as Frere explained, 'the best official returns were considerably below the truth', for at every place visited by his mission there were more Indian traders than the official figures accounted for. In fact Frere pointed out that during his 'circuit from Zanzibar around by Mozambique and Madagascar and up to Cape Guardafui' he hardly found 'half a dozen exceptions to the rule that every shopkeeper was an Indian'.[3]

Apart from their important role in the wholesale and distributive trade of Zanzibar, some of the leading Indian traders also provided the main banking and financial services available in Zanzibar during most of the nineteenth century, and the Indian rupee and pice currency gradually replaced the Maria Theresa dollars (thalers) as the principal currency in circulation in East Africa. As financiers the Indian traders invested their capital largely in loans and mortgages. Loans were extended largely to the Sultan, the Arab, Swahili, Indian, and European merchants; while many of the Arab and Swahili plantations in Zanzibar were mortaged to Indian bankers. Captain Hamerton explained in 1849 the role of the leading Indian firm in this respect: 'The best and only certain way of obtaining a supply of cash for immediate service is by getting it from the Imam's Custom Masters, who alone of all the merchants here would give a thousand dollars if required immediately . . . from the Custom Master Jairam Sewjee I can get in a few hours notice any reasonable sum even to the extent of five thousand dollars.'[4] Later Burton similarly referred to the Indian custom collector at Pangani, Trikindas, who evidently acted as a local banker and was owed 26,000 dollars.[5]

never left the seaboard, and later that one section of them, the Khojas, 'travel far and wide; several of them have visited the Lake Region.'

[1] F.O.C.P. no. 1936, Kirk's report on Zanzibar 1870–1, pp. 17–18.

[2] I.O. Political Dept., Letters from Zanzibar 1875–Aug. 1883, vol. i, report on Zanzibar Jan. 1875, by Frederic Holmwood, no. 2 of 1875, enclosure 48, p. 73.

[3] F.O. 84/1391, Frere to Granville, op. cit.

[4] Zanzibar Archives, Serial E. 11, Outward letter no. 12 of 1849, Hamerton to Bombay.

[5] Burton, op. cit., i. 331; ii. 147.

In fact Indian capital investment in Zanzibar steadily increased during the nineteenth century. Kirk reported in 1872 that while many of the Arab and Swahili plantations were heavily encumbered to Indian financiers, 'the single French house I have good reason to believe does not owe to Indians less than $4,00,000, the American consul (a trader) perhaps $2,00,000, and a second American firm not much less than the French. . . .'[1] Kirk further estimated that the total Indian capital invested in Zanzibar Island in 1873 was not less than £1,600,000.[2] A little later James Christie reckoned, probably with exaggeration, that over half the estates in the Island would be affected if the Indian merchants were 'to insist on the immediate realization of their outlying capital'.[3]

Apart from many of the estates being mortgaged to the Indian firms, much of Indian finance to the local caravan-traders took the form of loans and advances, on various kinds of security, of a variety of trade goods intended for exchange in the interior with local products—principally ivory, which formed the chief medium of repayment.[4] For example, the Swahili caravaneer Tippu Tib raised substantial loans in this way from two of the leading Indian merchants in Zanzibar—Ludha Damji and Tarya Topan.[5] With such experience of the methods of business in the interior, the Indian traders were able to extend valuable services to the European explorers—by acting as their local bankers, helping to equip their expeditions, and on occasions contracting to forward additional supplies of provisions and trade goods to them in the interior. Moreover, some of the explorers also spoke of the readiness with which the Indian merchants extended them hospitality both in Zanzibar and at the coastal settlements.[6]

In these circumstances, the Indian economic role in East Africa

[1] F.O. 84/1357, Kirk to Granville, 22 May 1872. Kirk reckoned the amounts in lacs, i.e. 4 lacs or 4,00,000, which is 400,000.

[2] F.O. 84/1391, Frere to Granville, op. cit.

[3] James Christie, *Cholera Epidemics in East Africa* (London, 1876), p. 346.

[4] F.O. 84/1391, op. cit.

[5] H. Brode, *Tippoo Tib* (London, 1907), pp. 26, 47–8.

[6] See, *inter alia*, Burton, i. 328, 485; ii. 11–12, 109, 121, 291, 343; Elton, op. cit., pp. 72–3, 76–106; Speke, *What Led to the Discovery of the Source of the Nile* (London, 1864), pp. 163–5, 169; V. L. Cameron, *Across Africa* (London, 1877), i. 12; *Livingstone's Last Journals* (London, 1874), i. 8; and Joseph Thomson, *Through Masai Land* (London, 1882), p. 12. Speke, for example, talked of 'the mingled pride and yearning pleasure these exotic Indians seemed to derive from having us as their guests. Being Indian Officers, they looked upon us as their guardians . . .' (p. 169).

assumed increasing importance during the later half of the nineteenth century. This was not entirely an isolated phenomenon but was closely related to the growth of Indian commerce all along the coast of the western Indian Ocean. Sir Bartle Frere pointed out in 1873 that along 'some 6,000 miles of sea coast in Africa and its Islands, and nearly the same extent in Asia' the Indian trader had become the most influential and permanent element of the commercial community: 'I doubt whether along the whole Coast from Dalgoa Bay to Kurrachee [*sic*], there are half a dozen ports known to commerce, at which the Indian traders are not, as a body, better able to buy or sell a cargo. . . .' Their enterprise also spread into every conceivable business undertaking, as Frere explained:

> Hardly a loan can be negotiated, or mortage effected, or a Bill cashed without Indian agency; not an import cargo can be distributed, nor an export cargo collected which . . . does not go through Indian hands. The European or American, the Arab or Sowaheli [*sic*] may trade and profit but only as an occasional link in the chain between producer and consumer, of which the Indian trader is the one invariable and most important link of all. . . .[1]

The Indian merchants most responsible for spearheading this commercial revival in East Africa were members of the traditional seafaring and trading castes and sects from Kutch and the surrounding districts of Surat, Porbundar, Jamnaggar, and Bombay; and they were commonly known as 'Hindi' or 'Banyan'. They had enjoyed an abundance of business experience in the western Indian Ocean from the earliest times, and familiarity with the traditional pattern of trade carried on with East Africa in small sailing vessels (dhows)— and with the aid of the monsoon winds. At the head of their ranks in Zanzibar stood the firm of Jairam Sewji[2]—belonging to the Bhattia Hindu caste—which farmed the customs at Zanzibar from 1835 to 1886, and held considerable influence in the commercial life of the East African Coast. The 'enterprising Bhattias' of Kutch were in fact generally regarded as the 'merchants par excellence of Zanzibar' and as 'probably the most important by wealth and influence'.[3]

---

[1] F.O. 84/1391, Frere to Granville, op. cit.

[2] Rigby, for example, described Jairam Sewji as leader of the Indian community in Zanzibar; see Zanzibar Archives, Serial E. 26, Outward letter no. 11 of 1859. See also F.O. 84/1357, Kirk to Bombay Govt., 27 Jan., 1872. For further information about this firm see pp. 15–17, below.

[3] F.O. 84/1391, Frere to Granville, op. cit., and Burton, i. 327. Sir Bartle Frere (F.O. 84/1391) explained that most of the Banyans (Indians) belonged to

Other Hindu trading communities active in Zanzibar were the Vanias and Lohanas—while there was also a sprinkling of Brahmins, and of lesser castes engaged as barbers, tailors, washermen, etc. Burton described the Indian traders with particular reference to the Bhattias, as 'Unarmed burghers' who appeared 'Right meek by side of the Arabs' fierceness'.[1] Among the Muslims, the Khoja, Bohra, and Memon sects[2] appear prominently; and in the latter part of the nineteenth century their population, especially that of the Khojas, far exceeded that of their Hindu counterpart.[3] This was partly due to the readiness of the Muslims, in contrast to the Hindus, to bring their families along with them from India—apart from their apparent advantages in a Muslim sultanate. The diversity of the Indian population was further accentuated by the settlement of a sizeable number of Parsees, Goans (Roman Catholics), Singhalese (Buddhists), and Baluchis (Muslims)—the last being chiefly members of the Sultan's army and police.

The steady expansion of the enterprise of these Indian trading communities in Zanzibar owed much to their commercial skills and

---

'four or five of the great trading classes of Western India'—with a few representatives of other castes such as goldsmiths, tailors, cooks, and washermen: 'The Indians we met were generally: Bhattias, Lohana, Wanias, Khojas, Memons, Bohras. The Bhattias are probably the most important by wealth and influence at Zanzibar. . . . The Bhattias are one of the very ancient, skilful, and important subdivisions of the Hindoo commercial castes . . . the Bhattias and Banians are most numerous at and near Zanzibar. The Khojas on the Island and the mainland of the equatorial regions and the Bohras to the South in Madgascar and to the north in Galla and Somaliland.' Frere further thought that the Khojas, Bohras, and Memons 'generally monopolize all that the Hindoo Bhattias and Banians do not possess of the trade in Cloth and cotton goods, ironmongery, cutlery and china and small wares . . .'. For further information about the various Indian communities in Zanzibar, see also Christie, op. cit., pp. 335–44; F.O.C.P. no. 2314, memorandum by Kazi Shahabudin, 14 Feb. 1870, pp. 14–15; and *Zanzibar Gazette*, 30 Nov. 1898, article on the Bhattias.

[1] Burton, op. cit., i. 105.

[2] The Khojas and Bohras belong to the Shia division of Islam and the Memons to the Sunni division; and they trace their origins to conversion to Islam of members of some of the Hindu trading communities. The Khojas split into two sects after 1866: The Ismailis, the majority, follow the Aga Khan as Imam, and the Ithna–Asheri do not. During the 1890s there was considerable friction between these two sects in East Africa; see Sir Arthur H. Hardinge, *A Diplomatist in the East* (London, 1928), pp. 99–100. The split among the Khojas in East Africa was finally confirmed by legal action in the Zanzibar High Court in 1905.

[3] Holmwood gave the following breakdown of Indian population by sects in 1875: Hindus 814, Khojas 2,725, Bohras 543, Memons 116, and Goans 59. See his report on Zanzibar in I.O. Political Dept., Letters from Zanzibar, 1875—Aug. 1883, vol. i.

business acumen. While contemporary observers made various adverse remarks about them, they equally emphasized their qualities of industriousness, frugality, and perseverance. Burton, for example, explained that the Indian traders 'rose in mercantile repute' by such qualities and because of commercial integrity—and added that 'they work all day, rarely enjoying the siesta unless rich enough to afford such luxury. . .'.[1] Frere compared them to the Marvari 'adventurers' who spread from their native state of Rajasthan to various parts of India—and subsequently also to East Africa—to engage very successfully in a wide variety of business undertakings. Further, Frere thought that for some of these trading classes, 'trade in East Africa seems to have the same charm as colonizing has for some of our own countrymen'.[2] But from some of the accounts of their life of isolation and insecurity in Zanzibar,[3] it would appear that it was not so much the 'charm' of foreign trade as the economic pressures of the dry and arid Kutch country that made such commercial enterprise a principal source of livelihood for these communities.

Some of the contemporary accounts[4] dealing with the Bhattia community reveal what was perhaps the normal practice among Indian traders seeking an opening in East African trade. The prospective trader generally arrived in Zanzibar in a dhow from Kutch–Mandvi at an early age to serve an extended period of apprenticeship with an old-established firm. This formed the basis for his setting up shop at a later date on his own or as an agent—with the help of goods advanced on credit by some large firm. Alternatively, the apprenticeship could lead by stages to appointment as manager or partner in existing firms. Only after some years of successful enterprise in Africa could the young trader hope to pay a visit to Kutch to marry and to establish fresh business connections. Both in business

---

[1] Burton, op. cit., i. 327–8, 332. The British Consul, Atkins Hamerton, noted in 1854 that 'Banians and India men as they are designated here . . . are all respected, even those from the Hon. Company's own parts—and the parts in the protected states.' Zanzibar Archives, Serial E. 19. Outward letter no. 9 of 1854, Hamerton to Bombay.

[2] F.O. 84/1391, Frere to Granville, 7 May 1873, op. cit.

[3] See, for example, Speke, *What Led to the Discovery of the Source of the Nile*, p. 169, where he refers, with obvious exaggeration, to the life of the Indian traders as being one of 'utter banishment' and 'worse than that of hermits'.

[4] F.O. 84/1391, Frere to Granville, op. cit.; and article on the Bhattias in *Zanzibar Gazette*, 30 Nov. 1898. See also Burton, op. cit. i. 329, where he writes: 'The Bhattia at Zanzibar is a visitor, not a Colonist; he begins his life before his teens, and, after an expatriation of nine to twelve years, he goes home to become a householder . . .'.

and in personal life there was thus a close interrelationship between Kutch and Zanzibar; and mutual good faith and trust apparently formed the corner-stone of the enterprise of these Kutch merchants. This was provided largely by ties of kinship, caste, and sect; and was perhaps best expressed in what Frere described as 'the marvellous system of private intelligence which is the keystone of native Indian commerce and by which every great Indian trader seems to hear of everything which concerns him wherever it may happen'.[1] Zanzibar, like Kutch–Mandvi and Bombay across the ocean, was the operational headquarters for the activities of the Indian merchants, and such a system of 'private intelligence' was no doubt indispensable in an age of primitive shipping when trade was still carried on in much the same fashion as in earlier times.

The leading pioneer among Indian merchants in Zanzibar during the nineteenth century was the firm of Jairam Sewji, based on Kutch–Mandvi and Bombay. In 1835 it acquired control of the important post of customs collectors after successfully outbidding the rival firm of Wat Bhima to an annual rental of $110,000.[2] Apart from the prestige attached to holding this high post of trust from the Sultans, the firm gained considerable advantages as the principal financial advisers to the Sultans—and this enabled Jairam Sewji to make rapid progress in his business enterprise in East Africa. With the assistance of his fellow Kutch merchants, who were appointed to act as his agents at various coastal ports,[3] he was able to develop an

[1] F.O. 84/1391, Frere to Granville, 7 May 1873, op. cit. In another account James Christie explained that the principal business meetings in Zanzibar were conducted at the customs house—with the Banyans, as the 'presiding deities of the place', appearing 'on the sphere of action at any early hour . . . with an air of supreme indifference, but with minds intent on business . . .'. See Christie, op. cit., p. 356.

[2] See Kirk's report on Zanzibar 1870–1 in F.O.C.P. no. 1936, pp. 17–18; Gray, *History of Zanzibar*, p. 143; and N. R. Bennett, 'Americans in Zanzibar 1825–1845', *Tanganyika Notes and Records* (Mar. 1961), p. 101. Because of their long association with the East African Coast (Swahil), members of this family acquired the surname, 'Sualy'—oral information. See also Bombay Archives, P.D. vol. 59 of 1844, Comp. 289, where Jairam signed his name in Gujerati, viz. Jairam Sewji Sualy.

[3] F.O. 84/1391, Frere to Granville, op. cit. and Burton, op. cit., vol. i. 328–9 give details of the organization of this firm and its agencies along the Coast. As Burton explained: 'Ladha Damha [*sic*] farms the Customs at Zanzibar, at Pemba Island his nephew Pisu has the same charge: Mombasah [*sic*] is in the hands of Lakhmidas, and some forty of his co-religionists; Pangani is directed by Trikindas and contains twenty Bhattias; including those of Mbweni; . . . Ramji, an active and intelligent trader, presides at Bagamoyo, and the Customs at Kilwa are collected by Kishindas. I need hardly say that almost all of them are

extensive business network. Similarly, as customs masters the firm was in an advantageous position to play a leading role in the import and export trade of Zanzibar. In fact between 1837 and 1841, the leading American firm of R. P. Waters and Jairam Sewji struck a close business partnership, which enabled them to dominate the import-export trade to their mutual advantage.[1]

Later, in 1844, Jairam was able to outbid a rival claimant to the custom-house,[2] and had by then apparently greatly strengthened both his financial position as well as his relations with the Sultan. This is evident from attempts made by the Rao of Kutch in 1844 to compel Jairam Sewji to part with two million dollars—being one-half of the total assets of the firm—which were claimed by his former partner, resident in Kutch. Seyyid Said came to Jairam's rescue, and appealed to the Governor of Bombay on his behalf.[3] The confidence of the Sultan, and later of the British Consul, enjoyed by Jairam was shared equally by his agent in Zanzibar, Ludha Damji. Sir John Kirk wrote of him, after his death in 1871:

> Ludha Damji was upwards of seventy years of age and had lived in Zanzibar for more than forty years. During the latter part of Syed Saeed and the whole of Syed Majid's rule he had held the important post of the head of the Agency of Jairam Sewji, Farmer of State Revenue, and no one was more esteemed for his upright conduct by all classes.[4]

connected by blood as well as by trade.' Sir Bartle Frere in his memorandum (F.O. 84/1391) stated that 'the Sultan's customs are farmed by one of the most eminent Indian houses (Jairam Sewji), and no doubt as is customary elsewhere, the profits and responsibilities are not confined to one house, but are shared by other houses in friendly correspondence with the principal. Specially salaried Establishments are rarely employed in such cases at the outposts; one or more of the leading firms at an outpost agrees to keep the accounts and pass documents, almost all cash payments being settled at Zanzibar.'

[1] F.O. 84/425, Hamerton to Aberdeen, 21 May 1842; J. Gray, 'Early Connections between the U.S. and East Africa', *Tanganyika Notes and Records* (Dec. 1946), p. 66; and C. T. Brady, *Commerce and Conquest in East Africa* (Salem, 1950), pp. 103, 107, 109.   [2] N. R. Bennett, op. cit.

[3] Bombay Archives, P.D. vol. 59 of 1844, Comp. 289, Said to Governor of Bombay, 21 Apr. 1844: 'The Rao of Kutch treats my friend Jeyram the agent deputed from Zanzibar with severity. . . . The sole cause of this treatment is the Rao's desire to exact money from him. I therefore beg Your Excellency will always regard Jeyram with kindness.' Jairam in turn seems to have maintained good relations with the Bombay Govt. and was in later years allowed to consign goods ordered by the Sultan duty free from Bombay. In 1873 he presented the Governor of Bombay with the gift of an elephant—especially shipped from Zanzibar for the purpose. See Bombay Archives, P.D. vol. 230 of 1873, Comp. 912 and P.D. vol. 136 of 1868, Comp. 1159.

[4] F.O. 84/1344, copy of Kirk to Bombay Govt., 24 Nov. 1871. An earlier dispatch from Rigby to Bombay, Zanzibar Archives, Serial E. 26, Outward

In the circumstances the firm of Jairam Sewji was able to maintain its control of the post of customs collectors after the expiry of successive five-year contracts, and at a steadily increasing annual rental. By 1860 the figure stood at $196,000; in 1870 the amount had increased to $300,000; and in 1880 to an annual rental of $500,000.[1] In addition, the constant indebtedness of the Sultans to the firm further strengthened its position; while the British Consul, Sir John Kirk, also supported the firm with a view to keeping 'the advantages and prestige of the control of the Custom-houses in exclusive hands of British subjects'[2]. In 1860 Seyyid Majid was indebted to the firm of Jairam Sewji to the amount of $327,000;[3] and by 1870 the debt had risen to $540,000—partly perhaps because of the amounts drawn upon the firm by the Sultan to pay the Muscat subsidy.[4] The constant indebtedness apparently compromised the Sultan's position to some extent. General Rigby reported in 1860 that 'The agent of the Custom Master acts as Treasurer and Banker and scarcely a dollar reaches His Highness or any of his family except through him. Being indebted to him in so large a sum, His Highness is entirely dependent on his goodwill for any money he requires. . . .'[5] However, Seyyid Bhargash, upon his accession to the throne in 1870, sought to repudiate the debt and to farm out the customs to the rival Indian firms of Wat Bhima and Tarya Topan. These two firms were in turn dissuaded by Kirk from becoming parties to the Sultan's unilateral repudiation of the debt. Eventually an arrangement was worked out whereby Jairam Sewji waived a greater part of the debt and the Sultan acknowledged a debt of $200,000 interest free, and once

letter no. 13 of 1858, also shows that Jairam enjoyed close relations with the British Consul. For, after Hamerton's death at Zanzibar in 1857, and before his successor's arrival, Jairam's agent, Ludha Damji, acted as caretaker of the British Agency. See also Zanzibar Archives, Serial E. 11. Outward letter no. 13 of 1848, Hamerton to Bombay, which refers to assistance given by Jairam for repairs to Hamerton's house. Burton similarly described Ludha Damji as 'a man of the highest respectability'; see Burton, op. cit. i. 271.

[1] Zanzibar Archives, Serial E. 28, Outward letter no. 3 of 1860, Rigby to Bombay; Bombay Archives, P.D. vol. 33 of 1861, Comp. 15, Rigby to Bombay, 18 Sept. 1860. See also below, p. 18, n. 3.

[2] F.O.C.P. no. 4637 (1880), p. 59, and Bombay Archives, P.D. vol. 143 of 1871, Comp. 1659, Kirk to Bombay Govt., 24 Aug. 1871.

[3] Bombay Archives, P.D. vol. 33 of 1861, Comp. 15, Rigby to Bombay Govt., 18 Sept. 1860.

[4] F.O. 84/1357, Kirk to Bombay, 10 Apr. 1872, and Bombay Archives, P.D. vol. 144 of 1870, Comp. 1198.

[5] Bombay Archives, P.D. vol. 33 of 1861, Comp. 15, Rigby to Bombay Govt., 18 Sept. 1860.

again entrusted the State revenues to the care of the Sewji firm.[1] In fact the relationship between the Sultan and the firm was not without a certain degree of mutual compensation, for as Kirk later explained, Ludha Damji 'would sooner have relinquished the whole debt than have allowed the Customs to pass into other hands.'[2]

Between 1875 and 1880, however, the firm of Jairam Sewji lost its control of the Zanzibar customs to another leading Indian trader, Tarya Topan, and was able to recapture its old position only by raising the annual rent by $100,000 to a total of $500,000.[3] The firm was now under the new management of Ibji Sewji and Damodar Jairam following the deaths of Jairam Sewji in 1866 and Ludha Damji in 1871. Its long ascendancy in the financial life of Zanzibar which began in 1835 was to continue until the very eve of the Partition of East Africa in 1886. In that year the Sultan abandoned the practice of accepting private tenders for the custom-house and entrusted the task of customs collection to what Frederic Holmwood, rather unfairly, described as a 'promiscuous staff of untrained and irresponsible retainers'.[4] For among their ranks were two leading Indian merchants—Nasser Lillani and Peera Dewji[5]—who were to have their brief moment of ascendancy before the declaration of British protection over Zanzibar ended the old system.

The important position held by the firm of Jairam Sewji in Zanzibar over this prolonged period reflected in part the extensive business network built by the firm over the years—extending from Kutch-Mandvi and Bombay to Zanzibar and the East African Coast. Some idea of the enterprise of this firm and of the large amount of capital commanded by it can be gained from the details of the transactions of an Indian firm in Zanzibar provided by

[1] Bombay Archives, P.D. vol. 143 of 1871, Comp. 1659, Kirk to Bombay Govt., 24 and 28 Aug. 1871. The Bombay Govt. was critical of Kirk's intervention in support of Jairam Sewji, see Bombay Govt. to Kirk, 24 Aug. 1871, F.O. 84/1357. But as Kirk explained in his dispatch of 24 Aug. 1871: 'it was immaterial to me who held the customs so long as they remained in the hands of a British subject'.
[2] F.O. 84/1357, Kirk to Granville, 10 Apr. 1872, and Bombay Govt. to Kirk, 24 Aug. 1871.
[3] F.O.C.P. no. 4637 (1880), p. 59, and India Archives, Foreign Dept.—Sept. 1880, Pros. 207, Pol. A, Kirk to Govt. of India, 24 Aug. 1880.
[4] F.O. 84/1774, Holmwood to Salisbury, 25 July 1886, and F.O. 84/1775, Holmwood to Salisbury, 23 Sept. 1886.
[5] F.O. 84/1910, Euan Smith to Salisbury, 22 Oct. 1888. For a popular account of these traders, see *Samachar* (Zanzibar), Silver Jubilee number, Dec. 1936.

Sir Bartle Frere—which refer almost certainly to the firm of Jairam Sewji:[1]

The books showed a capital of about £434,000 invested in loans and mortgages in East Africa. Of this amount £60,000 had been advanced in various ways to the Sultan and his family, a rather large sum to Arabs in the interior,[2] a somewhat smaller amount to Arabs in Zanzibar and on the Coast, but the total of advances and loans to Arabs and natives of Zanzibar . . . was little less than £200,000. This sum had been lent and advanced in various ways, by loans, advances and mortgages . . . by advances of goods for Trade etc. Loans and advances to Europeans[3] and Americans were set down at about £140,000, and those to Indians in Africa at about £100,000.

Frere further pointed out that these were the African assets of the firm and did not include the capital and stock in trade of the parent company in Mandvi and Bombay, which far exceeded the African investments—so that the total 'capital employed in African Trade and Banking by this one family' could be reckoned at a much higher figure.

Another outstanding Indian trader in Zanzibar during the later part of the nineteenth century was Tarya Topan,[4] a member of the Khoja Ismailia community. Kirk described him in 1871, during the scramble for the custom mastership, as the only merchant capable of entering into competition with the firm of Jairam Sewji.[5] And in 1875, Tarya Topan was in fact able to wrest this much coveted post for five years at a rental of $350,000[6]—although in 1880 the Sewji firm regained control. In their day both Sewji and Tarya Topan were

[1] F.O. 84/1391, Frere to Granville, 7 May 1873, op. cit.

[2] F.O. 84/1391, Frere to Granville, op. cit. Elsewhere in his memorandum on the Indians, Frere referred to an amount of £57,000 lent by this firm to Arabs in the Unyanembe area.

[3] The agent of the firm, Ludha Damji, also had financial dealings with the European firms, and in one case he invested $100,000, not knowing that the amount would later be employed by Capt. H. A. Fraser to supply fresh meat to the vessels of the Royal Navy visiting Zanzibar. This was to affect Damji's religious susceptibilities and he made a point of requiring his heirs to withdraw the association. See F.O. 84/1344, copy of Kirk to Bombay Govt., 24 Nov. 1871.

[4] Stanley referred to him as 'one of the richest merchants in town', and Cameron as 'one of the most influential of the Indian traders'. See H. M. Stanley, *Through the Dark Continent* (London 1878), vol. i. 63, and Cameron, op. cit., vol. i. 23.

[5] Bombay Archives, P.D. vol. 143 of 1871, Comp. 1659, Kirk to Bombay Govt., 24 Aug. 1871.

[6] India Archives, Foreign Dept.—Sept. 1880, Pros. 207, Pol. A, Kirk to Govt. of India, 24 Aug. 1880.

Zanzibar's pre-eminent businessmen and enjoyed considerable influence throughout the sultanate. This is exemplified by the statement of a contemporary explorer who wrote: 'Dr. Kirk obtained for us letters of recommendation from the Sultan and, what was perhaps still more important, from the Indian merchant who farms the Customs, to whom nearly every trader in the interior owes money, so that his injunctions could not be lightly disregarded.'[1] In fact both these firms provided a variety of services to the various European explorers—and, as the leading firms in Zanzibar, were better able to do so than others. Ludha Damji, agent of Jairam Sewji, acted as the local banker for Burton and Speke, and also, as Speke explained, 'found our outfit of beads, brass wire, and cloths, which is the circulating medium in inner Africa instead of money'.[2] Damji also helped to equip Livingstone's expeditions—contracting also to forward additional supplies to him in the interior.[3] Tarya Topan similarly acted for a number of explorers. Cameron found him 'more inclined to assist us than any other',[4] while Stanley wrote of him: 'I made Tarya's acquaintance in 1871, and the righteous manner in which he then dealt by me caused me now to proceed to him for the same purpose as before, viz. to sell me cloth, cottons. . . .'[5]

As a leader of the majority of the Indian community in Zanzibar, the Khojas, Tarya Topan was to play an important role in Zanzibar affairs during the 1870s and the 1880s; and his success was to provide an impetus to the Khoja Ismailia enterprise in East Africa generally. In 1881 he supported Kirk's efforts to establish a school in Zanzibar by undertaking to provide Rs. 200,000 for the purpose;[6] and as a leading property owner he endowed suitable buildings and a sum of money for the establishment of the first general hospital in Zanzibar in 1887.[7] He was also to assist British efforts in the final suppression of slavery in Zanzibar; and in view of his services was rewarded with

---

[1] Cameron, i. 24.

[2] Speke, *What Led to the Discovery of the Source of the Nile*, pp. 194–5 and Burton, i. 485.

[3] *Livingstone's Last Journals*, i. 8. See also R. Coupland, *Livingstone's Last Journey* (London, 1945), p. 37.

[4] Cameron, i. 23.   [5] Stanley, op. cit. i. 63.

[6] F.O. 84/1773, Kirk to Salisbury, 1 May 1886. Kirk's efforts to establish a school did not materialize until 1891.

[7] Bombay Archives, P.D. vol. 185 of 1887, Comp. 453. Topan stated in his letter to the Bombay Govt. that his offer was intended to coincide with the Diamond Jubilee celebrations and to form a memorial to the Queen's Jubilee. See also India Archives, Foreign Dept.—Apr. 1887, Pros. 156–62, Intl. A, and Aug. 1887, Pros. 97–9, Extl. A.

a knighthood in July 1890. Yet the enormous business interests in East Africa created by Tarya Topan were to be frittered away in the scramble for his fortunes among his descendants—in much the same way as the assets of the firm of Jairam Sewji were squandered.[1] This was perhaps a normal hazard of a family-based business and was typical of many other Indian traders. But local Indian tradition, both in Zanzibar and in East Africa generally, richly preserves the story of the success and influence enjoyed by these two prominent nineteenth-century Indian firms—which no doubt inspired the careers of many another Indian merchant in East Africa.

The rise of some of the Indian merchants to positions of affluence and eminence in Zanzibar and the overall growth of their economic activities in the area were to expose the Indians to increasing scrutiny. As the principal financiers and bankers and as economically one of the most important groups in the population—acting as creditors, wholesalers, and retailers—the Indians became the target of much hostile criticism from other sections of the population. The position of the Indian money-lenders particularly became rather anomalous. While on the one hand they were denounced as usurious and extortionate, on the other they continued to provide what was after all a basic and vital economic service—extending credit to land-owners and others against the security of their properties. The two aspects of the attitude towards the Indian financiers and traders generally are perhaps best exemplified by the policies Seyyid Bhargash pursued towards them. At first his attitude was one of hostility both to the Indians and to British policy generally.[2] Not only did he seek to repudiate the debt to Jairam Sewji which he inherited from his predecessor, but he also briefly attempted by a proclamation in 1870 to ban Indians from trading or holding estates outside the town of Zanzibar.[3] Yet later in his reign, Bhargash leaned considerably towards the Indians and a number of Indian merchants—Tarya Topan, Nasser Lillani, Ibji Sewji, Damodar Jairam, and above all Peera Dewji[4]—were among his closest associates and advisers.

---

[1] For disputes among the successors of Tarya Topan and Jairam Sewji, see *Zanzibar Gazette*, 9 and 16 Mar. 1892, 27 Apr. 1892, and 15 June 1892.

[2] Bombay Archives, P.D. vol. 145 of 1871, contains dispatches and minutes on this subject.

[3] F.O.C.P. no. 1936, pp. 17–18, Kirk's report on Zanzibar 1870–1. See also R. Coupland, *East Africa & Its Invaders* (Oxford, 1938), p. 91.

[4] Peera Dewji was described by Euan Smith as one of the Sultan's closest advisers, and one who wielded considerable influence in Zanzibar, F.O. 84/1910, Euan Smith to Salisbury, 22 Oct. 1888. Later Dewji was deported from Zanzibar

A series of critical comments about the Indians and popular conceptions and misconceptions about them gained considerable currency from the accounts of various contemporary observers. Elton, for example, described the Indian merchant as 'crafty, money-making, cunning, intensely polite, his soul bound to his body by the one laudable and religious anxiety of its helping him to turn his coin to better advantage'.[1] Burton described the Indian traders as the local Jews, and thought that one section of them were 'unscrupulous and one-idea'd in pursuit of gain', used false weights and measures, and were receivers of stolen goods;[2] while Speke in a similar vein provided a picture of a Banyan 'contemplating' his account book![3] On the other extreme, the Indian merchant was described as a monopolist: Frere talked of the 'completeness' of his monopoly of trade and thought that over the previous fifty years East African trade had been 'in a great measure recreated and silently monopolized by a few of the less prominent classes of Indian traders'.[4] Similarly, the Indians were described as mere 'birds of passage' who had no thought of settling down in Zanzibar. Rigby and Holmwood, however, felt that the Muslims came to Zanzibar as settlers—a view they based on the Muslims bringing their families with them.[5] But Frere dismissed this view and thought that both the Hindus and the Muslims had 'as little idea of settling or adopting the country for their own, as a young Englishman in Hongkong'.[6] Yet the Indians had created a substantial stake in the

for a year on charges of intriguing against the authority of the British Consul, see Bombay Archives, P.D. vol. 220 of 1889, Comp. 873.

[1] Elton, op. cit., p. 30. Another writer, H. S. Newman, *Banani, The Transition from Slavery to Freedom in Zanzibar and Pemba* (London, 1898), p. 70, thought that the Indian money-lenders were 'extortionate and held up to common execration'—but 'Still the Arabs flee to them for loans like flies to the flame.'

[2] Burton, i. 105, 338–9. The sect referred to were the Khojas.

[3] Speke, *Journal of the Discovery of the Source of the Nile*, p. 9.

[4] F.O. 84/1391, Frere to Granville, op. cit. Similarly, James Christie thought that the Indians were 'in many respects' 'the real ruling power' in Zanzibar, and held 'directly or indirectly . . . almost unlimited sway over the commerce of the place'. See Christie, op. cit., p. 345.

[5] Rigby, *Report on the Zanzibar Dominions*, and Holmwood's report on Zanzibar, Jan. 1875, in I.O. Political Dept. Letters from Zanzibar, 1875–Aug. 1883, vol. i. no. 2 of 1875, enclosure 48.

[6] F.O. 84/1391, Frere to Granville, op. cit. Similar views were echoed by Kirk, who accused the Khojas of collecting large sums of money for transmission to the Aga Khan; and the firm of Jairam Sewji of failing to leave any 'trace of their existence' in Zanzibar in spite of its extensive business interests in the place. See F.O. 84/1344, Kirk to Granville, 28 Sept. 1871, and F.O.C.P. no. 1936, pp. 22–3.

country, and the large sums of money invested by them in real estate, trade goods, and loans provided for what was in essence a virtually permanent commitment to the country.

The Indian traders were to come into greater disrepute following Burton's accusations that they were hostile to European exploration and spared 'no scruples in compassing their ends'.[1] Later Livingstone denounced them more seriously, accusing them of sabotaging his explorations by fraudulent practices, and, what was more important, singling them out as the worst offenders in the slave trade.[2] The accusations of Livingstone and Burton were denied by Speke, Rigby, and Kirk.[3] But Livingstone's highly coloured accounts of the slave trade and of Indian complicity in it aroused public opinion and led to the appointment of the Frere Mission in 1873 to investigate the whole issue. In the meantime, ironically enough, it was an Indian firm in Zanzibar that provided the *coup de grâce* for the old Slave Market in Zanzibar, which it purchased together with other property from Mwenyi Mkuu, the local chief, for the purposes of residential development.[4]

Sir Bartle Frere's detailed inquiry into the East African slave trade revealed, so far as the Indians were concerned, that they had been quite unfairly singled out for complicity in this traffic. As Frere pointed out:

The Slave Trade generally is in the hands of Arabs, or men of mixed Arab and African descent. Beyond furnishing the capital for it, I do not think that the Indian or other foreign traders are often directly implicated in it, and as regards the European merchants and the more respectable Indian houses, I doubt whether any case of wilful and direct participation in slaving ventures could be established against any of them, though probably few could escape implication for indirect aiding and abetting, often unconsciously, if all the ramifications of their commercial connections were laid open.[5]

[1] Burton, op. cit., i. 328.
[2] F.O. 84/1357, Livingstone to Kirk, 30 Oct. and 17 Nov. 1871, and Kirk to Bombay, 13 Sept. 1872.
[3] Russell, *General Rigby, Zanzibar and Slave Trade*, pp. 270–1, and F.O. 84/1357, copy of Kirk to Bombay Govt., 13 Sept. 1872.
[4] F.O. 84/1357, Kirk to Granville, 6 Aug. 1872 and 17 Dec. 1872; Bombay Archives, P.D. vol. 230 of 1873, Comp. 88, Kirk to Bombay Govt., 17 Dec. 1872; India Archives, Foreign Dept.—Oct. 1873, Pros. 225, Pol. A, Closing of Zanzibar Slave Market, and Feb. 1873, Pros. 338–44, Pol. A, Purchase of Zanzibar Slave Market by Kutchee. The site in question is today that of the Anglican Cathedral in Zanzibar.
[5] F.O. 84/1391, Frere to Granville, 7 May 1873, enclosed 'Memorandum on the Position and Authority of the Sultan', dated 17 Apr. 1873.

Frere concluded that in view of their position as customs collectors, financiers, and merchants the Indians were inevitably involved—especially indirectly—in the slave trade. The Muslims, he thought, more frequently committed themselves to direct slave dealing while the Hindus helped in 'aiding, abetting and concealing it'—especially as the 'collection and concealment of the Slave Cargo before shipment . . . are matters of everyday concern and business-interest to the Indian agent of the Indian farmer of the Sultan's Customs. He cannot help being aware of them, and taking part in them, at least by concealment of what he knows, and as an accomplice after the fact.'[1] Livingstone's accusations, however, tended to supplement a rather exaggerated popular picture of extensive Indian involvement in the slave trade. Even General Rigby's much-publicized measures against Indian slave-holding in Zanzibar drew only a one-sided picture—for in fact one of the largest single slave-holders among British subjects in Zanzibar during the 1860s was an English firm.[2] The only Indian point of view available on this subject at the time was provided by Kazi Shahabuddin, Minister of the Rao of Kutch, who accompanied Frere on his mission to East Africa. In his memorandum[3] he criticized as 'deliberate untruth' the view that slavery was a flourishing institution in Kutch, or that Indian traders—any more than the European or American firms—provided the sole finance for this traffic, considering that some of the trade goods and the entire supply of arms and ammunition originated from the European firms.[4]

In the final analysis, however, the adverse criticisms of the Indian

[1] F.O. 84/1391, Frere to Granville, 7 May 1873 enclosed 'Memorandum on Banians or natives of India in East Africa'.

[2] Bombay Archives, P.D. vol. 135 of 1868, Comp. 478, Churchill to Bombay, 22 Dec. 1867 and F.O. to Seward, 14 June 1867; P.D. vol. 280 of 1874, Comp. 1963, Kirk to Govt. of India, 12 Sept. 1874. India Archives, Foreign Dept.—Nov. 1866, Pros. 45–57, Pol. A, May 1867, Pros. 141–3, Pol. A, and June 1868, Pros. 54–7, Pol. A. These Proceedings reveal that in 1867, Fraser and Co. in Zanzibar held 711 slaves. See also Russell, op. cit., p. 141.

[3] F.O. 84/1391, Frere to Granville, memorandum by Kazi Shahabudin enclosed with Frere's memo. on the Indians in East Africa.

[4] See also R. W. Beachey, 'The Arms Trade in East Africa in the late 19th century', Journal of African History, iii. no. 3 (1962), 451–67. But allegations regarding Indian complicity in the slave trade continued virtually unchecked—notwithstanding the investigations of the Frere Mission. A popular contemporary view in this respect was expressed by Elton: 'Our Indian Banyan subjects are to be found in various localities on the Eastern seaboard;—anxious enough to "run" with the Arab slave dealer when dollars are tolerably safe, and forward enough to "hunt" with the representatives of our flag, and claim a British subject's rights if it serves their purpose . . .'. Elton, op. cit., p. iii.

community were to provide a precedent for the future and the tendency to use the Indians as a 'scapegoat' was to continue. But much more important in this respect was the legacy of nineteenth-century Zanzibar of a substantial Indian role in the life of East Africa. Already, on the eve of Partition, the Indians were an important element in the economic and political situation. From their small beginnings as seasonal traders, they had developed a vast network of commerce throughout the region by the later years of the century. The character of their association with East Africa had also undergone a gradual transition from the sporadic commercial contact of the early years to a more regular and committed association in the later years.

The interaction between the growth of the Indian role and that of British political influence in Zanzibar—since the establishment of the British Agency in Zanzibar in 1841, under the direction of the Bombay Government—attested to the political significance of the Indian 'factor'. Yet the predominance of British India in this interrelationship was to end in 1883, when the growing momentum of the scramble for Africa rendered the existing political arrangements untenable. In that year the prolonged control and patronage of the Zanzibar Agency by the Bombay Government from 1841 to 1873 and by the Government of India from 1873 to 1883 passed into the hands of the Imperial Government;[1] as also did the British Indian Post Office at Zanzibar a few years later.[2] An era seemed to have ended; but the new one was to build on the foundations provided by the former. The Imperial and British Indian link that had been forged in the nineteenth century was to persist well into the colonial period; and Indian enterprise followed, or sometimes preceded, the growth of British, and to a lesser extent of German, political influence in the interior of East Africa. The existing population of Indian merchants in Zanzibar and along the Coast was to provide the nucleus for such expansion of their activities into the interior. Already, on the eve of the Partition, Sir John Kirk was concerned that German paramountcy in Tanganyika would enable a 'rival nation' to utilize 'the trading capacities of our Indian subjects to advance and develop her commerce'—especially as Bagamoyo,

[1] India Archives, Foreign Dept.—May 1884, Pros. 29–71, A. Pol. E, I.O. to Govt. of India, 20 and 31 July 1883, and F.O. to Kirk, 19 July 1883.

[2] F.O. 84/2084, I.O. to F.O., 14 June 1890; and India Archives, Foreign Dept. —Nov. 1884, Pros. 520–5, Extl. A, July 1884, Pros. 161–2, A Pol. E, and May 1884, Pros. 29–71, A. Pol. E.

being the principal point for the arrival and departure of the ivory caravans, had a large concentration of the Indian merchants operating along the Coast.[1] In the British sphere, on the other hand, the existing British Indian role in East Africa formed the basis for major considerations of direct Indian involvement in the massive task of 'opening up' the interior.

[1] F.O. 84/1774, Kirk to Salisbury, 4 and 5 June 1886. In an earlier dispatch of 11 Mar. 1886 (F.O. 84/1773), Kirk referred to the German attempts to break the Arab domination of the ivory trade, and made the important observation that: 'Although Europeans are not likely to be able to compete with the Arabs in the ivory trade I am convinced that British Indians might open an advantageous business by dealing on the spot with those who now collect ivory in the distant interior and would gladly avoid the journey to the Coast if able to replenish their stores of goods at some central place inland.' This provides an important clue to the subsequent penetration of the interior of East Africa by the Indian traders during the 1890s.

CHAPTER II

Beginnings in the Interior

c. 1886 to c. 1902

THE Partition of East Africa in 1886 and the subsequent opening up of the interior under European administration was to have far-reaching implications for the traditional Indian association with the Coast. Indian economic activities in the Zanzibar sultanate had already greatly expanded during the nineteenth century, partly in association with the British diplomatic effort in the area. The direct British involvement in East Africa, while on the one hand replacing British Indian preponderance in Zanzibar affairs by the Imperial factor after 1883, on the other hand made the interior of East Africa accessible to Indian labour and enterprise to an unprecedented extent. While the old-established Indian firms rapidly took advantage of the protection afforded by European administration to extend their activities into the interior, other British Indian subjects were to be directly associated with the Imperial policy to open up and develop the territories. This in a sense marked a continuation and extension of the precedents set in Zanzibar during the nineteenth century, although the resources of the British empire in India could now be employed in East Africa on a much larger scale. The old British consulate in Zanzibar was a typical product of its times, and well up to the eve of the Partition its preoccupation lay largely with British Indian affairs. Apart from the fact that many of the Consuls were seconded from the Indian Civil Service, most of the clerks and subordinate staff were British Indian recruits—largely Parsees and Goans in the early days. In fact both in its organization and activities the consulate followed the British Indian pattern. The Partition of East Africa and the subsequent shift of emphasis to the interior enabled these precedents to be adopted on the mainland—providing as they did a ready-made framework for administrative policy. Many of the early officials, including those of the Imperial British East Africa Company, 1888–95, were men with British Indian experience and relied on the methods and precedents provided by such experience. The association of the British Indians in the massive task of opening up the interior was thus to proceed apace with the extension of British rule. And the resources of her empire in India gave Britain an initial advantage in Kenya and Uganda such as Germany lacked in Tanganyika.

The policy of Indian association with the Imperial effort in the interior received its first and rather tentative expression under the Imperial British East Africa Company. The Royal Charter in 1888 made specific mention of the fact that the possession of the mainland by the Company 'would be advantageous to the commercial and other interests of Our subjects in the Indian Ocean, who may otherwise become compelled to reside or trade under the government or protection of alien powers'.[1] In turn the Company's activities gained from the presence of Indian merchants and artisans—particularly at Mombasa. One of the Indian merchants who was later to distinguish himself in fact owed his career in East Africa to a contract with the Company in 1890 to recruit Indian workers and police for service in the Company's territories.[2] The Company also employed Indian administrative staff—usually Goan clerks and customs officials—at its various stations in the interior and along the Coast.[3] Similarly, while the Company largely depended on Sudanese and Swahili troops, a start was made in recruiting Indian troops. At first the Company employed the 17th Madras Sappers for military duties and during 1889–90 it sought the Government of India's permission to recruit 200 Sikhs for such duties as well as 200 artisans for telegraphic and railway works. The Indian Government opposed such sporadic recruitment—especially from the Punjab—but after Foreign Office urging permission was granted to recruit elsewhere in India.[4] Similarly Captain Lugard in his expedition to Uganda in 1891 was accompanied by a small escort of Indian troops; and Captain MacDonald during his survey for the Uganda Railway 1891–2 had an escort of forty-six Indians including soldiers, porters, a

---

[1] Extract from the *London Gazette,* 7 Sept. 1888, in C.O. pamphlet no. 1, ref. 10942.

[2] See pp. 53–5, below, and P. L. McDermott, *British East Africa or IBEA* (London, 1893), pp. 210–11.

[3] *Reports relating to the Administration of the E.A. Protectorate,* Cd. 2740 (1905), p. 2, and C.O. 533/19, Jackson to Elgin, 20 and 22 Dec. 1906, enclosures.

[4] F.O. 2/117, 'Employment of Indian Troops in the Protectorates, 1889–1896', I.O. to F.O., 24 Jan. 1890, and IBEA Company to F.O. 10 Feb. 1890; India Archives, Foreign Dept.—Oct. 1889, Pros. 10–15, Extl. A. See also p. 29, n. 3 below.

surveyor, a draughtsman, and a hospital assistant—although his original request to the Government of India for 100 Punjabi troops was turned down.[1] The Company also raised a contingent of Indian police for its expedition to Witu. Between 1891 and 1893 the contingent was stationed at Witu and some of it at other coastal ports— Mombasa, Kismayu, Lamu, and Malindi—and it functioned as the principal law-enforcing agency.[2]

Perhaps more significant in revealing the importance of the British Indian association were the series of proposals made by various officials at this time concerning the development of East Africa by Indian indentured workers and agriculturists. As early as 1890 the Company had made direct but unsuccessful representations to the Government of India seeking permission to import Indian labourers and asking for East Africa to be placed in the same category as Ceylon and the Straits Settlements to which such emigration was permitted under the Indian Emigration Act of 1883.[3] The request to the Government of India was later repeated by Sir Gerald Portal in September 1891, but owing to pressure of other work the matter was allowed to lapse until taken up again by Sir Arthur Hardinge in 1895, when he felt that the question of Indian immigration had assumed 'more vital importance than formerly to the future commercial welfare' of, particularly, Zanzibar.[4] Similarly the question of settling indentured Indian agriculturists in East Africa was much canvassed during this period—particularly as it was felt that both the climate and the presence of the Indian commercial community would facilitate the task of the Indian agriculturists. Sir John Kirk had in fact earlier discussed a similar scheme with the firm of Jairam

---

[1] F.O. 2/256, I.O. to F.O., 31 Jan. 1899, enclosing Govt. of India to I.O., 27 Oct. 1898—also printed in F.O.C.P. no. 7400, pp. 108–12; and J. R. L. McDonald, *Soldiering and Surveying in British East Africa* (London, 1897), pp. 3–5.

[2] H. Moyse-Bartlett, *The King's African Rifles* (London, 1957), pp. 96–8; *Handbook of Kenya Colony and Protectorate* 1920 (London, 1921), p. 457; and P. L. McDermott, op. cit., pp. 97–8.

[3] F.O. 2/671, I.O. to F.O., 23 Oct. 1895, enclosures: MacKinnon, Mackenzie, & Co. (IBEA Company agents in India) to Govt. of India, 25 Aug. 1890 and Govt. of India to Mackinnon, Mackenzie, & Co., 21 Oct. 1890; F.O. 2/256, I.O. to F.O., 31 Jan. 1899, enclosing Govt. of India to I.O., 27 Oct. 1898; India Archives, Foreign Dept.—Feb. 1889, Pros. 100–1, Extl. A, and Oct. 1889, Pros. 10–15, Extl. A. See also Bombay Archives, P. D. vol. 134 of 1895, Comp. 107, Govt. of India to Mackinnon, Mackenzie, & Co., 21 Oct. 1890 and related proceedings.

[4] I.O. Emigration—Jan. 1896, Pros. 7–8, file 63 of 1895, p. 19, Hardinge to Govt. of India, 6 Sept. 1895.

Sewji to finance Indian agricultural settlement in Zanzibar.[1] From the very beginning, the directors of the Company similarly contemplated 'the colonisation of the vast unoccupied areas adjacent to the Coast with British Indian families of the agricultural class'.[2] And the matter was raised again by the Company in 1892: 'The question of immigration from India appears to the directors to be one of great importance with a view to the colonization of trained agriculturists of the unoccupied districts of the Company's territories.'[3] Similarly Sir Charles Euan Smith, the Consul-General in Zanzibar, after a visit to the Kilimanjaro district in 1893, in which he was accompanied by an Indian surveyor, recommended the area for Indian agricultural settlement.[4] In Zanzibar also the question of importing Indian agriculturists, particularly in view of the decline of some of the larger Arab plantations, continued to be raised throughout the 1890s.[5] Perhaps the thinking of the time was best explained by Lugard:

> From the overcrowded provinces of India especially, colonists might be drawn, and this would effect a relief to congested districts. From them we could draw labourers, both artizans and coolies, while they might also afford a recruiting ground for soldiers and police. The wants, moreover, of these more civilized settlers would . . . very greatly add to the imports, and the products of their industry to the exports. . . . Moreover, the methods of agriculture . . . would soon be imitated by the African.[6]

Such considerations—and they did not of course materialize—were not confined to the British sphere alone. German authorities, perhaps taking their cue from British policy and from the advantages of Indian mercantile activity in the area, similarly sought the immigration of Indians to help in the process of the development of

[1] *Report of the Committee on Emigration from India to the Crown Colonies and Protectorates*, Part II, *Minutes of Evidence*, Cd. 5193 (1910), p. 238.

[2] P. L. MacDermott, op. cit., pp. 217–18.

[3] *Zanzibar Gazette*, 29 June 1892, p. 6.

[4] F.O.C.P. no. 6454, Euan Smith to Rosebery, 7 Apr. 1893, pp. 138–43.

[5] I. O. Emigration—Jan. 1896, Pros. 7–8, file 63 of 1895 and file 8 of 1896, part A; Jan. 1897, Pros. 3–4, file 18, part A; and Jan. 1898, Pros. 5, file 5, part B. In 1892, the Govt. of India 'expressed its willingness to allow under certain conditions the importation of coolies from India to Zanzibar'. See *Zanzibar Gazette*, 17 Feb. 1892, p. 1. Subsequent discussion for the importation of Indian coolies for plantation work in Zanzibar revealed that these conditions revolved largely around assurances of proper treatment—the Govt. of India insisting that the plantation workers be recruited on the same agreements as the Uganda Railway coolies. See I.O. Emigration—Oct. 1896, Pros. 1, file 8, p. 1067.

[6] F. D. Lugard, *Rise of Our East African Empire* (London, 1893), i. 488–9. See also Lugard, *The Dual Mandate in British Tropical Africa* (London, 1929), p. 41.

Tanganyika. The matter was taken up in earnest in 1894, when representations were made to the Foreign Office in London to encourage the emigration of Indian artisans and agriculturists to German East Africa in order to supplement the activities of the existing commercial population. In transmitting the request to the India Office, the Foreign Office wrote:

> The question of employing Indian labour in the German Protectorate in East Africa has been repeatedly advanced recently. . . . It is a well-known fact that, amongst the population engaged in connection with commercial enterprises in East Africa, the Indian element is largely represented, and Indian emigrants are therefore sure to meet countrymen with whom to find support, if necessary.

But the regulations relating to the 'Importation and Treatment of East Asiatic Labourers' issued in German East Africa included a clause that provided for flogging as a punishment, which was enough to deter the Government of India from sanctioning the emigration of Indian labourers.[1] The Indian Emigration Act of 1883, however, placed no restrictions on voluntary travellers, and skilled workers could still be recruited for German East Africa—especially for work on railway construction—as the German Consul in Bombay found in 1894. But later in the year he sought to ignore the ban on the emigration of indentured workers by attempting to ship 600 labourers from the Portuguese port of Goa. This caused considerable concern to the Bombay Government—especially in view of the subsequent report that twenty-one Indian artisans recruited from Ajmer for service on the German East Africa Railway had arrived in Zanzibar from Tanga in destitute circumstances[2].

The initial reluctance of the Government of India to sanction the emigration of indentured Indian workers—as evident in the unsuccessful bids by the Imperial British East Africa Company in 1890, by German East Africa in 1894, and one by the Congo Free State in

[1] As the F.O. wrote to the I.O., 11 Apr. 1894: 'There is one Regulation to which the Government of India would certainly not assent, and that is the provision . . . empowering an employer to inflict corporal chastisement on his male labourers.' See also F.O. to I.O., 10 Mar. 1894 in I.O. Emigration—Aug. 1895, Pros. 1–4, file 38, part A, and Bombay Archives, P.D. vol. 134 of 1895, Comp. 356, which contains detailed proceedings in this respect.

[2] I.O. Emigration—June 1895, Pros. 7, file 38, part B; Aug. 1895, Pros. 1, 3–4, file 38, pp. 409, 417, Hardinge to Bombay Govt., 8 Mar. 1895. See also Bombay Archives, P.D. vol. 134 of 1895, Comp. 356, Hardinge to Bombay Govt., 8 Mar. 1895 and attached papers.

1895[1]—owed much to the past abuses of the indenture system in other colonies and to the political difficulties created by such emigration.[2] But equally the precedent for the employment of indentured Indian labour in the colonies had existed since the system first began in 1834,[3] and with the growing demands for labour in East Africa the application of the system to the East African territories became increasingly irresistible. The Government of India finally sanctioned the emigration of indentured Indian labour to East Africa after the decision to construct the Uganda Railway was taken in 1895.

When the proposals for the construction of the Uganda Railway were first mooted, the question of labour caused considerable concern. Sir Guilford Molesworth pointed out in 1891 that the need for labour would be 'a factor of considerable doubt and difficulty . . . it is probable that, at all events for skilled labour, it will be necessary to depend on imported labour'.[4] In the following year Captain MacDonald recommended that 'for the first two years of construction the bulk of the labour would have to be imported from India'.[5] When the decision to build the Uganda Railway was finally taken in 1895 it was decided to construct it 'upon the Indian methods and chiefly by means of Indian coolies'.[6] In fact the Railway Committee appointed by the Foreign Office 'arrived at the conclusion that it would be hopeless to expect that the railway could be constructed at any reasonable cost and speed unless they were allowed to recruit Indian labour freely',[7] and also indent upon India for the various materials, rolling stock, etc. Accordingly, negotiations were opened in October 1895, with the India Office seeking every facility in the recruitment of labour in India for the Uganda Railway. These were to continue well into 1896 when the Government of India finally issued a Notification in May, amending the Indian Emigration Act, and legalizing emigration to East Africa—specifically for the

[1] F.O. 2/671, I.O. to F.O., 23 Oct. 1895, and enclosures, and Bombay Archives, P.D. vol. 134 of 1895, Comp. 107.

[2] For a detailed discussion, see I. M. Cumpston, *Indians Overseas in British Territories 1834–1854* (Oxford, 1953), pp. 174, 179, *passim*.

[3] Cumpston, ibid.

[4] *Final Report of the Uganda Railway Committee*, Cd. 2164 (1904), p. 3.

[5] Quoted in Hill, *Permanent Way* (1949), i. 86.

[6] Cd. 2164 (1904), op. cit., p. 7.

[7] F.O.C.P. no. 7040, F.O. to I.O., 30 Jan. 1897, p. 10. Copy of this letter and departmental minutes also in Bombay Archives, G.D. vol. 142 C of 1897, Comp. 671, part I, 'Emigration of Coolies to Africa'.

construction of the Railway and under three-year contract terms as approved by the Government of India.[1]

Meanwhile, however, preliminary arrangements were made by the Railway Committee with the Government of India to start immediate recruitment for labour in India. An experienced engineer and a medical officer with sufficient hospital staff were acquired on 'loan' from the Government of India; and these officers were in the first instance engaged in selecting labour. By January 1896 the first batch of about 1,000 Indian indentured workers—including a proportion of blacksmiths, carpenters, and masons—arrived in Mombasa. Another batch of Indian surveyors, draughtsmen, accountants, clerks, and overseers with a few European officers reached Mombasa in February 1896. These Indian recruits were engaged on contract terms approved by the Government of India.[2]

Subsequently, private Indian contractors took up the job of recruiting indentured workers for the Uganda Railway—mainly from the north-western areas, with Lahore serving as the principal recruiting centre. The most important among them were A. M. Jeevanjee and Hussein Bux—the latter operating on the basis of a letter from the Chief Engineer of the Railway, Sir George Whitehouse, to the British India Steam Navigation Company in Bombay, dated 28 February 1896, which stated: 'the Bearer Mr. Hossen Bux has been commissioned by me to bring more labour to Africa for the Uganda Railway. He will call upon you to arrange passages and dates of sailing and fares and freights will be paid here through Smith, Mackenzie & Co.'[3] Later, in April 1896 the Protector of Emigrants at Bombay reported that shiploads of coolies recruited by Jeevanjee were arriving in Bombay from Karachi for trans-shipment to Mombasa: 'I understand that one or two batches of coolies have

[1] F.O. 2/671, 'Coolie Emigration from India to African Protectorates 1895–1902', I.O. to F.O., 23 Oct. 1895, I.O. to Govt. of India, 31 Oct. 1895, and Hardinge to Salisbury, 24 Aug. 1900. See also F.O.C.P. no. 7040, pp. 11–12, and I.O. Emigration—Dec. 1895, Pros. 11–12, file 64 of 1890, part A, Govt. of India to I.O., 17 Dec. 1895. For details of discussions between the F.O., I.O., and the Govt. of India, see especially I.O. Emigration—July 1896, Pros. 9–17, file 38 of 1895, F.O. to I.O., 11 Oct. 1895, pp. 783–8; and July 1896, Pros. 18–55, file 2, pp. 789–853.

[2] I.O. Emigration—July 1896, op. cit., and F. L. O'Callaghan, 'Uganda Railway', *Professional Papers of the Corps of Royal Engineers, 1900*, xxvi, Paper VIII, C.O. pamphlet no. 7, ref. P. 10554.

[3] Bombay Archives, G.D. vol. 119 C of 1896, Comp. 671, Part I, copy of Whitehouse to B.I.S.N. Co., 28 Feb. 1896, and P.D. vol. 143 of 1896, Comp. 902, Protector of Emigrants, Bombay, to Bombay Govt., 27 Apr. 1896.

already been sent from Kurrachee . . . and that Messrs. A. M. Jeevanjee & Co. are actively recruiting in the N.W. provinces for more men.'[1] But during April–May 1896 a batch of coolies shipped by Jeevanjee from Karachi was held up in Bombay for irregular contracts and was allowed to sail for Mombasa only after telegraphic assurance from Whitehouse that they were intended for the Uganda Railway.[2]

The Government of India, however, objected to such haphazard recruitment and sought to enforce strict regulations—as it pointed out in a dispatch to the Bombay Government:

Cases have occurred in which native artizans have been recruited in India for service in the East African Colonies . . . under agreements, or promises which have not been fulfilled . . . although the Government of India have no desire to interfere with the emigration of native traders and others who are in a position to take care of their own interests . . . it is necessary to provide for the protection of artizans and labourers.[3]

Consequently in June 1896 the Government of India objected to the existing form of agreements under which labour was recruited for the Uganda Railway and laid down new conditions which included: (i) maximum term of service to be three years, (ii) the nature of work to be specified in the contract, (iii) a minimum wage of Rs. 15 per month plus rations—remuneration not to be based on task work, (iv) payment to begin no later than date of embarkation, and (v) an indefeasible right to return passage.[4] Detailed discussions were then held in connection with these conditions and finally in September 1896 a revised form of agreement for indentured workers was issued by the Foreign Office. This met most of the requirements of the Government of India except that the minimum wage was

[1] Bombay Archives, G.D. vol. 119 C of 1896, Comp. 671, Part I, Protector of Emigrants, Karachi, to Bombay Govt., 1 Apr. 1896. Similarly the customs officer at Mombasa reported to Bombay Govt., 5 Oct. 1896, that a large number of Indian coolies recruited by private contractors were arriving in Mombasa. See Bombay Archives, P.D. vol. 143 of 1896, Comp. 902.

[2] I.O. Emigration—July 1896, Pros. 18–55, file 2, p. 799; and Bombay Archives, G.D. vol. 119 C of 1896, Comp. 671, Part I, Protector of Emigrants, Karachi, to Bombay Govt., 1 Apr. 1896, and Protector of Emigrants, Karachi, to Commissioner of Customs, Bombay, 18 May 1896.

[3] F.O.C.P. no. 7040, F.O. to I.O., 30 Jan. 1897, p. 10; and Bombay Archives, G.D. vol. 120 C of 1896, Comp. 671, Part II, Govt. of India to Bombay Govt., 27 May 1896.

[4] *Final Report of the Uganda Railway Committee*, Cd. 2164 (1904), pp. 11–12.

fixed at Rs. 12 per month.[1] Meanwhile the Bombay Government had opposed the appointment of Hussein Bux as the recruiting agent in India for the Uganda Railway, and in June 1896 he was replaced by Messrs. Grindlay, Groom, & Co. as the Railway's agents in Bombay. Private contractors, however, evidently continued to recruit and ship workers to East Africa.[2]

The revised form of agreement for the Uganda Railway workers adopted in September 1896, however, soon came under attack for it was found to be 'wholly impracticable to induce the labourers to perform a fair and reasonable amount of work'. The Foreign Office, pressed on by the Railway Committee, urged the India Office to accept drastic changes in the existing terms of service in order to ensure greater efficiency of the labour force.[3] Further discussions between the India and Foreign Offices between October 1896 and March 1897 were then held and a new form of agreement was finally adopted. This gave the Chief Engineer powers of fine and dismissal in the case of unsatisfactory or incompetent coolies, and also allowed for their employment under a system of task- or piece-work whereby a premium was paid over and above the minimum

[1] I.O. Emigration—Sept. 1896, Pros. 12–23, file 2, pp. 1039–55, contain details of correspondence between F.O., I.O., and Govt. of India regarding the new form of agreement. See also Bombay Archives, G.D. vol. 120 C of 1896, Comp. 671, Part II, copy of F.O. to I.O., 31 July 1896.

[2] I.O. Emigration—July 1896, Pros. 18–55, file 2, pp. 789, 799; and Bombay Archives, P.D. vol. 143 of 1896, Comp. 902, and G.D. vol. 119 C of 1896, Comp. 671, Part I, Protector of Emigrants, Karachi, to Commissioner of Customs, Bombay, 18 May 1896. See also p. 37, below.

[3] F.O.C.P. no. 7040, F.O. to I.O., 30 Jan. 1897, pp. 10–11. As the F.O. explained, the average output of work by the coolies was only 24·4 cubic feet per man —'or less than half of what might fairly be expected of them' in India. The Chief Engineer of the Railway was unable 'to devise any means (under the existing contracts) by which the men can be got to perform a reasonable day's work. They have been offered petty contracts . . . and bonus for doing anything over a certain amount but without effect. The coolie . . . so far appears to be master of the situation'—for there was no provision in the agreement for punishment, except repatriation to India. This was hardly helpful: 'The right of repatriation being, within a period of six months from date of discharge, absolute, any dissatisfied labourer has only to provoke the Chief Engineer into dismissing him, can then engage in other works, and after this considerable period, can claim a free return passage, possibly without having done a single day's work for the railway. Engagements may even be entered into by persons with the sole object of thus gaining a free passage to Africa.' In the circumstances the F.O. urged that in the case of dismissal for misconduct or incompetency, the coolie should 'return to India at once, if at all, and not at his convenience'; while the Chief Engineer should be given additional powers to impose fines and other punishment. These conditions were subsequently accepted by the Government of India.

wage for extra work.[1] The new terms of employment proved to be satisfactory, for the Railway found that the system of task-work gave the coolies an inducement to work harder.[2]

Recruitment of Indian labour for the Uganda Railway was, however, severely affected by the outbreak of plague in India and the prohibition of emigration from the ports of Bombay and Karachi in March 1897. For a time, therefore, the Railway had to import labour from the distant port of Calcutta. In May, Grindlay, Groom, & Co. at Calcutta were appointed to act as the Railway's agents there and to recruit labour from Bengal and the eastern provinces, which were not subject to the plague prohibitions enforced by the Government of India.[3] But, because of difficulties in finding recruits in this area, special permission had to be obtained in July to recruit labour in the Punjab.[4] Subsequently, in August 1897, after further urging from the Foreign Office, emigration, specifically for the Uganda Railway, was permitted from the port of Karachi.[5] From then on, Karachi rather than Bombay became the principal centre for the recruitment and shipment of the coolies. The Railway Committee negotiated with the British India Steam Navigation Co. for a direct shipping connection between Karachi and Mombasa, instead of trans-shipment at Bombay as was the practice, and in December 1897 an agency of the Railway was established at Karachi.[6] Most of the work connected with the coolie emigration for the Railway and the supply of materials from India now came to be performed by the agent at Karachi. A sub-agency was also established at Lahore in order to exploit fully the resources of the 'coolie recruiting grounds

---

[1] I.O. Emigration—Mar. 1897, Pros. 7–11, file 10, p. 443; and Apr. 1897, Pros. 5–8, file 10, p. 101, contain copy of the revised form of agreement.

[2] *Report on the Uganda Railway by Sir Guilford Molesworth*, 28 Mar. 1899, C. 9331 (1899), p. 20.

[3] I.O. Emigration—May 1897, Pros. 10–39, file 10, p. 469, Govt. of India special Notification of 24 Apr. 1897; and Mar. 1897, Pros. 1–6, file 5, p. 435, Govt. of India Notification of 6 Mar. 1897.

[4] I.O. Emigration—July 1897, Pros. 35–7, file 10, p. 783, Messrs. Grindlay, Groom, & Co. to Bengal Govt., 7 July 1897, and details of departmental action thereon.

[5] I.O. Emigration—Sept. 1897, Pros. 8–14, file 10, p. 1009, F.O. to I.O., 2 Aug. 1897, I.O. to Govt. of India, 23 Aug. 1897, and Govt. of India Notification of 26 Aug. 1897.

[6] I.O. Emigration—Oct. 1897, Pros. 6–9, file 10, pp. 1097–9; Jan. 1898, Pros. 35–43, file 10, pp. 559–66, F.O. to I.O., 17 Dec. 1897; Feb. 1898, Pros. 7, file 21, pp. 591–6; and July 1898, Pros. 5–12, file 21, p. 791. See also Bombay Archives, G.D. vol. 178 C of 1898, Comp. 671, Bombay Govt. to Govt. of India, 15 Dec. 1897, and copy of F.O. to I.O., 17 Dec. 1897.

of the Upper Punjab'. The whole process of recruitment and shipment of labour was perhaps best explained by the Protector of Emigrants at Karachi:

In the early days paid recruiters were sent into the districts, but now that the popularity of the Uganda Railway amongst the Coolies has gained ground this is found to be unnecessary. Jemadars [headmen] apply to the Recruiting Agent [at Lahore] for work, and they are told to bring 100 men who, if passed by the doctor, are taken on, and the Jemadar is put in charge of the gang on a monthly salary of Rs. 25. The coolies get 3 annas a day till they embark and receive one month's pay in advance before proceeding to Budapur [the segregation camp]. The greatest care is taken . . . to prevent fraudulent enlistment . . . but it is impossible to stop youths who run away from home, or bad characters, from giving false names and addresses.[1]

From Lahore the coolies were carried in special trains to the segregation camp at Budapur and from there direct to their chartered steamers at Karachi.

In spite, therefore, of initial difficulties the recruitment and shipment of indentured workers for the Uganda Railway steadily increased after 1896 and was to continue until 1901. During this period about 32,000 Indian workers were recruited for service on the Uganda Railway on three-year contract terms and at an average overall cost of Rs. 30 per month per coolie.[2] The principal attraction for these voluntary recruits to proceed to East Africa lay of course in the prospect of obtaining employment and earning more than they could for the same kind of work in India. In fact notwithstanding the considerable hardships of construction work and the hazards of the ' Jigger' pest, or the man-eating lions of Tsavo,[3] about ten to fifteen per cent of the coolies renewed their contracts or returned later on fresh indentures. This was partly due to direct encouragement from the Railway officials, as the general manager of the Railway later explained: 'if he is a good man we tell him " you go back; if you wish

---

[1] Bombay Archives, G.D. vol. 278 of 1901, Comp. 120, report of the Protector of Emigrants, Karachi, for the year 1900-1. See also Cd. 2164 (1904), p. 12. An earlier report by the Protector of Emigrants, Karachi, for 1899–1900 showed that most of the emigration for the Uganda Railway now took place from the port of Karachi. Between 1895 and 1900, only 5,280 labourers and artisans for the Railway were shipped from Bombay, while 20,835 were shipped from Karachi. See Bombay Archives, G.D. vol. 245 C of 1900, Comp. 120.

[2] Cd. 2164 (1904), pp. 12–13.

[3] J. H. Patterson, *The Man Eaters of Tsavo* (London, 1907), pp. 340–1.

to come back to us, go to Karachi, come along and when you arrive in Mombasa we will refund you your passage".'[1]

The large-scale influx of Indian immigrants raised acute problems of organization. As Sir Guilford Molesworth explained in 1899: 'The construction of this railway involves an organization equivalent to the maintenance of an alien army, amounting now to 15,000 men, in a practically waterless country and devoid of resources, and of all means of animal or wheeled transport.'[2] At first supplies of provisions and rations had to be imported and a special commissariat was set up for the purpose. Similarly extensive medical facilities had to be organized and a police force raised. In fact every aspect of organization necessitated the employment of additional Indian staff ranging from assistant surgeons to water-carriers, so that both in the construction work and in the ancillary services there was an increasing demand for Indian staff. In fact about 5,000 subordinate Indian employees were recruited during this period in addition to the coolies—both to help the process of construction and later the running of the Railway in a variety of capacities. Similarly, a number of Indians came to East Africa on their own, mostly as traders, but some of them obtained employment on the Railway as petty contractors. As Whitehouse explained in April 1898: 'Masons, Carpenters, Blacksmiths, coolies are in constant request and there must be some 40 or 50 small contractors on the Railway with from 30 to 200 coolies each. The rates of Earth-work are high and the profits large but then on the other hand the discomforts they undergo are considerable and there are difficulties in obtaining food and water.'[3]

Most of the coolies and artisans employed on the Uganda Railway, however, were officially sponsored immigrants and came largely from the Punjab—a majority of them being Muslims. Others

---

[1] Cd. 5193 (1910), p. 70; see also pp. 236–42, Kirk's evidence, and *Report on the Uganda Railway by Sir Guilford Molesworth*, C. 9331 (1899), p. 20, where he states that many of the coolies applied to be re-engaged after the expiry of their three-year contracts.

[2] Cd. 9331 (1899), p. 13.

[3] Mombasa Provincial Archives, shelf 66, file 11: 'Uganda Railway Inward 1898–1900', Whitehouse to Crauford, 12 Apr. 1898, enclosed report on immigration of bona-fide immigrants into Mombasa. Copy of report also in I.O. Emigration—June 1898, Pros. 7–8, file 7, part B; and Bombay Archives, G.D. vol. 179 C of 1898, Comp. 671, Part III, enclosed in Hardinge to Govt. of India, 19 May 1898. For additional details regarding the growing demands for Indian manpower, see also Report of the Protector of Emigrants, Bombay, 1 Mar. 1899, in I.O. Emigration—Apr. 1899, Pros. 3–8, file 24, p. 667; C. 9331 (1899), op. cit., pp. 13–14; Cd. 2164 (1904), op. cit., p. 28.

originated from the Bombay Presidency, Sindh, Baluchistan, and the North-Western Frontier districts.[1] And it was this 'alien army' of Indian indentured workers, artisans, and subordinate staff generally that under the direction of British officials and experts executed almost all the work in connection with the construction of the Uganda Railway.[2] The indentured Indian immigrants, however, represented essentially a short-lived influx of Indians into East Africa. Of the 32,000 imported for the construction of the Railway, 16,312 returned to India at the expiry of their contracts, 2,493 died, while 6,454 were invalided home after being incapacitated by disease or mishaps at work—thus leaving a balance of 6,724 who failed to avail themselves of their contractual right to free repatriation to their homes.[3] But the real significance of their role in East Africa, apart from the construction of the Railway itself, lies in the impetus their officially sponsored immigration, and the Indian presence in the interior initiated by it, provided for the future Indian immigration into East Africa. For in addition to the coolies, and partly because of

[1] Whitehouse's report on the immigration of bona fide immigrants into Mombasa, Apr. 1898, in Mombasa Provincial Archives, op. cit., and Bombay Archives, G.D. vol. 245 C of 1900, Comp. 120, Administration report of the Protector of Emigrants, Karachi, for the year 1899–1900. These reports show that the Indian immigrants originated from various scattered parts of India— and occasionally from Afghanistan. An overwhelming majority of them—more than the combined total for all other areas—however, originated from the Punjab and the N.W. Frontier Province, with the Bombay Presidency taking the second place. Most of these immigrants were, of course, labourers; but there were also a large number of artisans who seemed to specialize in an interesting variety of jobs: blacksmiths, boilermakers, brickmakers, carpenters, fitters, firemen, hammer-men, jungle-cutters, masons, pointsmen, etc.

[2] See, for example, Col. T. Gracey's report on the Uganda Railway in *Correspondence respecting the Uganda Railway*, Cd. 670 (1901).

[3] *Final Report of the Uganda Railway Committee*, Cd. 2164 (1904), pp. 12–13. The detailed figures given in this report are:

Year	Number of coolies imported	Number repatriated	Number invalided	Deaths
1896–7	4,269	..	200	121
1897–8	7,131	..	705	340
1898–9	15,593	773	1,206	611
1899–1900	23,379	2,761	3,424	1,164
1900–1	31,646	4,109	5,811	1,984
1901–2	31,983	9,616	6,354	2,367
1902–3	31,983	16,312	6,454	2,493
	(Totals)			

them, the institutions of British India were increasingly transplanted along the Uganda Railway during this period: Indian laws, Indian police, Indian postal and currency systems, as well as Indian administrative practices. As Sir Harry Johnston explained in 1899:

I wonder if in England the importance of one aspect of this Railway construction has been realized? It means the driving of a wedge of India two miles broad right across East Africa from Mombasa to Victoria Nyanza. Fifteen thousand coolies, some hundreds of Indian clerks, draughtsmen, mechanics, surveyors and policemen are . . . carrying the Indian penal code, the Indian postal system, Indian coinage, Indian clothing, right across these wastes, deserts, forests and swamps. . . .[1]

This process was accelerated by the employment of British Indian troops and subordinate staff for the establishment and extension of British administration in Kenya and Uganda, and to a lesser extent in Zanzibar. The practice of employing Indian troops started rather tentatively with the I.B.E.A. Company, when some Indian soldiers and army surveyors were recruited for employment in East Africa. But the real precedent for the employment of selected British Indian troops, especially the Sikhs, had been established under Sir Harry Johnston in Central Africa.[2] And this precedent was followed in East Africa in August 1895, when a special Indian contingent was raised consisting of 300 Punjabi (Sikh and Muslim) volunteers from the Indian Army regiments. The main attraction of service in East Africa for these volunteers was, as with the coolies, the prospect of enhanced pay—in the case of the soldiers Rs. 18 per month. This Indian contingent arrived in Mombasa in December 1895 on a three-year tour of duty and was employed largely on police duties for the Uganda Railway, the Government caravans, and in the Coast Province—where the Administration had inherited the intransigence of the Mazrui and the Ogaden Somali from the Company.[3] Indian military presence in the country became particularly evident after the outbreak of the Mazrui rebellion towards

[1] F.O. 2/204, Johnston to Salisbury, 13 Oct. 1899. Also quoted in R. Oliver, *Sir Harry Johnston and the Scramble for Africa* (London, 1959), p. 293. Some idea of the extensive Indian presence generated by the construction of the Railway can also be gained from J. H. Patterson, op. cit., *passim.*

[2] R. Oliver, op. cit., pp. 195, 217, 257–8, *passim*; and F.O. 2/256, I.O. to F.O., 31 Jan. 1899, enclosing Govt. of India to I.O., 27 Oct. 1898—also printed in F.O.C.P. no. 7400, pp. 108–12.

[3] F.O. 2/117, I.O. to F.O., 23 Aug. 1895, 1 Apr. 1896, and 25 Mar. 1896, enclosing Govt. of India to I.O., 5 Feb. 1896; and F.O. 2/171, Hardinge to Salisbury, 24 Sept. 1898, enclosing report on the Indian contingent by Capt. W. Barratt, dated 17 Sept. 1898.

the end of 1895. The situation rapidly deteriorated early in 1896 after the Mazrui sacked Malindi and the local forces composed of the Swahili and Sudanese troops and the Indian contingent were unable to control the revolt. Reinforcements were then sought from India; and the 700-strong 24th Bombay Infantry was dispatched to Mombasa in March 1896—fully equipped for field service. From March to July the 24th Bombay Infantry was engaged in a series of operations against the Mazrui and their allies, and it returned to India in the latter month after the collapse of the Mazrui revolt.[1] Similarly in August 1896 Indian military reinforcements were dispatched to Zanzibar—consisting of an infantry detachment from the existing East Africa Indian contingent—and they helped to control the succession crisis there until November 1896.[2]

The most serious military problem at this time was raised by the mutiny of the Sudanese troops in Uganda in 1897. The forces in Uganda under Major MacDonald at the time consisted of thirty Sikhs, who had been recruited in May–June 1897 to form a military transport service for Uganda,[3] apart from a larger number of Swahili and Sudanese troops. In November 1897, 150 men of the East Africa Indian contingent were dispatched to Uganda to help contain the critical situation arising out of the mutiny of the Sudanese troops, and their arrival was greeted with obvious relief by the Uganda government officials.[4] At the same time additional reinforcements were sought from India; and the 27th Bombay Infantry was dispatched to East Africa in December 1897.[5] As its Commanding

[1] F.O. 2/117, F.O. to I.O., 20 Feb. 1896, F.O. to Cave, 21 and 26 Feb. 1896, Govt. of India to I.O., 25 Feb. and 3 Mar. 1896, Hardinge to F.O., 15 Mar. 1896: all telegrams; and F.O. 2/429, I.O. to F.O., 9 Aug. 1900, enclosing Govt. of India to I.O., 5 July 1900.

[2] F.O. 2/117, Cave to Salisbury, telegram, 26 Aug. 1896; and F.O. 2/143, Hardinge to Salisbury, 29 Mar. 1897, and F.O. to I.O., 30 Apr. 1897. See also F.O. 2/171, Hardinge to Salisbury, 24 Sept. 1898, enclosing Capt. Barratt's report on the Indian contingent, dated 17 Sept. 1898.

[3] F.O. 2/143, I.O. to F.O., 11 Aug. 1897, enclosing Govt. of India to I.O., 14 July 1897; and F.O. 2/170, Intelligence Division to F.O., 1 June 1898.

[4] F.O. 2/143, Salisbury to Cave, 21 Nov. 1897, and Cave to Salisbury, 22 Nov. 1897; Uganda Archives, Entebbe, 'Staff Correspondence Inward 1898', vol. i, Capt. Sitwell to H.M. Commissioner, 19 Jan. 1898, and P. C. Unyoro to H.M. Commissioner, 23 and 31 Jan. 1898. The Provincial Commissioner referred to the 'double effect' the arrival of Indian reinforcements had, both for the operations against the mutineers and in exercising 'a very good moral effect' on the other troops in Uganda.

[5] F.O. 2/143, I.O. to Viceroy, telegram, 22 Nov. 1897, Viceroy to I.O., telegrams, 26 and 29 Nov. 1897, and Salisbury to Cave, 2 Dec. 1897.

Officer later explained: 'At this time urgent appeals for help
from Uganda were received all along the line by successive detachments [of the 27th Bombay Infantry] who in order to save the
Protectorate . . . left their food rations behind and lived on roots and
plantations.'[1] The detachments reached Kampala during March to
July 1898; and until its return to India in May 1899, the 27th Bombay
Infantry engaged in a series of successful operations in the Protectorate.[2] In view of its services, its Commanding Officer later
recommended that the regiment be allowed to wear the motto
'Primus in Equatoria Africa'—which, however, did not meet with
the approval of the Commander-in-Chief, partly because of 'its
doubtful Latinity'.[3]

Meanwhile the revolt of Kabaka Mwanga and the threat of the
Ogaden Somali to Kismayu necessitated additional reinforcement
from India; and the Government of India dispatched a wing (360
troops—mostly Sikhs) of the 4th Bombay Infantry to East Africa in
March 1898. This wing was employed both in Jubaland and Uganda
until January 1899 when it returned to India.[4] The demands on the
military resources of India in fact greatly increased at this time. The
Imperial government decided to raise a special Indian contingent
for Uganda, while a new contingent needed to be raised to replace
the Indian contingent in East Africa at the expiry of its tour in 1898.[5]
The Government of India was reluctant to meet these increasing
demands; as the Commander-in-Chief pointed out: 'These calls on
India are increasing in frequency and in numbers asked for. . . .
We cannot spare Sikhs and Punjabi Mohammedans without in-
juriously affecting our own military establishments.'[6] At any rate

[1] F.O. 2/429, I.O. to F.O., 9 Aug. 1900, enclosing Govt. of India to I.O.,
5 July 1900.
[2] F.O. 2/429, ibid.; and F.O. 2/256, I.O. to F.O., 27 Mar. 1899.
[3] F.O. 2/429, op. cit.
[4] F.O. 2/170, I.O. to Viceroy, 18 Feb. 1898, Viceroy to I.O., 21 Feb. 1898,
F.O. to I.O., 22 Feb. 1898, and Crauford to F.O., 8 Mar. 1898: all telegrams;
F.O. 2/171, Hardinge to Salisbury, 8 Oct. 1898; and F.O. 2/256, Crauford to
Salisbury, 11 Jan. 1899.
[5] F.O. 2/143, I.O. to Govt. of India, 8 Dec. 1897; and F.O. 2/170, F.O. to I.O.,
25 Jan. 1898, and Hardinge to Salisbury, 9 Feb. 1898. A later report indicated
that the original object of enlisting a special Indian contingent for Uganda was
'to place at the disposal of the Government a loyal and reliable force which
formed the nucleus for defensive purposes'. See Entebbe Archives, Secretariat
Minute Paper no. 2974: 'Indian Contingent (1910).'
[6] F.O. 2/170, I.O. to F.O., 31 Mar. 1898, enclosing Govt. of India to I.O.,
10 Mar. 1898.

the recruitment of the Uganda Indian contingent was duly sanctioned —although public opinion in India generally seemed to resent having to bear 'the burden of empire' in this fashion.[1] The Uganda contingent consisting of 400 selected troops (200 Sikhs and 200 Punjabi Muslims) was dispatched to East Africa in June 1898; and in October of the same year another 200 Indian troops replaced the Indian contingent in Kenya.[2] But by the end of the century the practice of obtaining military reinforcements from India for service in Kenya and Uganda had virtually come to an end—especially as local African forces were organized as the King's African Rifles at the beginning of this century. However, the Uganda Indian contingent continued to receive replacements from India at the expiry of successive three-year tours of duty of the Indian soldiers until 1913, when it was finally disbanded.[3] The only Indian military presence in East Africa after that date was during the First World War, when two special Indian expeditionary forces were employed between 1914 and 1917 during the campaigns against German East Africa.

The employment of British Indian troops in East Africa during

[1] See, for example, *Zanzibar Gazette*, 1 June 1898, p. 3, which quotes a report in the *Times of India*, to the effect that: 'At the time of the outbreak in Uganda, we objected to the easy assumption that the strain of meeting the existing difficulties in the Protectorate must perforce fall upon the Indian army. . . . But when the despatch of the first reinforcements is followed by the formation of a Uganda Regiment in India—composed of picked men—and when simultaneously an Indian regiment is again ordered to garrison Mauritius, while Sikhs are holding Nyasaland . . . it becomes necessary to enquire whether India is not being called upon to bear more than her due share of the burden of empire.'

[2] F.O. 2/171, Viceroy to I.O., 6 Oct. 1898, and Hardinge to Salisbury, 23 Oct. 1898; Γ.O. 2/256, I.O. to F.O., 31 Jan. 1899, enclosing Govt. of India to I.O., 27 Oct. 1898; and *Zanzibar Gazette*, 8 June 1898, p. 4.

[3] F.O. 2/299, Johnston to Salisbury, 5 May 1900, strongly urged the sanction of replacements for the Uganda Indian contingent: 'The withdrawal of the Indian contingent for Uganda would in my opinion result in the speedy collapse of the Protectorate . . . at any rate for many years to come. . . . These Indian soldiers represent a core of absolutely loyal, brave, and practised soldiers whose retention in this country ensures the maintenance of our chief position.' See also Entebbe Archives, Class A. 29, Item 1: 'Correspondence with Govt. of India 1900–1906', especially no. 4 of 1905, memo. of the Military Dept. of Govt. of India, 12 Feb. 1901; and Uganda Secretariat Minute Papers nos. 1608, 2115, and 2974, which deal with the replacements for the Indian contingent in Uganda. For an account of the British Indian troop employment in East Africa generally, see also H. Moyse-Bartlett, *The King's African Rifles*, pp. 73–123. As in the case of Uganda, Indian military reinforcements also continued to be sent to Somaliland following the outbreak of a rebellion in Jubaland in 1900, led by the 'Mad Mullah', Haji Mohamed Abdulla. See F.O. 2/429, F.O. to I.O., 17 Dec. 1900; and F.O. 2/550, I.O. to F.O., 9 Jan. 1901, and enclosure.

the 1890s helped to strengthen the growing Indian presence in the interior and contributed to future immigration from the Punjab, where most of the soldiers originated from. In addition, the short-lived influx of a large number of Indian troops and their array of camp-followers boosted the enterprise of some Indian traders who established *dukas* in the vicinity of their camps, or became official agents for the supply of provisions or transport services, etc.[1] In Uganda Sir Harry Johnston even encouraged a scheme whereby to turn the Indian soldier, when not engaged in military operations, into a cultivator growing wheat for his own consumption—and imported corn-mills from India for the purpose.[2]

Both for the shipment of troops and the subordinate staff required by the East African Governments, the original agents at Bombay—Messrs. Grindlay, Groom, & Co., appointed in 1896—continued to act for the Railway as well as the Governments. In 1898, after the establishment of the Railway Agency in Karachi, the East African Governments—including Nyasaland and later Somaliland—decided to entrust the task of Agent in India to a government official at Bombay rather than to a private firm, and an appointment was accordingly made in January 1899.[3] This in part reflected the increasing demands for Indian subordinate employees in East Africa. From 1899 onwards recruitment of selected Indian personnel for a variety of appointments with the East African Governments steadily increased. While Karachi became the chief coolie-recruiting centre, drawing upon the resources of Sindh, Punjab, and the North-

[1] F.O. 2/257, Hardinge to Salisbury, 22 Aug. 1899, and Col. Broome to Salisbury, 13 Sept. 1899, enclosing report of the Commissariat Officer of the 27th Bombay Infantry Regiment; and F.O. 2/428, Hayes Sadler to Salisbury, 12 Apr. 1900, which shows that the firm of Cowasjee Dinshaw based on Aden—and later in East Africa—conveyed the Indian troops between Aden and the Somali coast, while also acting as general supplier of rations and stores. The camp-followers of the Indian troops included carpenters, hospital assistants, tailors, barbers, cooks, etc.

[2] F.O. 2/257, F.O. to Treasury, 1 Sept. 1899, and Treasury to F.O., 8 Sept. 1899.

[3] F.O. 2/431, 'Agency in India for African Protectorates 1896–1900', see memo. of 18 June 1896, 7 Dec. 1897, and Crown Agents to F.O., 20 Aug. 1898; and F.O. 2/552, 'Agency in India for African Protectorates 1901', which shows that the Bombay Agency was to be financed by the East African Governments in the following proportion: 7/14 of the expenses to be paid by the E.A.P., 4/14 by Uganda, and 3/14 by Nyasaland. See also I.O. Emigration—Apr. 1899, Pros. 9–14, file 27, p. 677, F.O. to I.O., 27 Jan. 1899, and Govt. of India to Bombay Govt., 26 Apr. 1899; and F.O. 2/671, Simson to Hill, 20 Feb. 1902, and minutes thereon.

Western Provinces, Bombay was to become the principal recruiting centre for skilled workers drawn mainly from the Bombay Presidency and to a lesser extent from the Punjab. With the completion of the Uganda Railway, the Agency at Karachi ceased to function after 1902; while the one at Bombay became the principal Agency in India for East Africa.[1] At first the recruitment of skilled staff for service in East Africa was not strictly legal as the Government of India Notification of May 1896 expressly applied to indentured emigration for the Uganda Railway. But for every batch of subordinate staff dispatched to East Africa by the Agent, the approval of the Government of India was generally forthcoming. The procedure was, however, rather cumbersome, and in 1900 the Foreign Office sought for general Indian emigration to East Africa to be made legal—pointing out to the India Office that 'in the present condition of the African Protectorates they are likely to be benefited by Indian Immigration. . . .'[2] Finally, in January 1901, the Government of India issued a Notification supplementing that of 1896 whereby emigration to East and Central Africa was legalized subject to the emigrants being recruited on specific forms of agreement for skilled and unskilled workers. These forms of agreement were later adopted in September 1901.[3] The recruitment of Indian staff for service with the East African Administrations could thus proceed virtually unhampered after this date. But already a large number of Indian administrative employees filled the subordinate ranks in the various government departments. The Goans particularly dominated the provincial administration as Sir Charles Eliot pointed out in 1901: the District Officers were usually 'assisted by a Goanese, or more

[1] I.O. Emigration—Nov. 1902, Pros. 1, file 20, p. 1425, F.O. to I.O., 30 Sept. 1902; and Bombay Archives, G.D. vol. 322 C of 1902, Comp. 50, Agent Simson to Bombay Govt., 15 May 1903, shows that the Karachi Agency of the Uganda Railway was taken over by the local associates of Messrs. Smith, Mackenzie, & Co. with headquarters at Bombay—the latter becoming the chief agents for the Railway in India. See also F.O. 2/431, op. cit.

[2] F.O. 2/671, I.O. to F.O., 9 Apr. 1900, enclosing Govt. of India to I.O., 8 Mar. 1900, F.O. to I.O., 16 May 1900; and Bombay Agent Simson to F.O., 24 Nov. 1899. See also I.O. Emigration—Mar. 1900, Pros. 13–18, file 7, p. 339; May 1900, Pros. 1–2, file 7, p. 435; Feb. 1901, Pros. 3–7, file 7, p. 153; and Bombay Archives, G.D. vol. 245 C of 1900, Comp. 94, Simson to Bombay Govt., 2 Oct. 1899.

[3] F.O. 2/671, Simson to Francis Bertie, 15 Feb. 1901, and Simson to Clement Hill, 13 Dec. 1901; and I.O. Emigration—May 1901, Pros. 12, file 41, part A, Govt. of India to F.O., 5 Mar. 1901. See also Bombay Archives, G.D. vol. 277 C of 1901, Comp. 40, Simson to Govt. of India, 15 Dec. 1900, and Govt. of India Notification of 24 Jan. 1901.

rarely by a European clerk. . . . In the coast towns there is also a Customs official, generally a Goanese.'¹ The important part played by the Indian administrative staff in the establishment and extension of British administration can hardly be over-estimated. German officials commented to Hardinge on one occasion: 'We envy you your subordinate staff of Indian baboo clerks, whether custom officers or tax collectors, who . . . have enough experience . . . to avoid incurring the distrust which so many of our men inspire.'²

On their side, the German authorities in Tanganyika similarly sought to encourage Indian immigration—in continuation of their efforts of 1894 seeking emigration from India to German East Africa to be made legal. A similar request to India was made by the German authorities in 1898—but to no avail. Subsequently, during 1900 and 1901, a scheme for the settlement of Khoja agriculturists in Tanganyika was mooted during the Aga Khan's visit to Berlin; while once again permission was sought to import indentured Indian labourers. The German Ambassador wrote to the Foreign Office that 'the Imperial Governor at Dar es Salaam has, in a report on the subject, expressed a very strong wish, in the interests of the Colony, that German East Africa might be added to the list of those countries into which, under the Indian Emigration Act of 1883, immigration under engagement is allowed'.³ In fact in an earlier memorandum, Hardinge had shown that there was considerable demand for Indian artisans and labourers in German East Africa, and that the Indians were well treated in so far as the law required proper contracts to be signed.⁴ But in 1902 the Government of India

---

¹ F.O.C.P. no. 7867, Eliot's report on the E.A.P., June 1901, p. 15.
² Sir Arthur H. Hardinge, *A Diplomatist in the East* (London, 1928), p. 91.
³ I.O. Emigration—Mar. 1901, Pros. 16–17, file 19, pp. 249–57, British Ambassador, Berlin, to F.O., 21 Nov. 1900, and Govt. of India to I.O., 21 Mar. 1901; Apr. 1902, Pros. 5–8, file 19, pp. 445–73, F.O. to I.O., 23 Mar. 1901, enclosing German Ambassador to F.O., 14 Mar. 1901, and I.O. to F.O., 30 Apr. 1901. In a report on German East Africa in 1901, Hollis explained the German scheme for the importation of Indian agriculturists into the territory: 'In order to develop the natural resources of the country, and especially the cultivation of rice and cotton, the immigration of agriculturists from British India would be welcomed. One of the items in the Estimates for the year 1901 is the demand for 1,500 l. to be used in grants to such immigrants. It is proposed, in order to defray the expenses of the journey and to enable the men to provide themselves with the necessary implements, to present 25 l. to each.' See F.O.C.P. no. 7690, p. 65. For the scheme to settle Khoja agriculturists in German East Africa, see also, I.O. Emigration—June 1900, Pros. 9–10, file 47, part B.
⁴ I.O. Emigration—June 1898, Pros. 7–8, file 7, part B, memo. from H.M. Consul-General, Zanzibar, 19 May 1898.

felt that such emigration should not be freed from the restrictions of the Act of 1883, explaining that

In an undeveloped and unsettled Colony, with a small and scattered European population, the administration of Government is not always sufficiently organized to ensure the full observance of the law; and admirable provisions may be made on paper for the protection of emigrants, but the machinery and the opportunity for enforcing them may alike be lacking.[1]

Sporadic recruitment of skilled workers in India for German East Africa was, however, sanctioned on occasions. In 1902, for example, a number of artisans—mechanics, blacksmiths, fitters, etc.—were recruited from Madras, and a similar request to recruit about forty artisans—including a chemical assistant and a gardener for work at the government botanical research station at Amani—from Bombay was approved. In addition about 100 Singhalese agricultural labourers were recruited at this time for service at Tanga.[2]

On the whole, however, German East Africa was left to depend largely on the services of voluntary Indian immigrants, who flowed into East Africa at a steadily increasing rate—aided, in addition to the dhows, by the steamers of the British India Steam Navigation Co. and of the German East Africa Line—the latter successfully competing for the Indian traffic with the aid of an Imperial subsidy.[3] These 'passenger' or 'free' Indian immigrants, as they were known, were not 'emigrants' under the Indian Emigration Act and were thus not subject to any restrictions; while the general process of opening up the East African territories, and the official sponsorship of indentured immigration, created opportunities of which these immigrants took advantage. A number of them penetrated into German East Africa to work on the railways or to set up as traders —their enterprise generally receiving encouragement from the

[1] I.O. Emigration—Apr. 1902, Pros. 5–8, file 19 of 1901, Govt. of India to I.O., 27 Mar. 1902, pp. 451–2.

[2] Bombay Archives, G.D. vol. 323 C of 1902, Comp. 54, German Consul to Bombay Govt., 14 Apr. 1902, Protector of Emigrants, Bombay, to Bombay Govt., 18 Apr. 1902, and German Marine Councillor to Bombay Govt., 14 Apr. 1903. On other occasions, however, German requests for Indian recruits were not successful. See, for example, Bombay Archives, G.D. vol. 245 C of 1900, Comp. 94 or P.D. vol. 63 of 1900, Comp. 1097, Bombay Govt. to German Consul, 21 July 1900—rejecting request for two Indian engineers and two Indian mates for service in the flotilla of G.E.A. at Dar es Salaam.

[3] *Report by Sir A. Hardinge on the Condition and Progress of the E.A. Protectorate . . . to the 20th July 1897*, C. 8683 (1897), p. 49.

authorities.[1] As early as 1896 the Protector of Emigrants at Bombay had reported that 'numbers of artizans go by every steamer to the various Ports in East Africa, men such as Tailors, shoemakers, Dhobis, cooks, shopkeepers and others all on their own responsibility'. A little later this official explained the process of voluntary emigration in further detail:

> The people are flocking to Africa of their own free will, at their own expense, and on the chance of doing better there . . . many classes and professions are represented in the exodus . . . numbers of Indians are going to East African ports, not as Emigrants, but as Adventurers, if I may venture to call them so . . . many have embarked for Mombasa . . . in the hope of finding work on the Uganda Railway, or in connection with the trade and wants that will spring up with the Railway construction.[2]

No reliable statistics are available about this voluntary emigration—but figures vary from over 600 in 1898 to about 2,000 in 1901.[3] The 'exodus', however, was not confined to East Africa alone, for a number of 'persons of trading, agricultural, labouring, artizan and clerical classes' were flocking to Zanzibar, British and German East Africa, Mozambique, and Natal during this period.[4] In East Africa there was an increasing demand for such immigrants at the time, and Hardinge showed in a memorandum in May 1898 that there were substantial openings for labourers and artisans in all the East African territories.[5] Later, in 1900, Hardinge explained that 'On

---

[1] F.O.C.P. no. 7403, Aga Khan's report on the position of Indians in German East Africa, Sept. 1899, pp. 54–5.

[2] Bombay Archives, G.D. vol. 120 C of 1896, Comp. 671, Part III, Protector of Emigrants, Bombay, to Bombay Govt., 11 July 1896, and to Commissioner of Customs, Salt, Opium, and Abkari, Poona, 8 Sept. 1896. Obviously, it was with the start of the Uganda Railway construction that Mombasa became the target for the voluntary emigrants—for an earlier report by the Protector of Emigrants, Bombay, 21 July 1896, showed that of the 286 'passenger' Indians on a ship bound for the east coast of Africa, 270 were destined for Natal, 10 for Zanzibar, and 6 for Mozambique. See Bombay Archives, P.D. vol. 143 of 1896, Comp. 902.

[3] Bombay Archives, G.D. vol. 278 C of 1901, Comp. 120, report of the Protector of Emigrants, Karachi, for the year 1900–1, and Judicial Dept., vol. 88 of 1904, Comp. 49, Protector of Emigrants, Bombay, to Commissioner of Customs, 3 Feb. 1904, and Commissioner of Sind to Bombay Govt., 11 Feb. 1904. For the general question of increased emigration of 'free' Indians to East Africa, see I.O. Emigration—Oct. 1896, Pros. 15–16, file 66, p. 1103; Aug. 1897, Pros. 4–6, file 37, p. 945; Dec. 1897, Pros. 4–7, file 37, part B; and July 1897, Pros. 9–32, file 5, pp. 761–7.

[4] Bombay Archives, G.D. vol. 142 C of 1897, Comp. 671, Part I, Govt. of India to Bombay Govt., 11 May 1897.

[5] I.O. Emigration—June 1898, Pros. 7–8, file 7, part B, memo. by Hardinge regarding openings for Indian artisans and labourers in Zanzibar, German East Africa, Mombasa, and on the Uganda Railway, 19 May 1898.

arrival in East Africa, to which they appear to have been mainly attracted by reports sent home by railway coolies, some engage as labourers on the railway, others are hired by private employers, in many cases, in quarries, or in connection with building works, whilst others again set up as petty traders.'[1] The prospects of employment coupled with those of enhanced earnings ranging from Rs. 20 per month for labourers to about Rs. 60 for artisans thus provided the main attractions for these voluntary emigrants.

It was, however, as traders that the Indian presence in the interior of East Africa became particularly marked during the early years of the colonial period. Apart from some of the skilled immigrants who established businesses as builders and contractors, the real pioneers of Indian commerce in the interior were the old-established merchants from Kutch and Bombay in Zanzibar and along the Coast. Their ranks steadily swelled—with new immigrants drawn from the Bombay Presidency and now particularly from Gujerat—as the prospects of trade advanced. The freedom of enterprise generally allowed them by the European Administrations accounted for the continued expansion of their historic mercantile connections with East Africa; while the influx of Indian immigrants and troops provided a stimulus for the rapid expansion of their activities into the interior—often into remote areas where the prospects of trade and the security assured by European rule were virtually non-existent. In a sense the penetration of the interior by the old Zanzibar merchants was also their response to the changing economic pattern, with the shift of emphasis from the Coast to the interior that followed the Partition of East Africa. The old predominance of Zanzibar as the chief entrepôt of trade came to be steadily undermined by the rise of the mainland ports of Mombasa, Dar es Salaam, Tanga, and Bagamoyo. Attempts were made by the British authorities to check the decline in Zanzibar's historic importance. In February 1892, Portal declared Zanzibar a free port, and at the same time called upon the four thousand merchants assembled for the ceremony— mostly British Indians—to help make Zanzibar a great commercial depot.[2] About six months later, in July 1892, a chamber of commerce

---

[1] F.O. 2/671, Hardinge to Salisbury, 24 Aug. 1900. See also I.O. Emigration— Feb. 1901, Pros. 3–7, file 7 of 1900, p. 153.

[2] *Zanzibar Gazette*, 10 Feb. 1892, p. 1. See also *Zanzibar Gazette*, 17 Feb. 1892, p. 2, which refers to an address presented by the British Indian merchants to Portal, hailing his decision to declare Zanzibar a free port: 'The port of Zanzibar, which from its geographical position, is the natural centre towards which the

was organized with the Indian merchants playing an active part in its activities.[1] By the end of the year the official *Gazette* reported with satisfaction that 'there has been considerable amount of building going on in the past year, and this method of investing his earnings is the best surety that the Indian trader will do all in his power to promote the success of trade and its retention in Zanzibar in preference to removing it to any of the Coast territories'.[2] But these attempts could hardly succeed as the political centre moved from Zanzibar to Mombasa and Dar es Salaam. By the turn of the century Zanzibar had in fact lost its old commercial predominance, and the policy of a free port was abandoned in 1899.[3] An increasing number of Indian merchants had meanwhile established agencies at the mainland ports—and from these coastal settlements some of them were to spearhead the expansion of 'legitimate commerce' along the old caravan routes, where the Arab and Swahili caravan traders had formerly operated, and later along the new lines of communications opened by the construction of the railways.

One of the earliest Indian merchants in Zanzibar to launch such expansion into the interior was Sewa Hajee Paroo,[4] who operated

---

trade of East Africa converges was in imminent danger of seeing it diverted and its prosperity thereby largely affected. By this wise decision the most serious obstacle to its material progress is removed. . . .'

[1] *Zanzibar Gazette*, 6 July 1892, p. 5.   [2] Ibid., 28 Dec. 1892, p. 5.

[3] For a few more years, after the free port policy was abandoned in 1899, Zanzibar continued to enjoy considerable commercial importance. For example, for the first few years of this century, about 50 per cent of the imports of German East Africa still passed through Zanzibar, but, as a report in 1905 indicated, the decline of Zanzibar as the principal commerical entrepôt of East Africa had virtually become an accomplished fact. See H. Brode, *British and German East Africa* (London, 1911), p. 15; W. E. Henderson, *Studies in German Colonial History* (London, 1962), p. 53; *Handbook of Kenya Colony and Protectorate 1920* (London, 1921), p. 576; and F.O.C.P. no. 8691 (1905), pp. 30–3, Vice-Consul Sinclair to Lansdowne, 23 March 1905, enclosure 1.

[4] For information about Sewa Hajee Paroo see F.O.C.P. no. 6454, pp. 207, 212, Rodd to Rosebery, 2 May 1893, enclosure 1, Sewa Hajee to Berkeley, 3 Dec. 1891, and enclosure 2; Tanzania Archives Dar es Salaam, file no. 7652: 'Sewa Haji, the will and property of'; H. Meyer, *Across East African Glaciers* (London, 1891), p. 41, and O. Baumann, *In Deutsch Ostafrika Wahrend des Aufstandes: Reise der Dr. Hans Meyerischen Expedition in Usambara* (Vienna, 1890), pp. 27, 198, 218–19; both quoted in J. A. Kieran, 'The Holy Ghost Fathers in East Africa 1863–1914' (University of London, Ph.D. thesis, 1966), pp. 355–6. Reference to Sewa Hajee as a leading trader in German East Africa is also made in *Deutsches Koloniale Lexicon* (Berlin, 1920). ii. 91; C. Gillman, 'Dar es Salaam 1860 to 1940 . . .', *Tanganyika Notes and Records* (Dec. 1945), pp. 1–23; and J. D. Karstedt, 'Beitrage zur Inderfrage in Deutsch-Ostafrika', *Koloniale Monatsblätter* (Berlin, 1913), pp. 337–55.

from Bagamoyo and chiefly in German East Africa. Sewa Hajee began his career initially as a supplier of trade goods and provisions to the late nineteenth-century European explorers and also recruited porters for their caravans. Subsequently, he established an agency of his Zanzibar-based firm at Bagamoyo, and began organizing his own caravans into the interior. Later he extended his operations all along the old caravan route—opening stores or agencies of his firm as far as the Lake region and Taveta—and was also reputed to have formed a brief partnership with the arms trader, Stokes. The various agencies in the interior were regularly supplied by Sewa Hajee's caravans from Bagamoyo with a variety of trade goods: cotton cloths, guns and ammunition, beads and brass wire, which were exchanged for the products of the interior—principally ivory. In 1891, for example, Sewa Hajee's store at Station Ukumbi on Lake Victoria held large stocks of imported articles: 1,000 guns, 10,000 lb. of gunpowder, over 60,000 lb. of cotton cloths, and 150,000 gun caps, etc.[1] Sewa Hajee apparently occupied an important position at Bagamoyo in the 1880s and 1890s—well up to his death in 1897—and local Indian tradition, especially among members of his Ismailia community, remembers him as a highly influential trader in Bagamoyo and Tanganyika generally during the late nineteenth century.

Bagamoyo was to produce another and far more important pioneer trader in Allidina Visram (1863–1916),[2] who carried the activities of his fellow Kutch merchant, Sewa Hajee, to their logical conclusion: his caravans penetrating beyond the borders of German East Africa into Uganda, Kenya, and parts of the Congo Free State and southern Sudan. Allidina began his career in East Africa in a fashion typical of the Kutch merchants of the time—arriving in Zanzibar in 1877 as a young apprentice to an old-established firm. It is probable that he moved to Bagamoyo in the same year as an assistant of Sewa Hajee; and after serving as an apprentice for some

---

[1] F.O.C.P. no. 6454, Rodd to Rosebery, 2 May 1893, enclosing Sewa Hajee to Berkeley, 3 Dec. 1891.
[2] For information about Allidina Visram see, *inter alia*, S. Playne and F. H. Gale, *East Africa (British)* (London, 1908–9), pp. 120–2; *Handbook for East Africa, Uganda and Zanzibar* (Mombasa, 1904); Y.S.A. Drumkey, *Drumkey's Year Book for East Africa* (Bombay, 1908); *Leader of British East Africa* (Nairobi), 8 and 15 July 1916; *Evidence of the Education Commission of the E.A.P.* (Nairobi, 1919), pp. 16–17; K. Ingham, *The Making of Modern Uganda* (London, 1958), pp. 98–9; Kenya Archives, file no. DC/MKS. 1/4/1: Nairobi District Annual Report for 1910–11; and *History of East Africa*, vol. ii. Ch. VIII. Additional sources are quoted in this chapter—and particularly in Ch. III, below.

years, struck out on his own—plunging inevitably into the business of organizing caravans into the interior. By the early 1890s, Allidina Visram had extended his operations all along the old caravan route, opening branches of his firm at Dar es Salaam, Sadani (near Bagamoyo), Tabora, Ujiji, and at Kilima in the Congo. In 1896 Allidina opened an agency in Zanzibar; while about the same time his caravans began penetrating northwards from Mwanza into Uganda, and he reached Kampala in 1898 to establish another branch of his firm there. Subsequently, Allidina extended his commercial activities to other parts of Uganda—opening stores at Jinja, Kisumu, and along the river Nile.

Before the Uganda Railway had reached Kisumu, Allidina's caravans bearing large quantities of goods from Zanzibar and Bagamoyo made their way to his growing chain of stores in Uganda by way of Tabora and Mwanza; and he also used a fleet of sailing vessels (dhows) to carry cargoes between various ports along Lake Victoria. At first Allidina's chief export from Uganda was ivory; as a contemporary account pointed out: 'One recollects many huge safaris of tusks wending their serpentine way through Uganda forests and swamps to Allidina Visram's store.'[1] But he was also among the first to purchase other local products: hides and skins, groundnuts and chillies, sesame and cotton; in fact 'anything and everything which tended to develop the country's resources'. Frederick Jackson reported from Uganda in 1902:

> Our present difficulty lies in the circulation of specie, but I am doing all I can to induce the people, through their chiefs, to cultivate sugar cane and simsim (sesame). An Indian trader, named Alidina Visram, is already prepared to buy up as much as the natives like to cultivate of each . . . and this should materially assist in the circulation of specie, rupees, and pice if the people can only be induced to cultivate.[2]

In addition to his role in the development of the import and export business of Uganda, Allidina's stores proved to be extremely useful to the Administration in the early years by acting as bankers and providing cash loans at a time when money was scarce. Allidina's 'primitive shop' was often 'the one and only, at which one could buy his provisions, his chairs and tables, his safari outfit. Alidina Visram advanced ready money to pay the Europeans, servants, and household expenses all against the monthly or tri-monthly cheques at

[1] *Leader of B.E.A.*, 15 July 1916.
[2] F.O.C.P. no. 7946, p. 197.

Mombasa.'[1] Perhaps his contributions in this respect were best summed up in a later government minute on the subject:

Allidina Visram, who was one of the pioneer traders in Uganda. I think he was one of the first Indians to take up trading in the Protectorate; certainly the first who did so on a large scale, about 30 years ago. He opened a store at nearly every Government station, and in the early days was of the greatest assistance to Government in many ways, such as transport, purchase of local produce, etc. Officers in out-stations were dependent, in those days, upon Allidina's agencies for the necessaries of life; nor did he abuse his monopoly by charging high prices.[2]

In 1899, Allidina Visram opened a branch of his firm in Mombasa, and subsequently built a chain of stores in Kenya on a pattern similar to the one adopted by him in Uganda. The completion of the Uganda Railway in 1901 greatly facilitated Allidina's enterprise, and his branch at Mombasa soon came to replace the one at Bagamoyo as his principal headquarters. Thus, by the turn of the century, Allidina Visram had established an extensive East Africa-wide business network and pioneered the development of trade and commerce in many districts. Sir Charles Eliot reported in 1902: 'At present, one merchant, Alidina Visram, supplies almost all the small traders with trade goods, &c.' and that these traders 'may repay him by monthly instalments, while trading under his name'.[3] Apart from some of these early Indian *duka wallas* who acted as his agents, most of Allidina's scattered stores were managed by Indian assistants—drawn particularly from his Ismailia community—so that Allidina Visram may well be regarded as the pioneer of Indian *duka* enterprise in the interior of East Africa.

Another outstanding Indian trader to launch expansion into the interior at this time was A. M. Jeevanjee (1856–1939).[4] He arrived in East Africa after a varied business career in India and during 1886 in Australia, where he established an agency in Adelaide for the import of Eastern goods. In 1890 Jeevanjee obtained a contract with

[1] *Leader of B.E.A.*, 15 July 1916.
[2] Entebbe Archives, file no. 4832: 'Miscellaneous, Allidina Visram', minute by the Chief Secretary's Office, 9 June 1925.
[3] F.O.C.P. no. 7946, p. 28.
[4] For information about A. M. Jeevanjee see, *inter alia*, Kenya Archives, Nairobi, file ARC(GH)—77; F.O.C.P. no. 7422, p. 269; *Leader of B.E.A.*, 7 May, 17 Sept., and 1 Oct. 1910, and 17 Apr. 1915; A.M. Jeevanjee, *Sanitation in Nairobi* (Bombay, 1915), C.O. pamphlet no. 214; and *Drumkey's Year Book for East Africa* (1908). Additional sources are quoted in this Chapter and Ch. III, below.

the I.B.E.A. Company—through its associates in Karachi—to recruit Indian workers, artisans, and police for service in the Company's territories. This provided Jeevanjee with an opening in East Africa which he was quick to grasp. In 1891 he established a branch of his Karachi-based firm at Mombasa and started business as stevedores and contractors. Later in 1896 his firm was hired by the Uganda Railway—which had just commenced construction—to recruit Indian workers, erect temporary buildings, undertake rock-cutting and other earth-works, fit up rolling-stock, and supply provisions for the Indian personnel. In 1899 Jeevanjee made a very profitable agreement with the Railway to supply foodstuffs for the entire Indian labour force employed by it as he could supply the rations cheaper than the Railway's own agent at Karachi! In the same year, he obtained another contract to build John Ainsworth's house in Nairobi[1]—and this gave him the opportunity to establish business in Nairobi just in time to be among the founding fathers of the future capital of Kenya.

The rapid expansion of his business activities in Nairobi and Mombasa apparently reflects Jeevanjee's business acumen and astuteness—a contemporary rightly described him as a 'hustler'.[2] An interesting insight into his business methods is provided by an incident in 1900 when his firm lost a contract to supply castor oil to the Uganda Railway to the Italian Trading Company, who outbid him by 4 annas to Rs. 2.8 per gallon. A. M. Jeevanjee immediately set himself up to undermine his rivals by buying out all the available oil in the country and at prices attractive enough to enable him to control the market: so that when in July 1900 the Railway called upon the Italian firm to deliver supplies of oil, the firm was able to supply only a few gallons. The Italian Company was thus obliged to buy oil from Jeevanjee, who promptly refused to sell it for anything less than Rs. 10 per gallon. This offer was later accepted, but Jeevanjee then insisted on selling the oil direct to the Railway. The eventual outcome of such tactics was that the Railway purchased 4,000 gallons of oil from Jeevanjee at Rs. 10 per gallon, and charged the difference of Rs. 30,000 to the Italian firm.[3] But such tactics notwithstanding,

---

[1] F.O. 2/795, Hardinge to Salisbury, 8 Jan. 1900, enclosing Ainsworth to Hardinge, 29 Dec. 1899.

[2] *Leader of B.E.A.*, 7 May 1910.

[3] F.O.C.P. no. 7732, pp. 253–6, 440. See also *East Africa and Uganda Mail* (Mombasa), 8 June 1901.

Jeevanjee's business activities in Kenya had greatly increased by the turn of the century. His firm undertook the construction of a series of the early buildings for government offices, staff quarters, post offices, and railway stations between Mombasa and Kisumu. Similarly he began investing in town land on his own account, and sometimes in partnership with other traders such as Allidina Visram, and was probably the leading property owner in Nairobi and Mombasa at the turn of the century. About the same time, he started a newspaper, the *African Standard*, at Mombasa which was later sold in 1903 to become the *Mombasa Times* and subsequently the *East African Standard* at Nairobi.[1]

A majority of the Indian traders who penetrated the interior during this period, however, had no such tales of large-scale and successful enterprise to tell. They were, typically, petty merchants who spread along the advancing railway lines, or moved to newly established administrative posts—while some of the more adventurous among them spread into remote districts. These petty Indian merchants were the real founders of Indian commercial enterprise in the interior of East Africa—and helped to create trade, first in a small way and then in a large way, in areas where none had existed previously. With considerable fortitude and perseverance, they pioneered the establishment of *dukas*, of local trading centres and Indian bazaars in different districts; and by introducing the local populations to a variety of imported goods and later the rupee currency, they provided an incentive to greater local production as well as the transition from a barter- to a money-based economy. Little is known of the life and work of these early petty merchants for they were less interested in the concerns of history than with the all-important task of eking out a living from the 'bush'.

Their activities in Kenya and Uganda began in earnest only after the construction of the Uganda Railway had started. While the demands of the Railway and generally of the Administration provided new prospects of large-scale business in the interior—especially for the old-established firms, a number of petty Indian merchants set up shops in temporary *dukas* along the expanding railway line where the presence of a large body of Indian immigrants, and later of African workers, provided a ready-made market for their goods. Some of the Indians, similarly, took up market-gardening along the

---

[1] *East African Standard* (Nairobi), 16 Nov. 1962, 31 Dec. 1965, and 1 Jan. 1966.

railway to meet the demand for fresh produce.[1] Hardinge pointed out in his report on Kenya for 1897–8 that 'Two Indian merchants have this year opened shops at Machakos, and the rupee currency is beginning to be understood and used by the Wakamba as a medium of exchange. Indian traders have also begun to settle at Voi in Taita and at Kibwezi and will doubtless establish themselves permanently at all the larger railway centres.'[2] Sir Guilford Molesworth similarly mentioned at this time that Indian traders were settling around the Railway's different stations and that Voi already had a flourishing Indian bazaar.[3] Ainsworth later explained that a temporary Indian bazaar was started at Kibwezi in 1898 and that about the same time he 'induced' some Indian traders to start a bazaar at Machakos, and that an Indian bazaar opened in Nairobi in 1899.[4] From the vicinity of the railway and the administrative posts, some of these traders spread into the countryside to purchase a variety of local produce— ivory, rubber, grain, gum copal, hides, horns, and copra—in exchange for their trade goods, consisting of the 'americani' and 'kaniki' cotton cloths, blankets, beads, and brass wire, etc.[5] A

---

[1] F.O. 2/569, Eliot to Lansdowne, 5 Jan. 1902, enclosed report of A. S. Rogers, dated 11 Dec. 1901; and Mombasa Archives, shelf 65, file 6: Uganda Railway, Outward File, 1898–1900 applications for market gardens, Jan. 1898, *passim.*

[2] *Report by Sir A. Hardinge on the B.E.A. Protectorate for the year 1897–8,* C. 9125 (1899), p. 17. For Hardinge's comments, 1 Feb. 1899, regarding the influx of Indians into the Ukamba Province, see also F.O.C.P. no. 7400 (1899), p. 269.

[3] C. 9331 (1899), op. cit., p. 2.

[4] *Reports Relating to the Administration of the East Africa Protectorate,* Cd. 2740 (1905), p. 18, and F.O.C.P. no. 8438, p. 255, or F.O. 2/916, Stewart to Lansdowne, 7 Mar. 1905, enclosed report by Ainsworth on the progress of the Ukamba Province. Similarly, Hobley later explained that in the early days 'wherever the Government founded a post, there the Indian went, often at the request of the district officer', and that much of the distributive trade of Kenya and Uganda—including in some of the remote areas—was carried on by the Indians. See C. W. Hobley, *Kenya From Chartered Company to Crown Colony* (London, 1929), p. 242. Similar views were echoed by another contemporary observer, who pointed out: 'The Indian trader was everywhere the first to take advantage of the extension of administrative influence on the mainland in order to begin the direct sale of trade goods to natives as one Administration Station after another was opened, even to the far remote localities down the Nile Valley. It is definitely the case in East Africa that *trade followed the flag.*' See W. M. Ross, *Kenya From Within,* p. 298.

[5] *Report by Sir A. Hardinge on the . . . East Africa Protectorate from its establishment to the 20th July 1897,* C. 8683 (1897), pp. 43, 47–8 and C. 9125 (1899), op. cit., p. 17. In these Reports, Hardinge also mentions that 50 per cent of the E.A.P.'s imports came from India—and that 30 per cent of the 'Americani' and 50 per cent of the 'Kaniki' cloths were produced in India. See also John

report from the District Officer at Rabai in March 1901, for example, indicated: 'There has been considerable trade in grain, and I am glad to say that an Indian merchant has opened a shop and commenced to trade at Samburu, where there is a large quantity of grain; moreover he has given the Chiefs some European potatoes to plant in order to do a trade in that article with Mombasa.'[1] This process was further explained by Whitehouse in a report of June 1902, which showed that for over two years Indian traders had been settled at Samburu, Kibwezi, and Masongleni and were sending grain procured from the Wakamba down to Mombasa. Similarly these traders obtained supplies of ghee (clarified butter) from Kiu and Machakos and of country salt and potatoes from Nairobi and Machakos.[2] In fact, as sections of the railway became operational their traffic at first consisted chiefly of Indian traders and their cargoes of import and export goods.[3] The Indians were of course not the only traders active in the East Africa Protectorate at this time, but as Ainsworth explained: 'The wholesale trade is mostly in the hands of Indians, and three or four British and German firms, while the retail trade is carried on by Indians . . . Swahilis.'[4] But the Indian petty merchant apparently filled a growing need for small traders and 'for middlemen who will buy the farmer's produce for cash on the spot'.[5] Further, because of the advantages of the old-established trading connection between Bombay and East Africa, the Indian merchant was better able to contribute to the transition in trade from its previous dependence on Arab-Swahili caravans to its concentration around local trading centres in the interior. In fact, after 1898, as Ainsworth pointed out in a later report:

By degrees the Indian traders created local centres of trade . . . the

Ainsworth: 'A Description of the Ukamba Province, E.A.P. 1900', C.O. pamphlet no. 6, ref. 10554, p. 193, where he mentions that most of the trade cloths used in East Africa came from India and Germany.
  [1] F.O.C.P. no. 7823, p. 174.
  [2] F.O.C.P. no. 7922, p. 200, report of the Chief Engineer, Uganda Railway, June 1902.
  [3] See, for example, F.O.C.P. no. 7422, p. 117, and F.O.C.P. no. 7212, p. 227, where a report indicated that already in 1898 traffic on the opened section of the railway consisted chiefly of Indian shopkeepers, 'who planted themselves down in small native built shops along the line where the population of the railway employes [sic] was large enough to give them sufficient trade'.
  [4] Ainsworth, 'A Description of the Ukamba Province . . . 1900', op. cit., p. 193.
  [5] C.O. 533/3, Stewart to Lyttelton, 9 Aug. 1905, enclosed memo. on prospects of trade by Ainsworth and Marsden

greatest and most important centre in the interior is Nairobi. The bulk of any native trade is . . . done by the Indians. The reason for this is that the Indian is a born 'small' trader, and for some time I think the 'small' trader will continue to be the principal factor in the trade transactions in the country. . . . Up to within quite recent times, European capital and enterprise have been almost entirely absent. . . .[1]

Similarly in Uganda and German East Africa, many small Indian traders penetrated into the interior in the footsteps of such pioneer traders as Allidina Visram; and helped to create trade and commerce in different districts. In German East Africa the population of Indian merchants had increased to about 3,000 by the turn of the century; and, while most of them were concentrated at the coastal settlements—principally Bagamoyo, Tanga, Pangani, Lindi, and Dar es Salaam—an increasing number of them had opened stores and agencies along the caravan routes and the advancing railways— with Tabora and Ujiji representing major concentrations of their population in the interior.[2] Similarly, before the Uganda Railway had reached Lake Victoria, the caravan routes through Tanganyika served as the principal means of communication for the Indian traders who penetrated into Uganda at an increasing rate during this period. Sir Harry Johnston noted that during his term as Special Commissioner in Uganda, 1899–1901,

Indian traders advanced their posts from Kampala (Mengo) to Toro, and all the posts at which European or native soldiers were established in the Nile Province, besides opening bazaars at all the stations in the eastern half of the Protectorate. The commercial enterprise of the Germans and British Indians . . . added largely to our revenues, and did a great deal to encourage the natives to embark in trade in the products of their country. To the British Indians I can only wish unlimited success, since they trade under the British flag, and create trade, first in a small way and then in a large way, where no trade had hitherto existed.[3]

[1] Cd. 2740 (1905), op. cit., pp. 18–19.

[2] F.O.C.P. no. 7690, report on German East Africa 1901, by Mr. Hollis, pp. 65, 80–7. Hollis's report provided the following details about the distribution of Indian traders in German East Africa in 1901: 1 Indian firm at Moshi and Marangu; 2 Indian shops in West Usambara; over 100 Indian shops in Tanga district as well as about 40 sugar mills owned by the Indians and Arabs; about 100 Indian shops at Pangani; 70 or 80 Indian traders at Lindi; 1 Indian shop at Dodoma; and relatively large concentrations of Indian traders at Dar es Salaam, Bagamoyo, Tabora, and Ujiji.

[3] Sir Harry Johnston, *The Uganda Protectorate* (London, 1902), i. 294. Sir Harry Johnston went on to say that the Indian as well as German traders 'give little or no bother; they ask for no guarantees and for no concession. They enter the country and pursue their trade under the laws in force, making the best

In fact at most of the principal settlements in Uganda—Kampala, Entebbe, Fort Portal, Eldama Ravine, and Kisumu—as well as the other outlying posts, Indian bazaars had been established by the beginning of this century. As Sir John Kirk later pointed out: 'When I was in Uganda, at Entebbe, the only large store where you could buy any respectable goods was an Indian store. . . . There was no European store then. This is six years ago. That was in Entebbe, at the farthest part beyond the railway, across the Lake.'[1] Looked at from the point of view of the early officials, this was a major advantage of the establishment of Indian *dukas* in the interior. The comment by the Chief Secretary's Office in Uganda regarding Allidina Visram— that 'He opened a store at nearly every government station, and in the early days was of the greatest assistance to the government in many ways, such as transport, purchase of local produce, etc. Officers in out-stations were dependent, in those days, upon Allidina's agencies for the necessaries of life . . .'[2]—could in fact be applied with some justification to the enterprise of the lesser Indian traders generally in East Africa. A report from Uganda in 1899, for example, indicated that 'should the (Indian) merchants retire from Uganda, the administration there would find it imperative to indent for their own goods, certainly until the cumbrous system of barter was abolished and people taught to recognise the value of currency as a medium of exchange'.[3] Similarly, Sir Harry Johnston pointed out in

of things as they find them.' Another contemporary account indicated that the caravan route from Mombasa through Mumias and Kisumu was also used by the Indian traders who penetrated into Uganda before the railway was completed— using donkey and cart transport to carry goods. A group of Mill Hill Fathers in 1899, for example, availed themselves of the transport facilities provided by the Indians in order to carry their goods from Nairobi to Uganda. See H. P. Gale, *Uganda and the Mill Hill Fathers* (London, 1959), pp. 185-8.

[1] Cd. 5193 (1910), op. cit., p. 238. Earlier in 1901, Sir Harry Johnston had similarly talked of the Indian role in Uganda: 'There are already several important European trading houses and a large number of British Indian traders and several respectable Arab merchants established in this Protectorate, and it is quite a mistaken notion . . . that the commerce of this Protectorate, remains to be created. At Entebbe, Kampala, Fort Portal, Eldama Ravine, Kisumu and most of the principal stations in Unyoro and along the course of the Nile there are shops or stores at which nearly all European necessaries can be purchased. . . .' See *Despatch from H.M.'s Special Commissioner in Uganda relating to Travellers in the Protectorate*, Cd. 590 (1901), p. 3.

[2] Entebbe Archives, file no. 4832: 'Miscellaneous, Allidina Visram', minute by the Chief Secretary's Office, 9 June 1925. See also p. 53, above.

[3] F.O. 2/431, see memo. by the E.A.P. Treasurer, 2 Apr. 1898, which quotes the views of Mr. Berkeley, Assistant Commissioner in Uganda.

1901: 'Thanks to the enterprise of British Indians and Germans, no important centre of European settlement is without its well-appointed store at which most things needful for European life in Africa can be purchased at reasonable prices.'[1]

The enterprise of the Indian merchants also contributed to the rapid spread of the rupee currency in Uganda—as also in the rest of East Africa. Sir Harry Johnston remarked in 1899: 'The rupee has circulated much more widely through the Uganda Protectorate than is probably known'; and again in 1901: 'cash in the form of rupees, thanks to the enterprise of British Indian and German merchants, is flooding Uganda'.[2] In fact since 1897 the Bombay Mint had been supplying copper coinage to the East African countries while the National Bank of India was the first to start business in East Africa.[3] The Administration in Uganda—and also in the East Africa Protectorate, and conceivably in German East Africa—had cause enough to welcome such a development. For, apart from its long-term significance in laying the foundations of a modern, money-based economy in the territories, the introduction of the rupee currency had the immediate result of solving some of the problems facing the establishment of Administration—especially as regards collection of taxes or the payment of employees. Ainsworth, for example, reported in 1905 that in Kenya,

Previous to 1898, the Government kept stores of trade goods, and trade goods formed the entire medium of exchange with the natives. Strings of beads, lengths of cloth, rings of wire, looking-glasses, umbrellas, bells, and similar articles had, at each place, a regular standard value. With the opening of the Indian bazaars, the Government began to close down their

---

[1] *Report by H.M.'s Special Commissioner on the Protectorate of Uganda*, Cd. 671 (1901), p. 7. In fact, as Johnston later commented, the Indian trader 'rendered further benefits to the European community by bringing down the German prices and by opening stores at places whither even a German hesitated to penetrate'. See Johnston, op. cit., i. 294. Similar views were later echoed by Hobley, who pointed out that in the early days the Indians 'filled a need' and that 'The heads of many of the old Indian firms in Mombasa were men for whom one conceived a regard, they would willingly cooperate with the Government, and no racial question ever arose.' See Hobley, op. cit., p. 242.

[2] Cd. 671 (1901), op. cit., p. 8; and F.O. 2/204, Johnston to Salisbury, Dec. 1899. Sir Charles Eliot in a dispatch to Lansdowne, 21 Jan. 1902, similarly referred to the increasing circulation of the rupee currency in East Africa—see F.O. 2/956. The same was true for German East Africa, where the rupee was also recognized as the official currency. See H. Brode, *British and German East Africa*, p. 12.

[3] Bombay Archives, P.D. vol. 132 of 1897, Comp. 1132; and F.O. 2/956, General Manager, National Bank of India, to F.O., 11 June 1900.

stores, and payment began to be made in rupees and pice, and now station trade goods are an unknown quantity.[1]

Similarly, in Uganda, until the turn of the century, taxes were paid in kind—in the form of local produce: ivory, india-rubber, and also in cowrie shells, and as one report indicated even wild animals.[2] But the spread of the rupee currency obviated the need to resort to such practices, and the Government was able to dispose of its accumulated stock of cowrie shells to 'native and Indian traders who (purchased) them at a reduced value to buy trade products in the far interior towards the Nile and the Congo Free State'.[3]

The early years of the colonial period—particularly the last decade of the nineteenth century—thus had great significance for the penetration of the interior of East Africa by Indian immigrants. This was essentially a three-pronged phenomenon—based on the association of Indian skilled and semi-skilled staff, of Indian troops, and Indian traders with the Imperial effort in the territories. As Sir Winston Churchill later explained it:

It was the Sikh (and Punjabi Muslim) soldier who bore an honourable part in the conquest and pacification of these East African countries. It is the Indian trader who, penetrating and maintaining himself in all sorts of places to which no white man would go or in which no white man could earn a living, has more than any one else developed the early beginnings of trade and opened up the first slender means of communications. It was by Indian labour that the one vital railway on which everything else depends was constructed. It is the Indian banker who supplies the larger part of the capital yet available. . . .[4]

Sir Harry Johnston echoed similar views at a later date when he recalled how he strove 'to open up East Africa to knowledge by the help of Indian troops, Indian doctors, and Indian clerks'; and pointed to the 'intermediary role played by the Indian sepoy, non-commissioned officer, surveyor, clerk, surgeon . . . trader and horticulturist, in all East Africa, from the Zambezi to Somaliland. . . .'[5] Similarly Herbert Samuel reporting on his visit to Uganda in 1902

---

[1] Cd. 2740 (1905), op. cit., pp. 18–19. See also Hobley, op. cit., pp. 79, 245–6, where he mentions the problems faced by the Governments in Kenya and Uganda —especially during the 1890s—due to the barter system, the need to make payments in trade goods, and the 'stupendous effort' required to keep Uganda provided with the necessaries of life.

[2] See R. Oliver, *Sir Harry Johnston and the Scramble for Africa*, p. 314.

[3] F.O. 2/956, Johnston to Lansdowne, 18 May 1901.

[4] W. S. Churchill, *My African Journey* (London, 1908), p. 49.

[5] *The Times* (London), 22 Aug. 1921, Harry Johnston to the editor.

referred to the extensive Indian role in East Africa—as the principal artisans and merchants, the 'backbone' of the military and police forces and of the subordinate staff in the various government and railway departments—and thought that the 'progress of these portions of Africa would have been slow indeed, had it not been possible to draw upon our Asiatic possessions for unlimited supplies of subordinate labour with brain and hand'.[1]

In the Imperial policy to draw upon the resources of the Indian empire for the opening up of these territories thus lay the seeds for the subsequent emergence of an Indian settlement in the interior of East Africa[2]—spearheaded by the indentured immigrants, the subordinate staff, and above all the traders.

[1] Herbert Samuel, 'The Uganda of Today', *Journal of the Society of Arts*, ii, no. 2626 (20 Mar. 1903), p. 395, C.O. pamphlet no. 15, ref. 10554.

[2] Indeed, as one official pointed out in 1906 in rebutting European opposition to the Indians as 'intruders' in East Africa: 'till three years ago East Africa was a purely Native Protectorate with settlements of Indians, and that it was the Indians who materially assisted the Administration in the early days of the development of the Protectorate by working on the Railway, building houses, and taking contracts at a time when there was practically no one else to do so. It is, therefore, somewhat irrational now to blame the Indians for having, under such circumstances, made a position for themselves in East Africa, or to blame the Government for having encouraged them.' See C.O.C.P. no. 879/92/844, p. 169.

CHAPTER III

Growth of the Economic Role

c. 1902 to c. 1921

THE last decade of the nineteenth century marked an important landmark in the growth of an Indian factor in the interior of East Africa. The officially sponsored participation of the Indians in the process of 'opening up' of the interior led to an increasing flow of Indian immigrants—skilled and semi-skilled employees, businessmen, and traders—into the East African territories. With these immigrants came also some of the institutions of British India—including the rupee currency which became the standard currency all over East Africa, and Indian laws—as well as British Indian methods of administration. These had the combined result of greatly strengthening the Indian presence in the territories. In fact, at the turn of the century, suggestions were not lacking that British East Africa had become a virtual 'appendage' of British India and was governed as one of its provinces.[1] Similarly, it was not entirely surprising that Sir Harry Johnston should describe East Africa as a possible 'America of the Hindu', or contemplate the growth of Entebbe as the future Calcutta, a new capital on the Mau plateau as the Simla, Mombasa as the Bombay, and Fort Portal as the Darjeeling of the new East African Empire.[2] In addition, official policy generally

[1] See, for example, C.O. 533/4, Jackson to Lyttelton, 7 Oct. 1905 and 18 Oct. 1905, enclosed petition of the Colonists' Association, Nairobi, dated 23 Aug. 1905; H. R. A. Philp, *A New Day in Kenya* (London, 1936), p. 105; and Norman Leys, *Kenya* (London, 1924), pp. 76–7. Among the British Indian laws applied to East Africa were: Indian Evidence Act, Indian Contract Act, Indian Post Office Act, and the Indian Criminal and Civil Codes. The rupee was recognized as the official currency by the East Africa and Uganda (Currency) Order-in-Council, 1905—see F.O. 2/956, 'Coinage and Currency in E.A. and Uganda 1900–1905'.

[2] F.O. 2/297, Johnston to Salisbury, 18 Feb. 1900; and Cd. 671 (1901), op. cit., p. 7. See also R. Oliver, *Sir Harry Johnston and the Scramble for Africa*, pp. 335–6. Johnston's views regarding Indian immigration into East Africa were somewhat similar to those expressed by Lugard in 1893—see p. 30, above. As Johnston explained: 'Indian trade, enterprise, and emigration require a suitable outlet. East Africa is, and should be, from every point of view, the America of the

continued to favour Indian association with the process of economic development. The question of encouraging time-expired coolies to settle in East Africa as agriculturists instead of returning to India at the end of their contracts was much canvassed at this time. Similarly, during 1900–1, when the Foreign Office was urging the Government of India to supplement the existing sanctions relating to indentured immigration for the Uganda Railway by legalizing emigration of skilled staff for service with the East African Administrations, the question of general Indian immigration into East Africa—which had rather languished since the Company's days—was also revived.

The Foreign Office comment in May 1900 that 'in the present condition of the African Protectorates, they are likely to be benefited by Indian immigration'[1] was perhaps symptomatic of the thinking of the time on this subject. In 1902, Sir Clement Hill further defined this view, stating that 'We are rather looking to India for our East African system and for development.' For, he added,

In the construction of the Railway and in the legal system which has been applied in the Protectorate H.M.'s Government have leaned towards Indian methods, and there do not at present appear to be any reasons such as have occasionally been urged in South Africa against the introduction of Indian labour. On the contrary, it seems likely to supply a much felt want and to stimulate the natives to work themselves.[2]

Similar views were echoed by the officials in East Africa. As early as 1899 Sub-Commissioner Crauford had stated that 'nothing would give me greater pleasure than to take steps to bring into this country suitable Indian agriculturists to develop its resources'.[3] In the following year Sir Arthur Hardinge reported that a number of Indian immigrants belonging to the agricultural class and some of the time-expired coolies were

Hindu. . . . I am aware that British Indian subjects carry on brisk trade in German and Portuguese East Africa . . . but . . . I regard it as a political necessity that a portion . . . of East Africa should be open to Indian enterprise under the British flag' (Cd. 671). Sir Winston Churchill echoed similar views a few years later, when contemplating the massive task of developing the East African territories with the help of Indian immigrants: 'The mighty continent of tropical Africa lies open to the colonizing and organizing capacities of the East.' W. S. Churchill, *My African Journey*, p. 52.

[1] F.O. 2/671, F.O. to I.O., 16 May 1900.

[2] F.O. 2/671, F.O. to Treasury, 28 Feb. 1902; and F.O. 2/569, minute by Hill, 25 Feb. 1902, on Eliot to Lansdowne, 5 Jan. 1902. Also printed in F.O.C.P. no. 7946, pp. 156–7. See also F.O. 2/433, Lansdowne to Eliot, 27 Aug. 1901.

[3] Mombasa Archives, shelf 76, file no. 50: 'Ukamba Outward 1899', Acting Commissioner C. H. Crauford to Ainsworth, 2 Aug. 1899.

already applying for plots of land for cultivation in various parts of the province of Ukamba, and I am of opinion that every encouragement should be given to them to settle there and form, it may be hoped, the nucleus of an industrious Indian Colony . . . the Government of India need have no apprehension as regards their welfare as they live under the protection of the Indian Codes which constitute the law in this Protectorate. . . .[1]

Sir Harry Johnston writing from Uganda a little later similarly favoured the immigration of Indian agriculturists, artisans, and traders, pointing out that East Africa 'affords great opportunities to the Indian agriculturist'; while as 'traders there is room for the Indian all over the Uganda Protectorate, and I might say with certainty that he is at the present time, and under like circumstances would be always, welcome to the natives. . . .'[2] Similar views were expressed by Sir Charles Eliot in 1901, when he pointed out: 'As Indian traders penetrate into the most distant and dangerous parts of the Protectorate, I do not see why agriculturists should not in time be induced to do the same', and that 'The Indians seem likely to become . . . intermediaries between Europeans and natives, and if they were allowed by the Indian Government to settle would probably do much to develop the natural resources of the country. . . .'[3]

But the much-canvassed schemes for large-scale Indian agricultural settlements in various parts of East Africa—including the Kenya Highlands—which were formulated at the beginning of the century were destined to remain still-born. The Government of India itself vetoed these schemes in March 1901 when it suggested that time-expired coolies might be encouraged to settle as agriculturists rather than undertake direct State-aided emigration, as the three East African Governments had recommended.[4] In fact about this time,

[1] F.O. 2/671, Hardinge to Salisbury, 24 Aug. 1900.

[2] F.O. 2/671, Johnston to Salisbury, 26 Oct. 1900. Copy of the dispatch also in I.O. Emigration—May 1901, Pros. 12, file 41, pp. 340–1. As Johnston further explained: 'The Indian trader is in fact more willingly received by the natives in this part of Africa than the European, who is apt to be too autocratic and unobliging in his methods of trading.'

[3] *Report by H.M. Commissioner on the E.A.P.*, Cd. 769 (1901), p. 6, or F.O.C.P. no. 7867, p. 7, Eliot's report on the E.A.P. June 1901. See also F.O.C.P. no. 7732, pp. 312, 369 B and C; and F.O. 2/443, Lansdowne to Eliot, 3 Aug. 1901.

[4] F.O. 2/671, I.O. to F.O., 5 Mar. 1901. Copy of the dispatch also in I.O. Emigration—May 1901, Pros. 12, file 41, p. 339. See also F.O. 2/443, Lansdowne to Eliot, 3 Aug. 1901; and I.O. Emigration—Sept. 1901, Pros. 12, file 41, p. 617, F.O. to I.O., 6 Aug. 1901, enclosing F.O. to Eliot, 3 Aug. 1901. In addition to the proposals for the settlement of time-expired coolies on land, tentative attempts were later made to encourage Indian soldiers to settle as agriculturists in East Africa. See F.O. 2/571, Eliot to Lansdowne, 25 Apr. 1902.

Eliot himself was prepared to favour Indian agricultural settlement in restricted areas of the Coast, Ukamba and Nyanza Provinces only, for he was moving towards a policy of encouraging White settlement in the Highlands. This he defined early in 1902, pointing out: 'Believing as I do that the East African Highlands are for the most part a white man's country . . . I doubt the expediency of settling large bodies of Indians in them, as even in Mombasa there is considerable friction between the European and Indian traders.'[1] Further, he suggested that 'the cool, grassy uplands so attractive to the white man were positively distasteful to the Hindu, and the Railway Coolies showed no inclination whatever to settle in the neighbourhood of Nairobi and similar localities'.[2] This, however, was an evident exaggeration for a number of Indian market-gardeners were already settled around Nairobi—comprising the main body of Indian agriculturists in the country.[3]

Eliot's sponsorship of the White Highlands policy, however, coincided with the growth of European hostility to the Indians which was expressed in demands for the restriction of Indian immigration and the encouragement of European settlement.[4] In these circumstances, the lengthy discussions of 1900–2 envisaging Indian agricultural settlement with a view to encouraging development and providing 'object-lessons' to the local people came to a rather inglorious conclusion—ending with the decision to subsidize a few Indian families to settle at Kibos in 1903.[5] The settlement at Kibos itself was hardly attractive to the Indians—the area was described as extremely unhealthy on account of swamps and mosquitoes—and only about a dozen or so coolies settled on the small plots of land alienated to them.[6] By 1906 only about half of the original allocation of £1,000 had been spent on the settlement— largely to replace some of the original settlers with a better class of

[1] F.O. 2/569, Eliot to Lansdowne, 5 Jan. 1902. Also printed in F.O.C.P. no. 7946. See also I.O. Emigration—Sept. 1901, Pros. 12, file 41, part A.
[2] F.O. 2/805, Eliot to Lansdowne, 21 Jan. 1902.
[3] F.O. 2/569, Eliot to Lansdowne, 5 Jan. 1902, enclosed report on Indian agricultural settlement by A. S. Rogers, dated 11 Dec. 1901.
[4] F.O. 2/805, Eliot to Lansdowne, 21 Jan. 1902.
[5] I.O. Emigration—Feb. 1904, Pros. 11, file 19, pp. 97–113; *Annual Report on the E.A.P. for 1904*, p. 16; *Annual Report on the E.A.P. for 1905*, p. 34. See also F.O. 2/569, Eliot to Lansdowne, 5 Jan. 1902, and enclosure.
[6] C.O. 533/4, Jackson to Lyttelton, 12 Oct. 1905, telegram and minutes thereon. See also *Kenya Land Commission, Evidence* (Nairobi, 1934), iii. 2176, evidence of the Nyanza Indian Farmers' Association.

agriculturists.[1] The settlement at Kibos, however, gradually made progress—by 1908, 1,000 acres were under cultivation—and the production of cotton, sugar cane, chillies, and corn had begun in earnest.[2] Kibos nevertheless remained a very minor achievement— ill befitting the masses of official paper that went into its creation.

Most of the Uganda Railway indentured workers who stayed behind, in fact, took to other occupations than farming at Kibos. Many of them continued to work for the Railway, while others became market-gardeners, itinerant traders, carpenters, and masons. Some of them also spread into Uganda, German East Africa, and Zanzibar.[3]

Official sponsorship of Indian immigration into East Africa was thus essentially a short-lived phenomenon—confined mainly to the indentured workers for the Uganda Railway between 1896 and 1901. But, while the much-discussed proposals of 1900–3 tended to degenerate into the settlement of Indians at Kibos, the issue as such was never quite closed. From time to time, in the early years of the century, the idea of State-aided Indian immigration was revived. This was partly due to the recurrent labour problems faced by the European settlers as well as to the political considerations arising out of the exclusive settlement of the Europeans in the Highlands. As Stewart explained in 1905: 'There are enormous tracts of land in the Protectorate perfectly suitable for Indians to develop without encroaching on the comparatively small area suitable for European settlement. There is no objection to the small plots and gardens which have already been leased to Indians and natives in the highlands, as they are generally far from European dwellings', but transfers of land 'ought to be absolutely barred to Indians or natives

---

[1] C.O. 533/3, Jackson to Lyttelton, 26 Aug. 1905, enclosed annual report of the E.A.P. Treasurer, dated 24 Aug. 1905; and *Annual Report on the E.A.P. for 1906.*

[2] *Correspondence Relating to the Tenure of Land in the E.A.P.*, Cd. 4117 (1908), p. 26, and *Report of the Committee on Emigration from India to the Crown Colonies and Protectorates*, Part III, *Papers Laid before the Committee*, Cd. 5194 (1910), p. 43, Jackson to Elgin, 12 Feb. 1907, and enclosure 8 (*b*), Protector of Immigrants, D. D. Waller, to Jackson, 8 Feb. 1907. For detailed information about the Kibos Indian settlement, see Kenya Archives, files no. PC/NZA. 3/22, 1/1 to 1/16, and PC/NZA. 3/22/2–3.

[3] I.O. Emigration—Mar. 1904, Pros. 2–3, file 92, p. 137, Cave to Lansdowne, 1 June 1903; *Report of the Committee on Emigration from India to the Crown Colonies and Protectorates*, Part I, Cd. 5192 (1910), p. 91; Part II, *Minutes of Evidence*, Cd. 5193 (1910), p. 68; and F. J. Jackson, *Early Days in East Africa* (London, 1930), pp. 325–6. See also M. F. Hill, *Permanent Way*, i. 255–6.

in the districts suitable for European colonization'.[1] A little earlier, in fact, the Director of Agriculture in Kenya had recommended Indian agricultural settlement in the lowlands—which he described as 'the unhealthy but richest parts of the country' or on account of their unhealthiness 'practically reserved for Indians'—where the Indians would raise valuable tropical crops and also demonstrate better cultural methods to the Africans.[2] Later, in November 1905, a committee on Indian immigration was appointed, and it similarly recommended Indian agricultural settlement in 'certain areas, unsuited to Europeans on account of climatic condition'. These the Committee defined as lying between the Coast and Kiu and between Fort Ternan and Lake Victoria.[3] The matter of Indian immigration was then taken up with the Colonial Office by Frederick Jackson, and later pressed on by Hayes Sadler in a dispatch of May 1906— in which he recommended Indian settlement at Kibos, Voi, and Malindi: these places being outside the Highlands, and 'in view of the help it is likely to give to native cultivation'.[4] In response to these developments, the official in charge of the Kibos settlement since its inception in 1903 was deputed to India in July 1906 in order to select about fifteen families for settlement—using the unexpended balance in the existing vote on Indian immigration.[5] But the so-called 'enormous tracts of land' and 'the unhealthy but richest parts of the country' proved rather illusory, and little came of these attempts.

Similarly the question of importing indentured Indian labour, in view of the general labour difficulties, was frequently canvassed at this time. There appears to have been a limited influx of such labour —particularly into German East Africa—during this period, through

[1] C.O. 533/3, Stewart to Lyttelton, 14 Aug. 1905.

[2] F.O. 2/914, Stewart to Lansdowne, 16 Jan. 1905, enclosed report on the cultivation of cotton in the E.A.P. by A. Linton and E. Brand, dated 13 Jan. 1905. Also printed in F.O.C.P. no. 8438, pp. 121–2.

[3] I.O. Emigration—Aug. 1906, Pros. 13–16, file 73, p. 499, Sadler to Elgin, 21 May 1906, and enclosures. The Committee also recommended 'reasonable inducement to be offered to secure the proper class of Indians', and fixed a maximum of fifty-acre plots and Rs. 300 in financial aid for each prospective settler.

[4] C.O. 533/4, Jackson to Lyttelton, telegram, 12 Oct. 1905; and I.O. Emigration—Aug. 1906, Pros. 13–16, file 73, pp. 499–501, Sadler to Elgin, 21 May 1906, and enclosed papers.

[5] I.O. Emigration—Aug. 1906, Pros. 13–16, file 73, I.O. to Govt. of India, telegram, 11 July 1906; Nov. 1906, Pros. 12–18, file 73, pp. 1329–31; and Bombay Archives, G.D. vol. 394 C of 1906, Comp. 55, Govt. of India to Bombay Govt., 15 Oct. 1906, and enclosures. See also C.O. 533/3, Jackson to Lyttelton, 26 Aug. 1905, enclosed annual report of the E.A.P. Treasurer, dated 24 Aug. 1905.

the agency of private contractors—notably A. M. Jeevanjee, who was convicted in the Bombay High Court in 1907 for such recruitment against the provisions of the Indian Emigration Act.[1] The demand for labour by the European planters and settlers was, however, insatiable, and in 1908 the question of importing Indian labour was taken up by Hayes Sadler—especially in respect of importing between 2,000 and 4,000 Indian workers for the plantations at the Coast.[2] The whole question, however, became part of the larger issue of general Indian immigration to the Colonies and Protectorates which came before a committee appointed by the Colonial Office under the chairmanship of Lord Sanderson. The Committee received a wide variety of memoranda and evidence during 1909—and it became clear that official opinion in Kenya was opposed to any scheme for State-aided Indian immigration to the country.[3] But proposals for the immigration of indentured Indian labour and of Indian agriculturists into the lowlands were much canvassed.[4] Official opinion in Uganda, on the other hand, was somewhat more favourable; and Sir Hesketh Bell echoed the earlier views of the Kenya officials when he pressed for State-aided immigration of Indian agriculturists into Uganda—as 'the settlement of such people, in the fertile districts of the Protectorate, would very soon become self-supporting and prosperous . . . [it] would afford valuable object lessons to the natives of the Protectorate and . . . contribute, in a notable degree, to the rapid development of this territory'.[5] The Sanderson Committee concluded in favour of continued Indian

---

[1] Bombay Archives, G.D. vol. 5 C of 1907, Comp. 64. See also P.D. Comp. 1335 of 1914 and Comp. 1684 of 1915.

[2] C.O. 533/59, Hayes Sadler to Crewe, 4 June 1908, and 12 Apr. 1909, telegram. See also Cd. 5194 (1910), op. cit., p. 49.

[3] C.O. 533/59, Hayes Sadler to Crewe, telegram, 12 Apr. 1909, and E.A.P., *Minutes of the Executive Council*, 12 Mar. 1909, which show that 'the Governor has already expressed his views to the Secretary of State against any system of state-aided Indian immigration, that the Government of this Protectorate has no desire to reconsider this point.'

[4] C.O. 533/59, Jackson to Crewe, 21 May 1909, and C.O. 533/62, Girouard to Crewe, 23 Sept. 1909.

[5] Entebbe Archives, file no. 386: 'Emigration from India to Crown Colonies', Hesketh Bell to Crewe, 15 Apr. 1909. See also Cd. 5194 (1910), op. cit., pp. 95, 152. Bell's views were supported by Hayes Sadler, who similarly pressed for Indian agricultural settlement in Uganda: 'Allidina Visram came to me sometime ago about taking up land in Uganda. I should like Indians there, because I look upon them as helping the people. They are thrifty, and they have a knowledge of agriculture, which, I think, would help the people very much.' See Cd. 5193 (1910), op. cit., p. 137.

immigration to help in the process of developing East Africa, pointing out that 'It may be safely affirmed . . . that the presence of a considerable number of Indian inhabitants has been and continues to be of material advantage to the British administration of the Protectorate.' But the Committee was opposed to the general question of importing indentured Indian labour.[1]

The demands for indentured Indian workers were, however, subsequently renewed by the Uganda Railway and in Zanzibar. In fact during 1906–7 the Railway had imported over 1,000 coolies from India on short-term indentures to work on the Mazeras realignment.[2] Later, in 1915, the Railway sought special permission to import Indian artisans for works connected with the Kilindini Harbour at Mombasa. But the Government of India, the Colonial Office reported, were 'obstinate as usual' in insisting upon proper contracts, etc. Permission was, however, obtained to import the required Indian labour as it was felt that the Sanderson Committee mainly objected to indentured immigration of Indian workers and agriculturists for private, as opposed to public, purposes.[3] Similarly in Zanzibar a scheme was mooted to recruit some Indian agricultural families as 'free settlers' and to engage labourers for public works— particularly road building—and an official was deputed to India for the purpose in 1912, but with little success.[4]

In essence, therefore, it is fair to say that after 1902 the previous policy of officially sponsored Indian immigration into East Africa— in respect of coolies for the construction of the Railway and subordinate staff for the Administrations—was for all practical purposes abandoned, and the weight of official policy directed to encouraging European settlement. As Alfred Lyttelton explained in 1905 in response to the anti-Indian views expressed by the European immigrants: 'Whatever decision may be eventually arrived at on these questions, it is obvious that the difficulty of arriving at a satisfactory solution will be increased, if the Indians in question have come to the Protectorate at the express invitation of the Government'—so that 'though we cannot well prevent them coming from their own accord I do not see why we should make trouble by helping them to

[1] Cd. 5192 (1910), op. cit., p. 92.
[2] *Annual Report on the E.A.P. for 1906–7.*
[3] C.O. 533/160, I.O. to C.O., 13 Jan. and 8 June 1915, and C.O. to I.O., 21 Jan. 1915, and minutes dated 10 June 1915.
[4] I.O. Emigration—Jan. 1911, Pros. 1–2, file 95 of 1910, part A, and May 1912, Pros. 9–14, file 29, part A.

come'.[1] Any scheme for State-aided Indian immigration into East
Africa was later finally buried by the Sanderson Committee; but at
the same time voluntary Indian immigration could continue virtually
unrestricted. And in such roles as artisan, subordinate staff, and
trader, in which the Indians had made an important beginning
during the 1890s, there was sufficient scope for new immigrants to
build on the foundations laid in the early years. In fact the key to
the settlement of Indians all over East Africa in the early years of
the century is provided by the growth of their role in the spheres
of subordinate employment, commercial enterprise, and as skilled
artisans—and the voluntary immigration that this encouraged. Yet,
interestingly enough, while official records are burdened with paper-
work relating to schemes for indentured Indian immigration that
never came to fruition, relatively little is known of what was essentially a much more significant phenomenon—the steady stream of
Indian immigrants that flowed along the channels of communication
opened during the 1890s and the opportunities they availed for a
variety of activities.

The demand for Indian skilled workers and subordinate staff
generated by the process of opening up the interior continued unabated into the present century. The indentured workers who
helped build the Uganda Railway largely returned to India, but the
Railway itself continued to depend heavily on Indian personnel for
its proper functioning. In a similar vein the demand for subordinate
Indian staff for the East African Administrations also steadily
increased. The Karachi Agency of the Railway ceased to function
after 1903 but a private firm then continued to act in a similar
capacity; while the Protector of Emigrants at Karachi maintained
a special establishment to deal with a variety of matters relating to
indentured emigration well up to the end of 1908.[2] Meanwhile the
functions of the principal Agency in India for the various East
African Administrations were exercised from Bombay, where an
agency had existed since 1896 and an official Agent since 1898.[3]

[1] C.O. 533/4, Lyttelton to Jackson, 25 Oct. 1905; Jackson to Lyttelton,
telegram, 12 Oct. 1905, and C.O. minutes thereon.

[2] C.O. 533/6, I.O. to F.O., 8 July 1905, enclosing Govt. of India to I.O.,
8 June 1905; I.O. Emigration—Apr. 1907, Pros. 2–4, file 44, p. 371; July 1908,
Pros. 23–4, file 70, part B; and Bombay Archives, G.D. vol. 322 C of 1902,
Comp. 50. Regarding the Uganda Railway's continuing dependence on Indian
employees, see also Cd. 5192 (1910), op. cit., p. 91.

[3] F.O. 2/791 and F.O. 2/894: 'Agency in India for the African Protectorates.'
See also p. 44, above.

Bombay thus became the principal recruiting centre and the port of departure for the variety of skilled workers that emigrated to East Africa during this period. The Railway itself appointed Messrs. Mackinnon, Mackenzie, & Co. at Bombay as its principal Agents in India after 1908.[1] But the process of recruitment and shipment of Indian emigrants did not always follow the official channels. In fact many Indian immigrants from the Bombay Presidency and Punjab arrived in East Africa during this period at the behest of their local contacts and obtained employment through local recruiting processes —although a majority of them took to private enterprise. This was partly due to the restrictions placed on emigration under contract by the Government of India, while emigration of 'free' or 'passenger' Indians could proceed without any official interference. The Protector of Emigrants in Bombay explained this situation in 1908 with reference to local recruitment in East Africa of Indian employees— particularly by the Railway: 'It appears . . . that the Uganda Railway authorities frequently import Indian labour without executing regular agreements in India. The men are induced to proceed to Uganda [*sic*] at their own expense, and on arrival in that country, agreements are made with them, the cost of their passages being refunded. . . .'[2] This official further pointed out that in the previous two years only 305 Indians had left Bombay under agreements executed in accordance with the emigration regulations, while 12,212 had similarly gone to East Africa but without any prior contracts—for, in addition to the Railway and the Administrations, private employers were also engaging 'free' Indian immigrants locally. The normal method adopted for such informal recruiting of Indian employees is perhaps best revealed by a letter from an executive engineer in the Public Works Department to a prospective Indian employee in the Punjab, dated 12 November 1909, which stated:

I have come back again to Naivasha. . . . I have not yet taken any man in your place and I shall be pleased if you will come, but you must *come at once* as I cannot wait longer than 1st January next. If you come I wish you to bring with you—4 good carpenters 3 good masons 1 good blacksmith. To the above men I shall give Rs. 2 per working day per man.

---

[1] I.O. Emigration—Apr. 1907, Pros. 2–4, file 44, p. 371, and July 1908, Pros. 23–4, file 70, part B.

[2] I.O. Emigration—Dec. 1908, Pros. 23–5, file 110, p. 861; and Bombay Archives, G.D. vol. 8 C of 1909, Comp. 9, Protector of Emigrants, Bombay, to Bombay Govt., 2 Oct. 1908. See also Girouard's report on British East Africa, May 1910 in C.O.C.P. no. 879/105/954, p. 84.

I shall want them to sign a stamped paper stating that they agree to work with me for 2½ years from date of arrival here. . . .[1]

The Indian authorities took objection to such informal recruiting methods since these infringed upon the provisions of the Emigration Act of 1908. It was felt that while the movement of 'free' Indians could continue unrestricted, that of skilled workers could not be freed from the existing restrictions—especially as there was 'no indication of any desire on the part of the Administrations of the East African Colonies that there should be a free movement of labour from India into their territories. On the other hand there are already symptoms of the growth of an anti-Asiatic feeling. . . .'[2] Consequently, steps were taken to check such recruitment of artisans from India by private invitation of officials in East Africa, but this hardly affected the voluntary emigration of artisans and traders, which far exceeded that of indentured emigrants—of whom it appears that only 107 went to British East Africa and 16 to German East Africa between 1909 and 1911.[3] In the circumstances, the need for an official Agent-General in India for the East African Governments steadily diminished; and in September 1912 the official Agency in Bombay was finally abolished—its much-reduced functions being taken over by a private firm, Messrs. Mackinnon, Mackenzie, & Co.[4]

Meanwhile, however, the Indian role in skilled and subordinate employment had assumed increasing importance in East Africa. In 1905, for example, the manager of the Uganda Railway reported that 1,254 Indians were employed on the Railway; and pointed out that:

[1] Bombay Archives, G.D. vol. 8 C of 1909, Comp. 9, Protector of Emigrants, Bombay, to Bombay Govt., 2 Oct. 1908, and Bombay Govt. to Govt. of India, 28 Oct. 1908, and G.D. vol. 59 C of 1910, Comp. 417. Details also in I.O. Emigration—Mar. 1910, Pros. 1–2, file 20, part A, and Aug. 1910, Pros. 1–2, file 20, part A.

[2] I.O. Emigration—Dec. 1908, Pros. 23–5, file 110, part A, copy of Govt. of India to Bombay Govt., 18 Dec. 1908. See also I.O. Emigration—Mar. 1910, Pros. 1–2, file 20, part A, and Aug. 1910, Pros. 1–2, file 20, part A; and Bombay Archives, G.D. vol. 59 C of 1910, Comp. 417.

[3] Bombay Archives, G.D. vol. 59 C of 1910, Comp. 1264, and vol. 71 C of 1911, Comp. 1199. An earlier report by the Principal Immigration Officer, Mombasa, in 1906 showed that of the 709 'free' Indian immigrants, three-fourths were carpenters and the remainder petty shopkeepers. See C.O. 533/19, Sadler to Elgin, 5 Dec. 1906, enclosed report.

[4] E.A.P., *Minutes of the Legislative Council*, 28 Nov. 1911; I.O. Emigration—Feb. 1913, Pros. 25–7, file 11, part B; Kenya Archives, file Mombasa 3/286, circular letter no. 63 from the Acting Chief Secretary, dated Aug. 12 1912; and Bombay Archives, P.D. vol. 129 of 1913.

At Mombasa, Nairobi and Port Florence (Kisumu), there are experienced European Station Masters with Indian Babus as Clerks and Signallers, while the menial staff is mixed Indian and African. . . . At the engine changing stations of Voi, Makindu and Nakuro [*sic*], there are Eurasian Station Masters, the other employees being as above described. At all other stations, the combined duties of station master and signaller are carried on by an Indian Babu and the menials are mixed Indian and African . . . the Guards are two-thirds European and one-third Goanese and Indian.[1]

Later in his evidence to the Sanderson Committee, the manager of the Railway stated that about 2,000 Indians were employed on the Railway as clerks and artisans and that 'almost entirely' all the station-masters were Indians—and explained that 'At the present moment we could not do without them'.[2] The importance of their role perhaps accounted for the successful strike action taken by the Indian employees of the Railway, in conjunction with those of the Public Works Department, in 1914.[3] But the number of Indian staff employed by the Railway did not much exceed the figure of 2,000 during this period—in 1921 they numbered 2,022.[4]

Similarly the role of subordinate Indian employees in the Administration steadily increased during this period in view of their competitiveness and the lack of qualified local candidates. In virtually every department of the central and provincial government, the subordinate ranks—clerks, artisans, etc.—were filled almost exclusively by Indian recruits. In 1904, for example, almost all clerical posts in the provincial and district administrations in Kenya and Uganda were filled by Goans—and in some of the remote and outlying districts the Goan clerk was often crucial to the smooth running of the administrative machine. In some of the central government departments—police, survey, and land—and particularly in the Railway, the Punjabi staff were particularly conspicuous; while, overall, Indian subordinates—especially the Goans—monopolized the middle posts in the various government departments. In Zanzibar the subordinate ranks of the Administration were filled largely by the Parsees—some of whom also rose to higher posts. In 1904 the Minister of Public Works in Zanzibar, the Registrar of the Court, and the Chief Sanitary Officer were all Parsees. In Kenya too a

[1] C.O. 533/2, Stewart to Lyttelton, 6 July 1905, enclosed report on the Uganda Railway, dated 5 July 1905.   [2] Cd. 5193 (1910), op. cit., pp. 66-8.
[3] C.O. 537/402, Belfield to Harcourt, 27 Aug. 1914.
[4] Kenya, *Report of the Census of Non-Natives*, 24 Apr. 1921.

Parsee held the post of head of the **Public Works Department** between 1896 and 1908.[1] The general dependence on Indian subordinate staff continued unchecked during this period, and the number of Indian employees in the central and provincial administrations of Kenya, Uganda, and Zanzibar steadily increased. In every department of government—including the ones newly established—the Indians filled the middle ranks in an extensive variety of capacities: as hospital assistants, surveyors, draughtsmen, clerks, cashiers, customs collectors, policemen, artisans, mechanics, carpenters, post and telegraph assistants, shorthand writers, typists, and compounders, etc.[2] The Blue Books of the East African Protectorates in fact published full details of the Indian staff in their Civil Lists well up to the eve of the First World War—an obvious reflection upon the importance attached to their role. In the field of provincial administration, for example, the importance of the Indian clerks—particularly the Goans—is best attested to in the report of the District Commissioner, Malindi, for 1911:

[1] F.O. 2/795, Ternan to Salisbury, 2 Nov. 1900; S. Playne and F. H. Gale, *East Africa (British)* (London, 1908–9), p. 305; and *Handbook for East Africa, Uganda and Zanzibar* (Govt. Printer, Mombasa, 1904). From the earliest times, the employment of Indian subordinate staff and artisans in East Africa tended to follow the patterns and precedents set in British India. The Goans and Parsees, for example, enjoyed a reputation for loyalty and efficiency that accounted for their extensive employment as administrative staff. Similarly the Goans had a reputation as caterers, stewards, wine merchants, chefs, and dealers in European groceries. The official caterers for the Uganda Railway during this period, for example, were a Goan firm; while some of the leading European stores were also run by the Goans (see p. 83, below). But the single most important community to be extensively associated with the Imperial effort in East Africa from the early days was the Muslims. Up until the eve of the First World War, they represented more than half of the Indian population in the territories. Most of the early Indian traders, the extension of whose enterprise in the interior coincided with the establishment of British Administration, were Muslims—especially Khojas (Ismailis). Sewa Hajee, for example, belonged to the Khoja community, so also did Allidina Visram; while A. M. Jeevanjee was a member of the Bohora (Muslim) community. Punjabi Muslims formed the majority of the labour recruited for the construction of the Uganda Railway—and were the principal artisans. They were also recruited into the local police forces, while at least half of the British Indian troops employed in East Africa during the early colonial period were Punjabi Muslims. The Sikhs enjoyed a reputation for being the backbone of the British Indian Army, and Sikh soldiers were frequently employed in East and Central Africa at the beginning of the colonial period—later they were often recruited into the local police forces. Sikh artisans, later conspicuous in East Africa, reflected the existing pattern in British India.

[2] *Handbook for East Africa, Uganda and Zanzibar 1904*; Official Blue Books, any volume before 1912; Playne and Gale, op. cit.; and *Drumkey's Year Book for East Africa* (1908).

As one of the two Administrative Officers is more frequently on safari than not the remaining one finds himself so busy . . . that he must rely to a very large extent on his clerks. . . . It speaks well therefore for the reputation and standing of our clerical staff that after 14 years' experience of District work in 5 provinces I have never once known one's confidence in the members of it to be misplaced or have had reason to regret the extent to which one has trusted them.[1]

An important feature of the growing role of Indian employees in the Administrations was their general competitiveness—the fact that they cost relatively little in salaries and benefits, which varied from a minimum of £40 to a maximum of £160 per annum in 1912.[2] Sir Percy Girouard had in fact pointed out in 1909 that

His [the Indian's] presence, in our existing financial conditions, makes government possible in that he provides the subordinate staff of nearly every department. It is urged that the white man could be substituted for him, but of the success of any such policy I have at present the gravest doubts, much as it appeals to me.[3]

Exact figures for the total number of subordinate Indian employees are not available. In Kenya they numbered 866 in 1912 and 1,447 in 1921; the comparable figures for Uganda and Zanzibar would probably be half this total. In Tanganyika, where the practice of employing subordinate Indian staff was adopted after the establishment of the British Mandate, a total of 804 Indian staff were employed by the Administration in 1921, while another 886 served the railways in that territory.[4]

[1] Mombasa Archives, shelf 1, file no. 37 of 1912: District of Malindi, report for the quarter ending 31 Dec. 1911. See also shelf 64, file no. 260 of 1912: Malindi District Annual Report for 1911–12, which similarly reveals the predominance of Goans in the Provincial Administration: 'There are no changes to record in the Clerical Staff other than the leave of absence of Mr. S. C. Fernandez District Clerk and Cashier. During his absence Mr. J. C. Braganza Jr. Assistant District Clerk acted for him and Mr. A. Ferreira filled the place of Mr. J. C. Braganza Junior. On the return from leave of Mr. S. C. Fernandes, Mr. J. C. Braganza reverted to his old post and Mr. A. Ferreira left the District. In February 1912 Mr. J. C. Braganza was transferred up-country and was relieved here by Mr. Menezes.' Needless to say all the names mentioned by the D.C. are Goan.
[2] *Terms of Service for members of the Non-European Clerical Staff of the Uganda and East Africa Protectorates,* 1912, C.O. pamphlet no. 33.
[3] C.O. 533/63, Girouard to Crewe, 13 Nov. 1909, enclosed interim report on E.A.P. and Uganda. See also Girouard's reports for 1909 and 1910 in C.O.C.P. no. 879/105/954, pp. 7, 84.
[4] Tanganyika, *Report on the Non-Native Census 1921;* Kenya, *Reports on the Non-Native Census, 1921 and 1926;* Uganda, *Census Returns 1911* and *Report of the Commissioner appointed to enquire into and report on the Financial Position and System of Taxation of Kenya,* Colonial no. 116 (1936), Appendix XI, p. 260 D.

The Indian role in middle-grade employment was, however, not restricted to government service alone. Both in private employment and in business their activities as skilled staff and as artisans steadily expanded during this period. Sir Hesketh Bell, for example, reported from Uganda in 1909 that 'Nearly all the artisans and skilled labourers employed by the Public Works Department and by private firms are Indians.'[1] The census returns for Kenya and Uganda in 1911 showed that a number of Indians were engaged as builders and contractors, masons, carpenters, blacksmiths, tailors, and shoemakers, etc; while a little later a local observer wrote that 'Most of the skilled and semi-skilled labour is done by Indian workmen'.[2] Similarly, in German East Africa about half of the Indian population of about 9,000 in 1912–13 were stated to be artisans and clerical staff engaged variously by the authorities or private firms or operating on their own account.[3] Many of these skilled immigrants were to launch a variety of business enterprises as contractors, outfitters, builders, and mechanics, etc., and helped to supplement the activities of the Indian commercial population in East Africa—which also witnessed a steady expansion during this period.

The enterprise of some of the pioneer Indian traders in the interior continued to develop upon the foundations laid in the early years. The most notable in this respect were the achievements of Allidina Visram, who had built up an extensive East Africa-wide business network by the beginning of this century. Various contemporary accounts describe the continuing expansion of his *duka*-based enterprise in different parts of East Africa. During the first decade of the century, his business 'empire' extended from Bombay through Mombasa and Bagamoyo to over thirty major branches in East Africa—at Dar es Salaam, Tanga, Tabora, Mwanza, Bukoba, Ujiji, Kilima, and other posts in Tanganyika and the Congo; at Kampala, Jinja, Mbale, Entebbe, Wadelai, Nimule, Gondokoro, Toro, Mbarara, Masindi, Hoima, and other posts in Uganda and southern Sudan; at Kisumu, Yala, Mumias, Kisii, Nairobi, Eldama Ravine, Nakuru, Naivasha, Maranga (Fort Hall), Laikipia, Kikere, Nyeri, and at other posts in Kenya. At the same time his firm employed over 500 Indian and many more African

---

[1] Cd. 5194 (1910), op. cit., p. 152.

[2] *The Leader Annual and Gazetter of B.E.A.*, 1914, C.O. ref. H. 12734.

[3] *Deutsches Koloniale Lexicon* (Berlin, 1920), ii. 91—quoted in India Archives, Emigration—Sept. 1925, Pros. 1–92, part A, departmental memo. on Indians in East Africa prepared by Mr. Ewbank.

assistants, apart from the traders who acted as his agents.[1] In fact the Land Office records in Kenya and Uganda reveal that Allidina's firm had invested extensively in plots of land in almost every early town or township in Kenya and Uganda. Meanwhile, the enterprise of this firm continued to expand. In 1909 Allidina was reported to have had seventeen agents operating in the Congo with about Rs. 400,000 worth of goods advanced by him—as he himself explained, these agents 'hold all my goods on credit, and we share profits on the sale of Ivory'.[2] In the same year his firm obtained a special licence from the Uganda Government to operate at Kilimi and send out caravans in search of ivory in the closed district of Karamoja.[3] In 1910 Allidina was reported to have agents spread as far as Addis Ababa, and to be importing fire-arms from Ethiopia into Uganda.[4] Similarly, his firm with 'customary enterprise' established two *dukas* in a remote district of the Northern Province of Uganda in 1912 in order to supply trade goods to the local population in exchange for ivory and other produce.[5] About the same time, Allidina Visram was described as the leading trader in the Mwanza and Bukoba area of Tanganyika and was reputed to have had substantial investments in the area at the time of his death in 1916.[6]

Meanwhile, Allidina had launched a diversification of his business activities in East Africa. The letter-heads of his firm reveal that about 1906 Zanzibar and Mombasa formed the headquarters, and that the firm acted in a wide variety of capacities—as importers of merchandise from Europe, India, and America, and as exporters of 'all kinds of East Africa and Uganda Produce'.[7] He also continued to use the telegraphic address 'Pagazi', which he had adopted at the beginning of his career—perhaps as a tribute to the one constant factor—the *mapagazi* or porters—in his rise from a small caravan trader to an East African commercial pioneer. Allidina also added

[1] *Handbook for East Africa, Uganda and Zanzibar, 1904*; Playne and Gale, op. cit., pp. 120–2; *Drumkey's Year Book for East Africa* (1908), p. 36. See also A. Visram's advertisement in 'Uganda Notes: A Journal of Missionary and General Interest', Dec. 1907, viii, no. 12 (Kampala, 1907).

[2] Entebbe Archives, file no. 72 (1909) and file no. 57 (1910).

[3] Entebbe Archives, file no. 1323 (1909): Bukedi, ivory trading at Kilimi.

[4] Entebbe Archives, file no. 1330, Eastern Province, Mbale: A. Visram's Agents, Importation of Firearms from Abyssinia.

[5] Entebbe Archives, file no. 2135 B: Northern Province Annual Report for 1912–13.

[6] Entebbe Archives, file no. 4832: 'Misc. Allidina Visram', and file no. 5677.

[7] Copy of letter-head in Kenya Archives, Nyanza Province Annual Report for 1906–7.

a small steamboat to his fleet of sailing vessels on Lake Victoria in order to cater for his growing cargo business between the various lake ports. His other interests included furniture-making at Kampala and Entebbe, soda factories, oil mills at Kisumu and at the Coast— obtaining oil from sesame and copra—a soap factory at Mombasa, two small cotton-ginning establishments at Mombasa and Entebbe, and saw-mills in Uganda and near Nyeri.[1] Perhaps the crowning achievement of his career was the cotton ginnery he established at Kampala during 1912–14, in association with other Indian merchants —which represented a substantial capital investment, and provided the foundations for the subsequent Indian role in the Uganda cotton industry. It was also fitting that Allidina Visram should thus invest his capital in the country where, in 1910, he was described by the Governor as 'the largest trader in the whole Protectorate, who is supposed to command a very large amount of capital'.[2]

An important feature of Allidina's business career was his relations with the Government and the public generally. In a variety of capacities he rendered valuable services to the Government in the early days. On occasions he was deputed by the Government to report on the conditions of trade in certain districts, or to assist in the establishment of transport services in the provinces. His firm, for example, pioneered cart transport services along the Mbale–Kumi road, between Kampala and Fort Portal as well as Kampala and Mbarara—in the latter two cases offering special facilities for the transport of government goods.[3] Other reports speak of his firm

[1] For A. Visram's various business interests, see Kenya Archives, file Mombasa 103/7, refers to soap factory 1907, and Nyanza Province Annual Reports for 1907–8 and 1910–11; Entebbe Archives, file no. 131 (1910), refers to erection of ginnery and oil factory at Entebbe; file no. 806 (1907), refers to Visram's leather tannery at Entebbe; files no. 569 (1908) and 146, 409, 483 (all 1909), refer to Visram's timber interests in Uganda; file nos. 553, 756, 4699, refer to Allidina's relations with his porters, and a large number of files—nos. 46, 87, 262, 578, 671, 990, 1016, 1322, and 5075—refer to Visram's extensive land holdings. See also Kenya Archives, file Mombasa 38/605, which refers to Allidina's commercial interests at Kisumu in 1915; and E.A.P., *Minutes of the Executive Council*, 14 Sept. 1912, which show Allidina's timber interests near Nyeri. For a general account, see Playne and Gale, op. cit., pp. 120–2.

[2] Cd. 5193 (1910), op. cit., pp. 318–19; *Leader of B.E.A.*, 8 July 1916; and C.O. 533/79, Confidential Report on the Uganda Cotton Industry by S. Simpson, Director of Agriculture, dated 31 July 1912, and comments thereon.

[3] Kenya Archives, Nyanza Province Annual Report for 1906–7 and Nairobi District Annual Report for 1910–11 (file no. DC/MKS. 1/4/1); and Entebbe Archives, file nos. 703 and 703 B: Eastern Province Annual Reports for 1909–10 and 1911–12; file no. 1972 C: Buganda Monthly Reports 1914.

being asked by the Government to supply oil presses at Mbale and Balulu—in order to facilitate the extraction of oil by the local people from sesame, ground-nuts, and castor seed; or that his 'enterprising firm' should be encouraged to set up a flour-mill in Toro, as it had previously done at Kampala to supply the Indian troops. The regard in which his firm was held is best exemplified in the District Commissioner's report on Hoima for 1912–13: 'I regret to report that Allidina Visram'—'the old pioneer trader'—'closed his business at the end of March.'[1] In a subsequent minute on the subject in June 1925, the Chief Secretary's department in Uganda perhaps best recalled the various services Allidina Visram had rendered to the Government:

He was always ready to help the encouragement of local industries by buying native crops which no one else would touch, at prices which meant a loss for him. I remember myself that when natives on Elgon were encouraged in 1909 to make beeswax, and made it in large quantities, no buyer could be found except Allidina, who paid locally a higher price per lb. than the product would fetch delivered at Liverpool. The same thing happened in the early days of the cotton industry in the Eastern Province.[2]

Similar views were expressed by an earlier Chief Secretary in a tribute to Allidina Visram following his death in June 1916. This recalled the 'long and prosperous career' of Allidina in Zanzibar, Tanganyika, Kenya, and Uganda, and the 'universal regard' in which he was held; and pointed out that: 'During his many years of close association with the Protectorate he played a very important part in its development and always rendered most willing and valuable assistance to the Government whenever it was in his power to do so.'[3] The relations of Allidina's family with the public generally were

---

[1] Entebbe Archives, file no. 831 (1907), refers to Visram's assistance regarding Toro Produce; file no. 1145 (1909), refers to the oil industry in Bukedi; file no. 4304, Acting Treasurer to Chief Secretary, 23 May 1918, suggesting that Allidina Visram be asked to transport hoes to various stations; and files no. 2135 B and 2135 C: Northern Province Annual Reports for 1912–13 and 1913–14.

[2] Entebbe Archives, file no. 4832, 'Misc. Allidina Visram', memo. by the Chief Secretary's office to the Governor, 9 June 1925.

[3] Entebbe Archives, file no. 4832, Chief Secretary to A. A. Visram, 6 July 1916. Another official account similarly commented on Allidina's close relations with the Government as carried on under his son: 'Mr. Allidina Visram has a large and well-kept establishment at Mambrara where Officers Administering the Governments of East Africa and Uganda frequently visit him. . . . During the early part of the war he placed his Entebbe house at the disposal of the Government, rent free.' Minute by the Acting Governor, 1 Nov. 1917 in Entebbe Archives file no. 1016, 'Land, A. Visram'.

based on considerable munificence—expressed in the substantial donations he made to the Namirembe Cathedral, the local hospital and the Red Cross at Kampala, and to the Indian school at Mombasa which bears his name.[1] Allidina Visram was also among the founding members of the Chambers of Commerce in Mombasa and Kampala, and played a leading role in their activities in the early years. Perhaps, above all, it was in recognition of his various services to early Uganda that members of the Protectorate and Kabaka's Government joined in mourning his death;[2] while Indian merchants in Nairobi, Mombasa, and Kampala closed their shops for a day as a tribute to the man whose success as a pioneer trader had provided the foundations on which Indian *duka* enterprise in various parts of East Africa, and especially in Uganda, was built.

But the entrepreneurial skills which enabled Allidina Visram to play such an important role in the economic history of East Africa are necessarily qualities in short supply. His son and successor, A. A. Visram, continued to operate the extensive business network he had inherited, and the firm's predominance in the commercial life of Uganda and to a lesser extent of Kenya and Tanganyika was to continue. But shortly after the latter's death in 1923, Allidina Visram's remarkable business empire rapidly disintegrated. In 1918 his estate was worth well over Rs. 3 million; by 1925 his successors had become 'practically penniless' and sought the Government's assistance on the strength of Allidina's services to the Administration in the early days. This was granted to them in the form of two sites, where members of the Indian community undertook to help build two ginneries. Finally in 1926 the creditors of A. A. Visram's bankrupt estate had to content themselves with the payment of a mere 2 per cent dividend.[3] However, a few streets in a number of East African towns named after Allidina Visram, or his statue at Mombasa (which was recently removed), act as reminders of his pioneering commercial ventures; as also do the personal recollections of many old Indian traders in East Africa who knew him or, more important, began their business careers in Allidina's service. From

---

[1] Entebbe Archives, file no. 4832 and *Leader of B.E.A.*, 15 July 1916. See also W. M. Ross, *Kenya from Within*, p. 303.

[2] *Leader of B.E.A.*, 8 and 15 July 1916.

[3] Entebbe Archives, file no. 4832, Attorney-General to Chief Secretary, 14 Sept. 1918, Minutes of the Cotton Board, 26 Mar. 1925, Governor to Chief Secretary, 10 Mar. 1925, minute of 25 Jan. 1927 and *passim*. See also *Handbook of German East Africa* (London, 1920), p. 178.

such men one learns how Allidina Visram, starting as a minor caravan trader in Bagamoyo during the 1880s, pioneered the commercial penetration of Uganda and built in the process an extensive network of *dukas* and other business interests—which made him not only the largest early trader in that country, but, in their estimation, virtually an 'uncrowned King of Uganda'.

In Kenya the firm of A. M. Jeevanjee also made substantial progress during this period. By the early years of the century its operations covered a wide field, and Jeevanjee acted as a builder and contractor, stevedore, estate agent, general merchant, importer and exporter, and as a shipowner—operating two lines of steamships between Bombay and Mauritius and Bombay and Jedda. He also continued to build a series of offices and quarters which were leased by the Administration; while the branches of his firm spread from Bombay, Karachi, Goa to Mombasa and Nairobi.[1] In 1905 A. M. Jeevanjee built the municipal market in Nairobi which was described as 'the most up-to-date structure of its kind in East Africa'.[2] He also laid the first public gardens in Nairobi, which still bear his name. In fact his firm's business interests and investments in Nairobi had greatly increased so that Ainsworth was able to describe him in 1906 as 'a gentleman who has done much for the prosperity of this town'.[3] Later accounts speak of the continuing expansion of his business enterprise and investments in Kenya; while during the First World War he specially offered his services to the Government as well as a financial contribution to the British military hospital in Nairobi.[4]

A number of Indian firms similarly pioneered the exploitation of the commercial potential of East Africa. Most of them were small traders, who by the very nature of their enterprise have left few records; but from scattered bits and pieces of information available about them—including the personal reminiscences of some of them who are still alive—a picture of steady growth, sometimes in the face of numerous odds, and of valuable contribution to economic development clearly emerges. Some contemporary sources[5] reveal the

[1] *Handbook for East Africa, Uganda and Zanzibar 1904*; C.O.C.P. 879/87/772, p. 188; *Leader of B.E.A.* 1 Oct. 1910; and *Drumkey's Year Book for East Africa* (1908).
[2] *Reports Relating to the Administration of the E.A.P.*, Cd. 2740 (1905), p. 12.
[3] A. M. Jeevanjee, *Sanitation in Nairobi*, C.O. pamphlet no. 214, enclosures. See also Ross, op. cit., p. 303.
[4] *Leader of B.E.A.*, 17 Apr. 1915; and I.O. Emigration—Jan. 1915, Pros. 37, file 163 of 1914, part B.
[5] Playne and Gale, op. cit.; *Drumkey's Year Book for East Africa* (1908);

enormous variety of functions performed by the Indians in the economic life of East Africa during this period—when other similar agencies were not available. There were, for example, such early caravan traders, who operated in the fashion of Allidina Visram but on a much lesser scale, as Dewji Jamal at Mombasa, or Waljee Bhanjee in Uganda, and perhaps more important, Nasser Virjee in German East Africa—particularly in the Mwanza area.[1] There were the old-established firms of Cowasjee Dinshaw and Esmailji Jivanji who operated a number of steamers and virtually controlled the coastal communications of East Africa;[2] or the highly successful firms of Karimjee Jivanji operating in Zanzibar, Mombasa, and, particularly, along the Tanganyika Coast.[3] In Kenya, Suleiman Virji and Beliram Parimal had launched successful commercial enterprises; while J. A. Nazareth acted as the official caterer to the Railway and Souza, Junior, & Dias were distinguished for the 'enterprise with which they cater for all sorts of [household] needs'.[4] Similarly the carriages and rickshaws of the horse-dealer Ali Khan provided the principal transport service in Nairobi at the time.[5] There were in fact a large number of old-established Indian firms and new immigrant traders, too numerous to be mentioned, engaged at this time in a wide variety of business undertakings, ranging from miscellaneous contractors to importers and exporters, estate agents, and hardware dealers, etc. But among the newcomers of particular importance were such firms as Narandas Rajaram of Bombay, who pioneered the introduction of Uganda cotton to the Bombay market in 1914, or Vithaldas Haridas, the progenitor of the vast enterprise of

Handbook for East Africa, Uganda and Zanzibar 1904; and advertisements in various contemporary editions of the *E.A.S.* and the *Leader of B.E.A.*

[1] *Tanganyika Herald* (Dar es Salaam), 13 Nov. 1947, p. 7 and oral information.
[2] Mombasa Archives, shelf 1, file no. 37 of 1912: District of Malindi report for the quarter ending 31 Dec. 1911; *Annual Report on the E.A.P. for 1910–11*; H. Brode, *British and German East Africa*, p. 28, refers to a 629-ton steamer owned by an Indian firm in Zanzibar, which carried on the Coastal trade between Mombasa, Tanga, Dar es Salaam, and Zanzibar. The Parsee firm of Cowasjee Dinshaw, based on Aden and later Zanzibar, had earlier helped equip Lord Delamere's expeditions into East Africa during the 1890s—see E. Huxley, *White Man's Country*, i. 31–2.
[3] For these various firms, see *Handbook for East Africa, Uganda and Zanzibar 1904*; and *Drumkey's Year Book for East Africa* (1908).
[4] *E.A.S.*, 24 Dec. 1910; Playne and Gale, op. cit., p. 185; Ross, op. cit., p. 321; and Entebbe Archives, file no. 1138: Buganda Annual Report for 1909–10—enclosed report by the D.C. Entebbe shows that Allidina Visram and Souza, Junior, & Dias were the principal traders at Entebbe in 1910.
[5] Playne and Gale, op. cit., pp. 172–3; and *E.A.S.*, 24 Dec. 1910.

the Madhvani and related families in the cotton and sugar industries of Uganda; or Nanji Kalidas Mehta who similarly pioneered
what was later to become an extensive East Africa-wide business network based on the Uganda cotton and sugar industries; and, among
many others, Kanji Naranjee, a later business magnate in Nairobi.[1]

But less heard of—and more important for the growth of the
Indian economic role in East Africa—were the increasing number of
petty traders who had moved along the railways, the caravan routes,
to the newly established administrative posts and into some remote
districts. They were the traders who pushed the frontiers of commerce into new regions and created fresh opportunities for commercial enterprise—while also forming the backbone of the emerging
Indian bazaars in various parts of East Africa. In Kenya, the Indian
bazaars at Nairobi and Mombasa developed into the major centres of
Indian commercial enterprise; while those at Machakos and Kisumu,
established from the early days of the colonial period, grew in
importance as local centres of Indian trade. In addition, during the
early years of this century new Indian bazaars were progressively
established in various parts of the country. By 1910, for example,
there were forty-four Indian *dukawallas* operating in the African
reserves of the Ukamba Province, while thirty of them were settled in
Machakos. Similarly, another thirty Indian traders had established
shops along the railway and Indian bazaars existed at Kibwezi, Ulu,
Kitui, and Sultan Hamud. Most of them were engaged in selling an
increasing variety of imported goods—blankets, lamps, cloths, and
provisions—and purchasing local produce—grain, hides and skins,
and ghee. In some areas barter trade still continued in spite of the
rapid spread of the rupee currency, but now it was the hoes that
formed the principal article of barter.[2] In the Coast Province, apart
from the old settlements at Mombasa, Malindi, and Lamu, Indian
bazaars were established at Rabai, Mazeras, Samburu, Mariakani,
Mackinnon Road, Taveta, Vanga, and Voi by 1911; while a few
Indian traders penetrated into the 'out-back' to engage in trade

[1] For Narandas Rajaram, see the correspondence with Govt. of India in
I.O. Emigration—June 1919, Pros. 35–40, part A. For an obituary on Kanji
Naranjee, see *E.A.S.*, 1 Oct. 1964. See also Minutes of the Uganda Chamber of
Commerce, 29 Jan. 1915 to 10 Dec. 1926, *passim*. For further information about
the Madhvani and Mehta firms, see Ch. V, below.

[2] Kenya Archives, file no. MKS/57: Machakos District Political Record
Book, 1910–11, vol. ii, and file no. MKS/1: Machakos District Annual Reports
for 1910 and 1913. See also *Reports Relating to the Administration of the E.A.P.*,
Cd. 2740 (1905), pp. 18–19, and *Annual Report on the E.A.P. for 1908–9.*

based on local produce—especially in the country around the old-established bazaar at Voi. By 1911 some of the Indian traders were also carrying on commercial traffic between Voi and Moshi in Tanganyika with the help of carts and donkeys.[1] Subsequent reports reveal a steady growth of Indian commercial enterprise in this area. In 1913–14, for example, an Indian firm at Mwatate, near Voi, shipped 7,000 lb. of beans and 6,000 lb. of maize purchased from the local producers, while Indian shops had been established at the smaller settlements of Bura, Tsavo, Kedai, etc.[2] A later report showed that in spite of fluctuations in trade during the war, Indian commercial predominance in the Voi area and along the railway continued unchecked.[3]

The same process of steady growth applies to other provinces of Kenya. In the Central Province, Indian bazaars were progressively established at the various emerging townships well before 1911—at Nyeri, Limuru, Kikuyu, Fort Hall, Ruiru, Thika, and at Embu and Meru; while a number of Indian traders spread into the districts in search of increasing quantities of local produce.[4] The District Commissioner at Nyeri, for example, reported in 1908 that the Indian traders in the Nyeri bazaar and their agents purchased substantial quantities of local produce from the Kikuyu and sold it to passing caravans or shipped it to Nairobi, Naivasha, and Rumuruti. Further he added that 'their trade goods are in demand with the Kikuyu natives of the District and their presence here, therefore, serves a useful purpose.'[5] Similarly a later report from Limuru indicated that an Indian trader had exported twenty tons of maize from the place during 1912–13, while about fifty other Indian shops were engaged in similar business.[6] By 1921 in fact much of the trade in local produce was 'chiefly in Indian hands' and the Indian traders had penetrated into the various outlying settlements. Their enterprise contributed to increased local production in the area—in 1921, for example, the

[1] E.A.P., *Census Returns 1911*; Mombasa Archives, shelf 1, file no. 37 of 1912: Quarterly Report of the D.C., Rabai, Dec. 1911, and Quarterly Report on Voi District, Dec. 1911.

[2] Kenya Archives, file no. TTA/5: Political Record Book, Taita District 1913–25, vol. i, Report on Taita District for 1913–14.

[3] Ibid., Report on Taita District for 1922.

[4] Kenya Archives, file no. KBU/3: Kiambu District Annual Report for 1911–12, and file no. KBU/4: Kiambu District Annual Report for 1912–13. See also E.A.P., *Census Returns 1911*.

[5] Kenya Archives, file no. PC/CP. 9/3/1: D.C., Nyeri, to P.C., 11 Sept. 1908.

[6] Kenya Archives, file no. KBU/4, op. cit.

African producers in the Nyeri District alone sold about 180,000 loads of maize to the Indian dealers. In addition a number of Indian traders operated on the European farms, or established temporary camps on them during the harvest season, in order to purchase local produce, which was then sent by rail to Nairobi and Mombasa. Some of them also established flour mills on these farms to meet the demands of the local workers.[1] The importance of Indian enterprise generally was best summed up in a later report of a missionary in the Fort Hall district:

> The Indian trader has done much to open up the Reserves . . . he has set the example of trading, transport, the use of water power for maize mills, etc., and the native's tentative attempts to begin his own wagon transport, to open shops, and to build maize mills in his Reserve are modelled on an Indian original.[2]

In a similar fashion the Indian traders expanded their activities in the Rift Valley Province during this period. Indian bazaars were progressively established at the various settlements of Nakuru, Naivasha, Eldoret, Eldama Ravine, Molo, Kijabe, Gilgil, Londiani, Baringo, and other places. A number of the Indian traders also operated on the European farms, while some of them established scattered *dukas* in the districts.[3] In the Nyanza and Western Provinces, Kisumu at first served as the principal base for the expansion of Indian commercial enterprise into various districts. By 1911, however, flourishing Indian bazaars had been established at Mumias, Kisii, Kapsabet, and Kericho; and as a report indicated: 'the people are daily finding fresh wants and the local Indian traders are endeavouring to meet them'. A little later the Provincial Commissioner pointed out that 'the Indian continues to be the predominant trader in the Province'.[4] Perhaps the general nature and method of Indian enterprise in the countryside was best explained by Professor

[1] Kenya Archives, file no. Mombasa 42/797: Chief Secretary's circular letter no. 11 of 22 Feb. 1917, and file no. PC/CP. 4/1/2: Kikuyu Province Annual Report for 1920–1.

[2] International Missionary Council, Edinburgh House, London, Papers of Dr. J. H. Oldham, file: 'Kenya Indians, General Correspondence', Revd. H. D. Hooper to J. H. Oldham, 27 Mar. 1923.

[3] Kenya Archives, file no. PC/RVP. 2/8/1–21: Uasin Gishu District Annual Reports for 1913–14, 1914–15, and 1919–20.

[4] Kenya Archives, file no. PC/NZA 1/2: Nyanza Province Annual Reports for 1910 and 1914. See also W. J. Simpson, *Report on Sanitary Matters in the E.A.P., Uganda and Zanzibar* (Colonial Office, 1915), p. 62.

Simpson in a report of 1915, which included a reference to trade at Yala near Kisumu:

> Yala is the great collecting centre for the grain and produce of the country north of the Yala River. To this station the natives bring their baskets of grain and sell it to the Indians, who store it . . . until it is convenient to send it in bags or carts to Kisumu. The road between Yala and Kisumu is thronged with carts passing to and fro. Those from Yala are loaded, according to the season of the year, with sim sim, maize, beans, hides, and skins and those from Kisumu with rice . . . cloths etc.

Similarly, Professor Simpson explained the role of the old-established Indian bazaar in Kisumu as the local base for commercial operations in the interior—pointing out that Kisumu was the principal emporium for retail articles and the distributing centre for the cart-loads of grain, maize, millet, and sim sim brought into the bazaar daily from the country.[1] Elsewhere in Kenya, a few Indian traders engaged in the livestock business in the Northern Province—sending out caravans into the remoter districts and also on occasion employing Swahili and other local intermediaries.[2]

The Indian traders in Kenya, as elsewhere in East Africa, thus built steadily on the foundations of Indian commercial enterprise in the interior laid towards the close of the nineteenth century. Their competitiveness and the general absence of any local agency to perform similar economic functions further facilitated their enterprise. The question of encouraging European traders, as against the Indians, was frequently raised during this period. But, as Ainsworth had explained in an earlier memorandum in 1905, there was

> small inducement for the European to set up as a storekeeper or trader on a small scale except in a centre of European population such as Nairobi; and even there he would have to contend against serious and overwhelming competition from the Goanese, Indians and others. In fact it may be said that at the present stage of the country's development no white man can compete with the Indian in the same goods as a small trader.[3]

No wonder therefore that in another report in 1905 Ainsworth stated: 'I think I am not exaggerating when I say that fully 80 per cent of the present capital and business energy of the country is

[1] Simpson, op. cit., p. 26.
[2] See, for example, Kenya Archives, file no. Mombasa 37/576: Permits to open shops 1915–16, and file no. MKS/57: Machakos District Political Record Book 1910–11, vol. ii.
[3] C.O. 533/3, Stewart to Lyttelton, 9 Aug. 1905, enclosed memo. by Ainsworth and Marsden. Also printed in C.O.C.P. no. 879/87/772, p. 165.

Indian.'[1] This view was shared by other officials. Jackson referred to the fact that 'the greater part of the trade of the country has been created by and still remains in the hands, either directly or indirectly, of Indians'; while Hobley pointed out at the same time that nearly three-quarters of the produce sent by rail on the Uganda Railway was supplied by the African producers and handled by Indian merchants.[2] Later, in 1908, Hayes Sadler explained that the Indians

have for years been intimately connected with the trade and development of the Protectorate; their numbers are increasing; a large part of the trade and commerce of the port and towns is in their hands, and they almost monopolize the retail business with the natives in the districts, where they are able to thrive under conditions which would be impossible for a European.[3]

In the circumstances, Indian commercial enterprise in Kenya represented a 'continually extending' process—and a majority of the Indian population of about 12,000 in 1911, which rose to about 23,000 in 1921, was engaged in commerce and industry. As a report in 1919 showed, Indian traders were 'firmly established' in all the leading towns and districts of the country, and were particularly active at Mombasa, Nairobi, and Kisumu, 'the three most important towns'—'It is at once apparent that the European trading element is much in the minority.'[4]

In Uganda, the enterprise of Allidina Visram provides a glimpse of what lesser Indian traders were doing in the wake of his pioneering ventures. By the turn of the century a number of the leading Indian firms at Mombasa had opened branches at Kampala, Entebbe, and Jinja, where Indian bazaars had been established. At first Indian traders penetrated into Uganda along the caravan route through Mwanza and Hoima, and to a lesser extent via Mumias through Kenya. But the construction of the Uganda Railway changed the old pattern of communications and facilitated commercial traffic on

---

[1] *Reports Relating to the Administration of the E.A.P.*, Cd. 2740 (1905), p. 19. See also C.O. 533/5, Jackson to Lyttelton, 11 Nov. 1905, enclosed minute by Ainsworth expresses similar views.

[2] C.O. 533/5, Jackson to Lyttelton, 11 Nov. 1905, enclosure no. 2, minute by Hobley. Also printed in C.O.C.P. no. 879/87/771, pp. 88–114.

[3] I.O. Emigration—Sept. 1908, Pros. 5–6, file 79, pp. 589–95, copy of Hayes Sadler to Crewe, 10 May 1908, and enclosed Sadler to Indian Association, Nairobi, Apr. 1908.

[4] T. Sleith, *Report on Trade Conditions in B.E.A., Uganda and Zanzibar* (Capetown, 1919), p. 13; and Kenya, *Report on the Census of Non-Natives*, 24 Apr. 1921.

Lake Victoria—from the railhead at Kisumu to the Uganda ports of Entebbe, Jinja, and Kampala. Lake traffic from Mwanza to the Uganda ports, however, also continued to operate. Elsewhere in Uganda, as in Kenya, the small Indian trader pushed the frontiers of commerce into the countryside—introducing wagon transport to develop the first slender means of communication, and undertaking the purchase of a variety of local products while retailing trade goods and provisions. Much of the country produce especially from the outlying trading and collecting centres—such as those of Hoima, Mbale, and Soroti—had at first to be exported to Kampala and Jinja by means of carts and porters, and posed considerable difficulties.[1] The introduction of cotton cultivation in Uganda—first in Buganda and later in Busoga—provided an impetus to the enterprise of the small Indian traders. Being already on the scene, they were the first to undertake virtually all the purchase and collection of the cotton crop when production began in 1903.[2] This in fact marked a continuation of their existing functions whereby they obtained an increasing quantity of local produce—ivory, sesame, chillies, groundnuts, ghee, beeswax, grain, hides and skins—and introduced a growing variety of imported goods to the local populations in the different districts—cloth, beads, lamps, kerosene, hoes, and bicycles. An observer in 1909, for example, referred to the petty Indian trader 'disappearing into the country' with a quantity of hoes and returning eventually with 'loads of hides and skins' and evidently of other products.[3] Similarly another report pointed out that the Indian traders 'who study the needs of the natives, and stock the articles they want have every chance of developing a profitable business . . .'.[4]

The participation of the Indian middlemen in the Uganda cotton industry was particularly stimulated by the growth of the industry's connection with the Bombay market—especially following the

[1] Entebbe Archives, file no. 409/1906: 'Usoga, trade prospects of', and file no. 2135 A: Northern Province Annual Report for 1911–12. See also file no. 703: Eastern Province Annual Report for 1909–10; file no. 1138 A: Buganda Annual Report for 1910–11; and file no. 2135: Northern Province Annual Report for 1910–11.

[2] C.O. 536/79, Confidential Report on the Uganda Cotton Industry, by S. Simpson, Director of Agriculture, 31 July 1912, minutes thereon, and memo. by J. A. Hutton, Chairman of British Cotton Growing Association; and Uganda, *Report of the Commission of Enquiry into the Cotton Industry of Uganda* (Entebbe, 1929), p. 2.

[3] J. B. Purvis, *Through Uganda to Mount Elgon* (London, 1909), p. 55.

[4] Entebbe Archives, file no. 703 B: Eastern Province Annual Report for 1911–12.

establishment of the firm of Narandas Rajaram at Kampala in 1914, and the ginnery built by Allidina Visram which became functional in the same year. As a result, the Indians were able to play an important role in the purchase and export of a large proportion of the Uganda cotton crop. In fact the annual report for Buganda in 1915 showed that 'The European ginners have done little as they are unable to give the prices offered by the Indian ginners who bought most of the cotton for shipment to Bombay.'[1] This tendency was to continue, and the share of Bombay in the cotton crop to increase. By 1919, for example, about fifty per cent of the crop was imported by the Bombay mills. In the circumstances, the Indian role in the Uganda cotton industry steadily increased and by 1919 they had established seventeen ginneries in the country where they had only owned one in 1914.[2] The growth of Indian enterprise in this respect was explained by Professor Simpson in his report of 1915. This showed that Mbale was the principal collecting and distributing centre for the cotton trade. From there petty Indian merchants and buyers of cotton spread into the district and Indian *dukas* were 'dotted over the main roads'. The cotton was stored in the Indian bazaar in Mbale and then transported by means of carts and porters to the ginneries.[3] Another contemporary visitor observed a few years later:

When we reached Iganga I found it had become an Indian village, with shops and houses on each side of the road. It is a centre for the cotton trade and here the natives for miles around bring their cotton for sale, and it is ginned, packed, and pressed into bales for despatch to the Coast. The [Indian] shops contain cotton cloth, kerosene oil, lamps, etc. which are sold to the natives. . . .[4]

After 1903, therefore, cotton played an important part in the growth of Indian commercial activities in Uganda—although other local products continued to feature prominently as articles of trade.

[1] Entebbe Archives, file no. 1138 F: Buganda Annual Report for 1915–16, p. 4.
[2] *Handbook of Uganda Protectorate* (London, 1921), p. 263; and Entebbe Archives, file no. 1138 H: Buganda Annual Report for 1917–18, p. 10—which showed that the increase of the Indian role in the Uganda cotton industry was also due to 'the better facilities of the Bombay market'; so that the European ginners had to 'broaden out their methods if they wish to hold their own'. See also Uganda, *Report of the Commission of Enquiry into the Cotton Industry of Uganda* (1929), pp. 3–4; and C. Ehrlich, 'The Marketing of Cotton in Uganda 1900–50' (London Ph.D. thesis 1958), pp. 146–50.
[3] Simpson, op. cit., p. 32.
[4] John Roscoe, *The Soul of Central Africa* (London, 1923), p. 289.

Busoga district was a particularly 'favourite field' for the petty Indian merchants; and during this period they developed important centres of trade at Jinja, Mbale, Kumi, and Balulu, while at the various townships and trading centres in the Eastern Province Indian *dukas* had been built.[1] Similarly in Buganda, apart from the important Indian bazaars at Entebbe and Kampala, petty Indian traders spread to Masaka and Mubende and the surrounding districts. The District Commissioner at Masaka reported in 1911 that 'The trade at Masaka has largely increased and there are now in this district 78 Goanese and Indians engaged in trading, Cotton, native ghee, hides and skins, and groundnuts being the principal items.' And in 1914 he further reported that a large number of excellent buildings had been put up during the year by the Indians and that a ginnery was also under construction.[2] Similarly the District Commissioner at Mubende showed in his report for 1909–10:

there are a fair number of Indian traders buying up cotton and skins. Near Bujuni in Buyaga trade appears very flourishing. Two Indians there pay as much as Rs. 10 per month for a small plot on one of the Chief's [holdings]. . . . There is considerable trade between Buyaga and Mboga where there are said to be 6 or 7 Indians settled.[3]

A later report in 1919 showed that in every district of Buganda, except Entebbe, there was a marked increase in the number of trading licences issued and in the demand for building plots required for the purposes of trade.[4] In the Northern and Western Provinces of Uganda, the number of Indian traders was relatively small compared to Buganda and to the Eastern Province. But at the trading centres of Hoima, Masinde, Nimule, and generally in the Nile District—and to a lesser extent in Toro and Ankole—there were scattered Indian shops and *dukas* engaged in local trade based mainly on ivory, hides and skins, and the provision of retail goods.[5] The growth of

---

[1] Entebbe Archives, file no. 5426, Part I, D.C., Jinja, to P.C. Eastern Province, 11 July 1918, and P.C. to Chief Secretary, 19 July 1918, and file no. 703 A: Eastern Province Annual Report for 1910–11. See also Cd. 5193 (1910), op. cit., p. 421; and Uganda: *Census Returns 1911*.

[2] Entebbe Archives, file no. 1138 A: Buganda Annual Report for 1910–11, enclosed Report of the D.C., Masaka, and file no. 1138 D: Buganda Annual Report for 1913–14, p. 12.

[3] Entebbe Archives, file no. 1138: Buganda Annual Report for 1909–10, enclosed Report of the D.C., Mubende.

[4] Entebbe Archives, file no. 1138 I: Buganda Annual Report for 1918–19.

[5] Entebbe Archives, files no. 2135, 2135 C, and 2135 D: Northern Province Annual Reports for 1910–11, pp. 25–6; 1913–14 and 1914–15, pp. 70–1, respectively; and Uganda, *Census Returns 1911*.

Indian enterprise generally is also shown by the census reports of this period. Of the total Indian population in Uganda of 2,216 in 1911, which rose to a figure of just over 5,000 in 1921, a majority of the working population was engaged in commerce and industry—and was concentrated mainly at Kampala, Entebbe, Jinja, and Mbale, with lesser settlements at Masaka, Kumi, Hoima, and Masinde.[1] But notwithstanding the relative smallness of their population, the Indian merchants played an important role in the commercial development of Uganda during this period. In 1907 an authoritative observer commented: '. . . this country could not have been in its present prosperous condition, if it had not been for the Indian merchants.'[2] Similarly a subsequent report in 1919 pointed out that 'The Indian Trader is prominent everywhere throughout Uganda where business is to be done either in a large or a small way, and is a very important factor in the commercial life of the place.'[3] The Uganda Development Commission in its report published in 1920 endorsed these views of the importance of the Indian economic role in the country—in marked contrast to the Kenya Economic Commission's report of 1919, which included a bitter denunciation of the Indian role in that country.

In Zanzibar, although the island had lost its former predominance in the commerce of East Africa, with the result that a number of Indian merchants had moved to the new entrepôts of trade at Mombasa, Tanga, and Dar es Salaam, Indian enterprise continued to follow and develop along the traditional pattern of commerce. Their role in the clove industry, in the import and export of goods, and as agents for the European firms as well as retailers and wholesalers continued to expand. But there was obviously no scope for the pioneering ventures of the type that took an increasing number of Indian traders into the interior. A report in 1919, which ascribed 'practically the whole of the commerce of the island' to the Indians, however, showed that the historic predominance of the Indians in the commercial life of Zanzibar continued unchecked during this period.[4] Indian population in the island, nevertheless, tended to

---

[1] Uganda, *Census Returns 1911* and *Report on the Non-Native Census 1921.*
[2] Minutes of the Uganda Chamber of Commerce, 12 Apr. 1907, address by Vice-President, A. E. Bertie-Smith.
[3] T. Sleith, *Report on Trade Conditions in B.E.A., Uganda and Zanzibar* (1919), p. 49.
[4] Sleith, ibid., p. 63. See also R. N. Lyne, *Zanzibar in Contemporary Times* (London, 1905), pp. 242, 244—which showed that the Indians 'possess the trade

remain static and there was no comparable or proportionate increase as elsewhere in East Africa. But a majority of the Indian population of about 8,500 in 1910, which rose to about 13,500 in 1921, was engaged, as elsewhere, in commerce and industry.[1]

In German East Africa, where the Indian traders had earlier launched expansion into the interior, their enterprise continued to expand—largely because the authorities allowed them freedom of enterprise, considering the Indian traders 'indispensable in mediating trade between European firms and the natives'. Apart from the Indian merchants who penetrated the interior along the old caravan routes, other Indian traders spread along the advancing railways, as they had done in Kenya, and engaged in very similar forms of trade. Some of them had also penetrated into Burundi by 1905, while a few others were expressly invited to Kigali, the capital of Rwanda, by the German Resident in 1907.[2] The whole process of the expansion of Indian economic enterprise in German East Africa during this period was explained by Dr. Heinrich Schnee, Governor of the territory from 1912 to 1914, in an article on the subject:

> With the gradual pacification of the country under German rule, the Indians moved towards the interior and settled in all commercial centres of the Protectorate. The Indian trading community in German East Africa have now completely freed themselves from the larger Indian firms in Zanzibar. Their export and import trade accounts for the German East Africa line running a special service to Bombay and other Indian ports. The Indians now buy up in the interior products of every sort—rubber, wax, hides, skins, cotton, grain and foodstuffs, ivory, copra, copal and supply natives with cotton cloth, beads and earthen ware, glass and simple household furniture. . . . The Indians flourish by dint of their acquisitiveness, their diligence, their astuteness in business. . . . For the present the Indians are indispensable as middlemen between the larger European firms and the natives.[3]

of the island, either as shop-keepers, money-lenders, merchants, small traders or skilled mechanics.'

[1] *Zanzibar and Pemba Census 1921.*

[2] W. R. Louis, *Ruanda-Urundi, 1884–1919* (Oxford, 1963), pp. 169–70; and John Iliffe, 'The German Administration in Tanganyika 1906–1911' (Cambridge Ph.D., thesis 1965), p. 191.

[3] Article by H. Schnee in *Deutsches Koloniale Lexicon* (Berlin, 1920), vol. ii, quoted in India Archives, Emigration—Sept. 1925, Pros. 1–92, part A, departmental memo. on Indians in East Africa. For the growth of Indian commercial enterprise in German East Africa, see also J. D. Karstedt, 'Beitrage zur Inderfrage in Deutsch-Ostafrika', *Koloniale Monatsblatter* (Berlin, 1913), pp. 337–55; and Cd. 5194 (1910), op. cit., p. 163, where Sir Harry Johnston commented that 'a great volume of German trade' coexisted 'on friendly terms with the enterprise of British Indians in German East Africa'.

In these circumstances, the Indian population in German East Africa increased from about 3,000 at the turn of the century to over 9,000 on the eve of the First World War—by 1921, owing to the war, it had increased to only about 10,000, and probably represented the pattern of Indian settlement as it had existed before the war. From this it would appear that the majority of the Indian population was engaged in commerce and industry and was concentrated along the Coast—particularly at Dar es Salaam and Tanga. But in the interior there were a substantial number of Indians at Tabora and Mwanza, while Indian trading centres existed at various other settlements: Bukoba, Dodoma, Iringa, Morogoro, Moshi, Usambara, Ujiji, and lesser places.[1]

During the course of the early colonial period, therefore, Indian traders had carried trade to the remotest parts of Kenya, Uganda, and Tanganyika. Most of them were engaged in trade on a small scale, but there were a few wealthy and successful merchants among them. The Indian bazaar had become a feature of all the emerging East African towns and townships, while Indian *dukas* were established in various trading centres and outlying posts. The services that the petty Indian traders provided to the local African producers—in marketing their surplus produce and introducing them to a wide variety of manufactured goods as well as the rupee currency—were of far-reaching significance. For the gradual extension of the commercial frontier by the Indian traders contributed to greater local production in various areas, and thereby set into motion the whole process of modern economic development in the countryside. As one contemporary Kenya official later commented:

> If an abrupt clearance of the Indians had been effected . . . one certain result would have been that the native tribes would have suddenly ceased to receive many supplies to which they were becoming accustomed, and the volume of trade would have abruptly declined. . . . It has been, and still is, the Indian who delivers the goods and pushes trade in the interior of Kenya.[2]

But the growing role of the petty Indian trader and middleman was to expose him to frequent abuse for resorting to sharp practice and dishonest business methods—mainly in respect of unfair price dealings and the use of false weights. Such charges, however, as the Hilton Young Commission later reported,

---

[1] Tanganyika, *Non-Native Census 1921* and *Handbook of German East Africa* (London, 1920), pp. 46, 72, 76.

[2] W. M. Ross, *Kenya from Within* (1927), pp. 416–17.

are brought against middlemen all the world over, and no doubt the ignorance of the African offers special opportunities to the unscrupulous. But the middleman generally survives as a necessary link in the chain of distribution, and it must be recognised that the Indian middlemen are doing useful work for which no other agency is at present available. The European cannot afford to trade on the small scale and with the small margins on which the Indian subsists, and the African generally is not yet sufficiently advanced to do so.[1]

The first two decades of the twentieth century thus witnessed a rapid growth of the Indian role in the interior of East Africa—spearheaded by the old-established traders and the officially sponsored artisans and subordinate staff. A steady stream of new Indian immigrants, originating mainly from Gujerat and the Punjab, flowed into East Africa during this period along the channels of communications opened up during the 1890s. And these immigrants were to build upon the twin foundations for middle-grade employment and commercial enterprise laid during the process of opening up the interior. While subsequent schemes for State-aided Indian immigration into East Africa came to nothing, they revealed at least official recognition of the contribution of Indian enterprise to the general process of development. And in view of this, Indian immigration into East Africa remained largely free of any restrictions during this period—in fact it was informally encouraged by the continuing employment of Indian staff and the freedom of enterprise generally allowed to the Indian traders. In the circumstances, the Indian economic role in the interior acquired crucial importance during this period—particularly before the First World War, when private European capital resources and skills had yet to make a sufficient impact in the territories. A mass of contemporary evidence testifies to this. Winston Churchill (later Sir) commented on it in 1908; while Sir John Kirk stated in his evidence to the Sanderson Committee: 'Drive away the Indians and you may shut up the [East Africa] Protectorate. . . .' Even Colonel Grogan conceded at this time that the Indians' intermediate role between the African and European communities was a 'fundamental factor' in the economic life of the country—and that, without it, the Protectorate would 'collapse like a puff ball'![2]

---

[1] *Report of the Commission on Closer Union of the Dependencies in Eastern and Central Africa,* Cmd. 3234 (1929), p. 27.
[2] W. S. Churchill, *My African Journey,* pp. 49, 52; Cd. 5192 (1910), op. cit., p. 91, for Kirk's comment; Cd. 5193 (1910), op. cit., evidence of Grogan under Q. 8107, see also evidence of Sir Edward Buck under Q. 4622.

In its subsequent report, the Hilton Young Commission assessed the importance of the Indian economic role in somewhat similar terms:

... the Indian community has played a useful, and in fact an indispensable, part in the development of these territories. Apart from the construction of the Kenya–Uganda Railway, the services of the Indian artisans and mechanics have been widely used by the public at large on works for which European agency would have been too costly and which the native is not yet fitted to perform. The Indian trader has been a potent factor in the process of Civilising. . . . The 'dukawala', or petty shopkeeper, has carried his wares far and wide into remote areas. . . . By increasing their [African] wants he has created an incentive to effort and thus sown the first seeds of economic progress. The Indian dealer has performed another useful function in marketing the products of native agriculture . . . their activities have undoubtedly stimulated the spread of Cotton civilisation in Uganda.[1]

The growth of the Indian role in East Africa during this period also accounted for the rise of a variety of Indian institutions in the territories. The immigrants had begun to settle down—opening up schools, building social and cultural facilities for members of their different communities; while some of the leading traders and the few professional men among them—mainly doctors and lawyers—provided leadership in the informal Indian associations established at various settlements to protect the rights and interests of the Indian community.

But already the process of growth had been severely influenced by the increasing European hostility towards the Indian immigrants—expressed in the demands for the restriction of their immigration and in various legal and administrative disabilities imposed on them. The momentum that Indian immigration and enterprise in East Africa provided by the large-scale influx of the officially sponsored immigrants in the early years of the colonial period could not so easily be reversed. But if an Indian settlement grew in East Africa during this period, its character was largely shaped by the political and racial controversies generated by the conflicts between the European and Indian immigrants. The process of growth came to be restricted to Indian participation in the limited fields of subordinate employment and commerce—and provided the pattern for the future.

[1] Cmd. 3234 (1929), op. cit., p. 27.

CHAPTER IV

The Political Consequences
1902 to 1923

THE growth of the Indian role in the interior of East Africa during the early colonial period was largely the outcome of their official association—as skilled and semi-skilled staff—with the colonial governments, and the voluntary Indian immigration that such association encouraged. The freedom of enterprise generally allowed them stimulated the extension of their historic commercial activities along the Coast into the interior and provided opportunities for new Indian immigrants to follow the fresh trails of trade blazed by the old-established firms. The fact that the Indians served the interests of colonial policy thus helped their penetration of the interior; and more important, in the years that followed a steady stream of Indian immigrants flowed into East Africa, largely on their own initiative, to avail themselves of the growing opportunities for employment. In a sense the new immigrants helped to fill the gap created by the departing coolies and troops. In these circumstances, the Indian role in East Africa steadily increased, as also did their stake or vested interest in the territories.

Meanwhile, however, Imperial policy did not merely envisage Indian participation in the general process of development—for in Kenya and German East Africa especially this period also witnessed a rapid growth of the European role. In Kenya, where official opinion in the early years tended to be preoccupied with schemes for the immigration of Indian artisans and agriculturists to facilitate the rapid development of the Protectorate, official support for European immigration did not begin in earnest until after 1902, when a policy of European settlement in the Highlands was launched. After this date, therefore, the settlement of Europeans in Kenya made rapid progress. By 1911 their population in the country had increased to a total of 3,175 and their enterprises had also expanded. In the following decade their numbers increased threefold, reaching a figure of 9,650 in 1921. Similarly in German East Africa, the European role steadily increased and there were well over 5,000 Europeans in the territory on the eve of the First World War.[1] The population of the East African territories had thus rapidly acquired a multi-racial character; and during this period the political problems arising out of the divergent interests and aspiration of the immigrant communities formed an important feature of East Africa history. As in Zanzibar in the nineteenth century, so in the interior in the twentieth, the extensive Indian role in East Africa came under increasing European scrutiny and criticism. While the overall contribution of Indian enterprise to the general process of development received substantial official support—as shown in the previous chapter—it tended generally to be overshadowed by the growth of European hostility towards the Indians and the mounting criticism of the community, which found practical expression in the imposition of several racial disabilities upon them.

The first major indication of a conflict of interests between the Europeans and the Indians in Kenya was provided by a petition submitted in January 1902 by a committee of the European settlers in Nairobi. This called upon the Government to 'encourage European colonization' and restrict Indian immigration—pointing out that

the further immigration of Asiatics into this country is entirely detrimental to the European settler in particular and to the native inhabitant generally, it being considered that such importation creates unfair competition to Europeans and natives, the latter being in every way superior in physique and morality, and more amenable to European supervision. Further the money earned by the native of the country remains here whereas the Asiatic takes away all his earnings to his native country. . . .[2]

About the same time Eliot also reported that there was 'considerable friction' between European and Indian merchants in Mombasa; while Herbert Samuel reporting on his visit to Uganda similarly referred to 'a certain hostility on the part of the small unofficial population of whites to . . . Asiatics, a certain jealousy of their competition'.[3] However, the petition of the European settlers found little favour in official quarters. Eliot himself dismissed it—as he reported to the Foreign Office:

[1] See Kenya, *Census Returns 1911* and *Census of Non-Natives 1921*; Tanganyika, *Census of Non-Natives 1921* and *Handbook of German East Africa* (1921).

[2] F.O. 2/805, Eliot to Lansdowne, 21 Jan. 1902, enclosed petition of the European settlers' committee, dated 4 Jan. 1902.

[3] F.O. 2/569, Eliot to Lansdowne, 5 Jan. 1902; and Herbert Samuel, 'The Uganda of Today', *Journal of the Society of Arts*, ii, no. 2626 (20 Mar. 1903), 395, C.O. pamphlet no. 15.

I said that the interests of Indians and Europeans were less likely to clash than the Committee supposed, for the cool, grassy uplands so attractive to the white man were positively distasteful to the Hindu. . . . It was true that at present the Asiatics send their earnings out of the country, but that was because their families are in India. . . . Though a few speakers agreed with my remarks, it was evident that the sense of the meeting was very hostile to the Indian element.[1]

The Imperial Government in turn could hardly entertain the demand for the restriction of Indian immigration, as it was at the time considering proposals for increased Indian participation in the development of the country.[2]

The Europeans were, however, able to make political capital out of other issues than the economic competition and rivalry between the Indians, in order to strengthen their demands for European paramountcy in the country generally and in particular for the reservation of the Highlands for exclusive European settlement. The 6,000-odd Uganda Railway coolies who opted to remain in East Africa after the expiry of their contracts had already exposed themselves to considerable official criticism for their activities as itinerant traders, etc. As Frederick Jackson later pointed out:

They thought they could continue as they pleased, and go where they liked, outside the limits of the Railway Zone. Provincial and District Commissioners, including myself, at that time resident at Ravine, took a different view, when they began roaming about as petty traders and without permits.[3]

Similarly in Zanzibar, the influx of some of these time-expired coolies —mostly as destitutes looking for employment—led to strong official opposition in 1903 and to proposals for the restriction of Indian immigration.[4] These coolies were later to become a favourite target of European criticism against the Indians generally—notwithstanding the fact that they represented only a small section of the Indian population in East Africa. Similarly, the haphazard way in which some of the early Indian bazaars were set up in the interior— notably at Nairobi—created a number of problems. The ramshackle

[1] F.O. 2/805, Eliot to Lansdowne, 21 Jan. 1902. See also F.O. 2/576, Eliot to Lansdowne, 31 Mar. 1902.
[2] F.O. 2/671, F.O. to I.O., 16 May 1900; F.O. 2/671, F.O. to Treasury, 28 Feb. 1902; and F.O. 2/569, minute by Hill, 25 Feb. 1902, on Eliot to Lansdowne, 5 Jan. 1902—see p. 64. above.
[3] F. J. Jackson, *Early Days in East Africa*, pp. 325–6. See also p. 67, n. 3.
[4] I.O. Emigration—Mar. 1904, Pros. 2–3, file 92, p. 137, Cave to Lansdowne, 1 June 1903.

structures that formed the early *dukas*, built on small plots of land alienated under temporary ownership licences, the general over-crowding in the Indian bazaars, and the lack of modern sanitary facilities presented a picture of extremely unhygienic conditions. The outbreaks of plague—notably at Nairobi at the turn of the century, which led to the existing Indian bazaar being burnt down and another built on a new site after 1902[1]—only helped to aggravate the growing official and unofficial objections to the Indians generally—political capital being made of the insanitary and over-crowded conditions in the Indian areas. Sir Donald Stewart, for example, in August 1905 supported European demands for the reservation of the Highlands not only because these comprised a 'comparatively small area' while there were 'enormous tracts of land' suitable for Indian settlement, but also because, 'Owing to the insanitary habits of Asiatics and Africans, they are not fit persons to take up land as neighbours of Europeans.'[2] Such views had been expounded in greater detail and an extreme form earlier in that year by some of the members of the Land Committee—notably Colonel Grogan, who attacked the Indian settlement in the country and asked for their exclusion in the same way as in South Africa.[3]

Meanwhile the Colonists' Association in Nairobi formed by the European settlers spearheaded their political campaign in Kenya. In August 1905, the Association presented a petition to the Government attacking the Indian role in the country and the prevalence of British Indian methods of government—pointing out: 'The East Africa Protectorate is governed as if it were a province of India. . . . The sooner the sorry farce of Indian Laws [Indian currency], and Indian methods of Government is abolished, and the white community are given their share in the Government of the country' the better.[4] The European demands for the restriction of Indian immigration, the reservation of the Highlands, and the abolition of the British Indian methods of government apparently made a consider-

---

[1] F.O. 2/795, Ternan to Salisbury, 2 Nov. 1900, and Eliot to Lansdowne, telegram, 2 Dec. 1902.

[2] C.O. 533/3, Stewart to Lyttelton, 14 Aug. 1905.

[3] E.A.P. *Report of the Land Committee* (Nairobi, 1905), Appendix A, p. 3.

[4] C.O. 533/4, Jackson to Lyttelton, 18 Oct. 1905, enclosed petition of the Colonists' Association, dated 23 Aug. 1905. A later report expressed the European opposition to the prevalence of British Indian laws and methods of government more colourfully—'this exotic Eastern veneer over a European settlement sits as badly upon the social fabric as a part in a coloured Eastern garb would on the shoulders of a London Cockney'. See *Leader of B.E.A.*, 11 June 1910.

able impact in official circles.[1] But equally, the Indian role in the country generally found strong support in official quarters. Jackson pointed out that 'the leaders of the Colonists' Association are for the most part either South Africans by birth or men who have resided for a considerable time in South Africa. Their strong prejudice against all black men is obvious to any unbiased person who reads the address. . . .' Similarly Ainsworth explained that 'most of the people belonging to the Colonists' Association are Anti-Native and Anti-Indian', and pointed out:

I do not think it has occurred to the promoters of the address to consider the position of the Indians (beyond possibly their absolute non-recognition of any representative rights) in the event of a Legislative Council being formed, yet the Indians are an important factor in the country and own a very considerable part of the trading and other capital (possibly 60 to 70 per cent).

Similar views were echoed by other officials, who criticized the petitioners for ignoring the wishes of the Africans and the Indians. As Hobley stated in his minute on the European petition:

The address omits a factor of no small moment in this country, I refer to the Indian community . . . which contains numerous merchants and others of capital and great enterprise . . . and they contribute very considerably to the revenue of the Protectorate. As an instance I may mention that they contribute no less than 25 per cent of the total Municipal rates at Nairobi whereas the European settler only contributes $6\frac{1}{2}$ per cent, . . . The old stock argument against encouraging Indian immigration is that Indians always transmit their savings to India . . . but if one considers for a moment, that accusation may with some weight be laid against Europeans.

The officials concluded their comments on the European petition with the prophetic remark that—in the words of Jackson—'To endeavour by legislation or otherwise to make this country exclusively a white man's country is in our opinion doomed to failure' in view of the overwhelming predominance of the African population and the important role of the Indians in the trade and commerce of the country.[2]

[1] C.O. 533/4, Jackson to Lyttelton, 7 Oct. 1905, and Lyttelton to Jackson, 25 Oct. 1905.
[2] C.O. 533/5, Jackson to Lyttelton, 11 Nov. 1905, enclosed minutes on the address of the Colonists' Association by Jackson, Hobley, and Ainsworth. A number of contemporary observers similarly ascribe the growth of the anti-Indian bias to South African influences. Hobley talked of the 'profound influence' that the South African 'outlook' had in the early days; while Ross

The European settlers were, however, able to make progress in their aspirations when a Legislative Council was established in 1906 with nominated unofficial European representation, while at the same time the Colonial Secretary, Lord Elgin, gave assurances concerning the reservation of the Highlands—that 'in view of the comparatively limited area in the Protectorate suitable for European civilization, a reasonable discretion will be exercised in dealing with application for land on the part of natives of India and other non-Europeans'. By 1908 such assurances were confirmed by what came to be known as 'the Elgin pledge'—that 'it is not consonant with the views of His Majesty's Government to impose *legal* restrictions on any particular section of the community, but as a matter of administrative convenience grants in the uplands area should not be made to Indians'.[1] The reservation of the Highlands was, however, only the principal manifestation of a larger and increasing anti-Indian campaign of the European settlers. In 1908 Hayes Sadler reported that

There is a growing tendency among the white settlers in the uplands to keep the Indian, not only out of the uplands, but of the country altogether. The spirit is akin to that prevailing in Natal and elsewhere, and is due to the fact that the White cannot compete in the east with the Indian shopkeeper for supplies of provisions and articles in daily use, or as a petty trader.[2]

In the following year Jackson similarly showed that, while at the Coast European opinion generally favoured the immigration of Indian labourers, and to a lesser extent of agriculturists, the main body of the European settlers were 'much opposed to Indians being allowed to settle in the country as they anticipate that this Protectorate will eventually become a white colony with responsible government in which case the Indian would find himself in the same position as he now is in the Transvaal and Natal'.[3] Such expressions of hostility towards the Indians, coupled as they were with the steady application of various racial disabilities upon them, were to have far-reaching political repercussions in Kenya. Well before the First World War the Indian Question in Kenya was raised at the highest

explained: 'Public aspersion to the Indian population as a whole, which was to rise to such heights of extravagance by the year 1922, began with a small group of South African Colonials in Nairobi.' See Ross, op. cit., pp. 302–3; and Hobley, *Kenya from Chartered Company to Crown Colony*, p. 242.

[1] *Correspondence relating to the Tenure of Land in the E.A.P.*, Cd. 4117 (1908), p. 33.

[2] Ibid., p. 25.   [3] C.O. 533/59, Jackson to Crewe, 21 May 1909.

level by both the Europeans and Indians, and it was tentatively settled by Imperial arbitration in a manner that provided a marked precedent for the subsequent settlement of 1923.

Indian political opposition to the discriminatory policies adopted in Kenya did not begin in earnest until 1906, when A. M. Jeevanjee, as President of the Indian Association, Mombasa—which had existed since the turn of the century[1]—called a 'mass' meeting of the Indians at Mombasa on 1 April 1906. The meeting was attended by most of the leading Indian professional men and merchants of the time, and its proceedings were dominated by the need to protect Indian rights in view of the European campaign for the reservation of the Highlands as well as of selected areas in the towns for exclusive European occupation—the point that particularly irked the Indians being that non-British Europeans would thus have 'preference in public matters over British Indians in a British Protectorate'. An amount of Rs. 20,000 was pledged at this meeting by the various Indian representatives in order 'to fight against the principles adopted by the Colonists' Association of Nairobi'.[2] Later in the same year, A. M. Jeevanjee led an Indian delegation to London to make direct representations to the Imperial Government; while at the same time he wrote a series of letters to Indian newspapers appealing for the support of Indian nationalist opinion against the anti-Indian policies pursued by the European settlers.[3] Subsequently, in 1907, a British East Africa Indian Association was formed as a representative body of the Indians in various parts of the country, and it made direct representations to Winston Churchill (later Sir) during his visit to Kenya. Churchill's views, which were later published in his book, *My African Journey*, and frequently quoted by the Indians, tended to reassure Indian opinion:

The Indian was here long before the first British Official. He may point to many generations of useful industry on the Coast and inland as the white settlers, especially the most recently arrived contingents from South Africa (the loudest against him of all) can count years of residence. Is it possible for any Government, with a scrap of respect for honest dealing between man and man, to embark on a policy of deliberately squeezing out the native of India from regions in which he has established himself under every security of public faith.[4]

[1] Ross, op. cit., p. 167.
[2] *E.A.S.*, 7 Apr. 1906; and Ross, op. cit., p. 303.   [3] *E.A.S.*, 15 Dec. 1906.
[4] W. S. Churchill, *My African Journey*, p. 49. See also Ross, op. cit., p. 308; and *Kenya Land Commission, Evidence*, iii, 2891.

Subsequently, in 1908, the Indians petitioned the Government for the grant of equal rights to them and of representation on the Legislative Council. The Governor, Sir James Hayes Sadler, who had excellent relations with the Indians and spoke their native language, Gujerati,[1] supported the Indian demand for representation. He informed a meeting of the Executive Council that the Indians' 'long connection with East Africa, their increasing numbers, and their influence on the trade of the Protectorate, constitute a legitimate claim to repre-sentation'.[2] Later, in a dispatch to the Colonial Office, Hayes Sadler pointed out that 'European non-official feeling in the Uplands will doubtless be opposed to the Indians being represented, but I do not consider that any such feeling should outweigh the legitimate claims' of that community, and he did not 'anticipate any difficulty in making a suitable nomination'.[3] But it was not until 1910 that Jeevanjee was appointed to the Legislative Council as an unofficial Indian member after a prolonged Indian campaign for representa-tion both on the Legislative Council and on the municipal council established in Nairobi since 1907.[4] A meeting of the Indian Associa-tion in Nairobi held after his appointment pressed Jeevanjee to work for equal rights for the Indians in Kenya—particularly in respect of land and education policies of the Government and trial by jury.[5]

But in the face of European hostility Jeevanjee's solitary position on the Legislative Council proved untenable; whereupon he travelled to London to make a direct appeal to British public opinion. In separate interviews in London, first with the *Daily Chronicle* and later with the *London Standard*, Jeevanjee denounced the anti-Indian bias of the European settlers, stating *inter alia*: 'A deliberate attempt is being made to debar us from any share in the commerce and agriculture of the country. We are marked down because of our race and colour. . . . I say nothing about the action of the South African Union towards us. But the case of British East Africa is entirely different. We are already there. . . . We have created

[1] See *E.A.S.*, 6 Jan. 1906; and Ross, op. cit., p. 303.
[2] E.A.P. *Minutes of the Executive Council*, 13 Apr. 1908. See also *Leader of B.E.A.*, 27 June 1908.
[3] C.O. 533/43, Sadler to Crewe, 10 May 1908. For this dispatch and minutes thereon, see also I.O. Emigration—Sept. 1908, Pros. 5–6, file 79, pp. 589–95.
[4] I.O. Emigration—Aug. 1910, Pros. 43, file 84, part B, Appointment of A. M. Jeevanjee; and *Leader of B.E.A.*, 29 Jan. and 2 Apr. 1910.
[5] *Leader of B.E.A.*, 26 Mar. and 2 Apr. 1910.

enormous interests there.'[1] Jeevanjee's outbursts in London caused an uproar in Nairobi, where some of his exaggerated claims that the Indians paid most of the taxes and owned most of the urban land were officially rejected in the Legislative Council.[2] Following this, Jeevanjee appears to have avoided attending any of the subsequent sessions of the Legislative Council; and after the expiry of his term in 1911, the appointment of an Indian member to the Legislative Council was allowed to lapse until 1919.

Meanwhile, however, Jeevanjee's public pronouncements in London were supplemented by direct representations to the Imperial Government on behalf of the Kenya Indians by the London branch of the All India Muslim League. In a lengthy memorandum in October 1910, the League traced the history of Indian association with the Imperial policy and the subsequent reversals in their position in Kenya. Apart from the reservation of the Highlands, which it described as the 'root-cause' of Indian discontent, the memorandum complained of government sponsorship of European immigration as against the Indian, the grant of the right to trial by jury to the Europeans and not the Indians, the legal exclusion of Indians from appointments as Justices of the Peace and, among other disabilities, racial discrimination in the sale of certain township plots in Nairobi which virtually restricted their purchase to the Europeans.[3] Such Indian representations to the Imperial Government were, however, countered by strong opposition to their demands by the local officials. Sir Percy Girouard, the Governor, in a memorandum rebutting Indian representations, dismissed Jeevanjee as an illiterate who had personally stated to him that the Highlands were not suitable for Indian settlement. Further the Governor pointed out that

this East Africa Colony is going to be controlled by our own kith and kin, and that their first charge in it is the civilisation, expansion and progress of its native millions, which is not incompatible with their own progress, though it is diametrically opposed by the introduction of the Indian agriculturist. . . . I am prepared to hazard the prediction that, if any such declaration [of policy] contained the announcement of grant of agricultural

---

[1] Ibid., 1 Oct. 1910 and 24 Dec. 1910. See also E.A.S., *The Indian Problem in Kenya* (Nairobi, 1922), p. 30.

[2] E.A.P. *Minutes of the Legislative Council*, 31 Oct. 1910. See also I.O. Emigration—May 1911, Pros. 1–2, file 48, part A, Jackson to Harcourt, 25 Nov. 1910, and memo. by Girouard.

[3] I.O. Emigration—May 1911, Pros. 1–2, file 48, pp. 225–63, see especially, I.O. to Govt. of India, 24 Mar. 1911, enclosed petition from the Muslim League, dated 13 Oct. 1910, and additional note from the League, dated 6 Jan. 1911.

lands to them [the Indians] in the Highlands, mob law would be in vogue within twenty four hours.[1]

Such views were echoed in a more extreme form by Frederick Jackson, who, in a remarkable display of the prejudice that until then had been prevalent mainly among the European settlers, regretted the continuing presence of the Indians in the interior after the railway had been constructed, and dismissed them as mere 'hucksters and usurers'. Further, foreshadowing the defamatory remarks later published in the Economic Commission report in 1919, Jackson accused the Indian community of unscrupulous business methods and of acting as carriers of disease. Similarly he explained that the influence of the Indians on the Africans had been 'deplorable'— pointing out that 'Missionary evidence is unanimous in regard to the ill-effects of intercourse between the Asiatic and African races'. Considering the anti-Indian bias of the missionaries in the country, it is hardly surprising that such should be their 'evidence'—but unfortunate that it received the weight of official credence. What was perhaps more significant was Jackson's attempt, quite falsely, to distinguish between the Indian traders on the Coast, whom he regarded kindly, and those in the interior, whom he dismissed as mere low-caste coolies—Jeevanjee himself being similarly described.[2] Such hostile official reactions to Indian representations showed the remarkable change in policy and attitude towards the Indians that had occurred since European settlement began in 1902—and in fact

[1] I.O. Emigration—May 1911, Pros. 1–2, file 48, part A, memo. by Sir Percy Girouard.

[2] I.O. Emigration—May 1911, Pros. 1–2, file 48, part A, Jackson to Harcourt, 25 Nov. 1910. As Lord Cranworth later pointed out, Jackson was 'on the best personal terms' with the old-established Indian traders—'for he well realized from personal experience all that they had done for the country'. But in dismissing most of the Indian population as low-class coolies, Jackson was apparently influenced by the erroneous view, commonly held by the Europeans, that most of the Indians were ex-coolies. See Lord Cranworth, *Kenya Chronicles* (London, 1939), p. 292. The official views against the Indians as expressed by Jackson and Girouard reflected in effect the growing anti-Indian bias of the European settlers in the country. This was in part due to the picture presented by the Indian settlement in the country generally—a picture of an 'East with all the allurements left out'—'The corrugated iron shanty by the roadside, the cheap, insanitary and utilitarian structures of a congested bazaar . . . the [Indian] trader, courteous but cute, a master at his calling, a trifle obsequious but nevertheless self-reliant and successful; in some ways a rival, and even, in cases, a disdainful rival. Outside the merchant and professional circles, most of the working Indians were poor, and many of them disregardful of appearances and of cleanliness. . . . If of British stock, one had to be a sportsman or a statesman or a Christian not to acquire a prejudice against it. . . .' Ross, op. cit., p. 414.

since as late as 1905 when Jackson himself defended Indian presence in the country against European opposition. Such a change of attitude may in part be accounted for by official antipathy towards the growth of political demands by the Indians, who, until aroused by the European settlers, had been largely apathetic to politics; and the possible implications for the future of such demands—especially as the Indian case was strengthened by the fact that Kenya, unlike South Africa and some other parts of the Empire, was not a self-governing colony and thus subject to direct Imperial control. At any rate, in view of official opposition to them, the Indians' demands for the redress of their grievances in Kenya met with quite the opposite reaction from the Imperial Government than they might have expected—although the India Office interceded on their behalf. The Colonial Secretary, Lewis Harcourt, was unable to 'accept without qualification' the Indian contention that 'any onerous or odious restrictions' had been imposed against them; or that Kenya was 'not, nor ever will be, a white man's country'. The reservation of the Highlands was justified for, while this area was 'on the whole unsuited to the Indian agriculturist', it comprised a 'comparatively small area in the Protectorate which is suitable for European residence and effort'. Similarly, the enforcement of racial segregation in the towns was necessitated by the need to maintain proper sanitary standards—especially in view of the information that the Secretary of State had received that most of the Indians were of low caste origin and prone to insanitary habits. But more important the Indian demands for equal treatment could not be entertained for

the interests of the four to five millions native inhabitants of British East Africa and the four millions inhabiting Uganda whose material progress and civilisation are now being mainly effected by the efforts of the European administrative staff aided by a large number of mission bodies . . . cannot but be the primary care of the Government of the country.[1]

Such a reply could hardly be expected to allay Indian fears of European paramountcy in the country, for, apart from the ideal of trusteeship for the Africans, most of the arguments used against the Indians were obviously much exaggerated by the local officials for political reasons. Indian political activity in Kenya was consequently

[1] I.O. Emigration—May 1911, Pros. 1–2, file 48, part A, Harcourt to Muslim League, 30 Mar. 1911, and I.O. to C.O., 22 Mar. 1911. See also Harcourt to Crewe, 17 Jan. 1913, in I.O. Emigration—June 1913, Pros. 13–15, file 45, part A.

intensified and demands for Indian representation on the Legislative
Council were renewed—the Government being petitioned in 1912 to
fill the vacancy created by Jeevanjee's retirement in 1911. But the
request was turned down on the grounds that there were 'no prominent Indians of sufficient educational qualifications' for appointment
to the Legislative Council![1] The Indians countered such official
rebuffs by taking up a campaign for the non-payment of the poll-tax
introduced in 1912;[2] while in Bombay a public meeting was convened
in July 1912 to protest against the disabilities imposed against the
Indians in Kenya and elsewhere in the Empire. In a memorial to
the Government of India the meeting expressed its opposition to the
introduction of the poll-tax without Indian representation, and the
policy of land reservation both in the Highlands and in the towns
whereby the Indians were restricted to the 'insalubrious' localities.[3]
The memorial, however, elicited a reply from the Government on the
same lines as given to the Muslim League by Harcourt in March
1911.

Meanwhile A. M. Jeevanjee published *An Appeal on Behalf of
Indians in East Africa*—a document whose importance lies chiefly in
the expression it gave to Indian grievances that were to form the
basis for the post-war political agitation in Kenya. In this *Appeal*
Jeevanjee pointed out that the real Indian case was not, as the Europeans sought to suggest, a design to achieve political dominance but,
on the contrary, simply the demand for elementary human rights.
In an impassioned attack on the racial restrictions 'lying like a

[1] C.O. 533/102, Girouard to Crewe, 19 Feb. 1912; and E.A.P. *Minutes of the
Executive Council*, 17 Feb. 1912.

[2] The Indian campaign against the poll-tax—based apparently on the slogan:
'No Taxation without Representation'—lacked consistency, and only sporadic
recourse was taken to the non-payment of the tax: as for example in 1914, when
Indian employees of the Railway and the Public Works Dept. refused to pay the
tax. See C.O. 537/402, Belfield to Harcourt, 27 Aug. 1914; E.A.P. *Minutes of
the Executive Council*, 16 Jan. 1915; and I.O. Emigration—Oct. 1919, Pros. 3,
part A.

[3] I.O. Emigration—Oct. 1912, Pros. 11–13, file 111, pp. 741–58; June 1913,
Pros. 13–15, file 45, pp. 409–35 (Harcourt to Crewe, 17 Jan. 1913, p. 411);
Bombay Archives, P.D. vol. 122 of 1912, Comp. 1541, Sir Jamsetji Jeejebhoy
(chairman of the public meeting) to Bombay Govt., 2 Aug. 1912, and P.D. vol.
113 of 1913, Comp. 1282, Govt. of India to Bombay Govt., 4 June 1913. For
Indian grievances over land reservation in the towns, see also Kenya Archives,
file no. Mombasa 2/126 of 1912, which reveals the practical implications of the
policy in the case of land purchased by an Indian merchant in 1904, where he was
later prohibited from residing under a restrictive covenant reserving the area for
European residence.

mill-stone around the necks of Indians', Jeevanjee stressed the Imperial significance of such policies: 'Now I ask is it right, that those very British subjects . . . who have done the pioneer work . . . should be regarded . . . as undesirables . . . to be boycotted and got rid of? It is not a cause in which Indians in East Africa alone are concerned; but it is a matter in which the large questions of the status and position of all Indians in the Empire are involved.' Jeevanjee then called for the annexation of Kenya to the British Indian Empire and its administration upon the principles adopted in India.[1]

Indian political activity in Kenya prior to the First World War was, however, largely disorganized and unsuccessful, while the Convention of European Associations formed in 1910 rapidly gained political importance during the period—and provided in the process an example in successful pressure politics that the Indians were to follow. The various Indian attempts to organize themselves politically culminated in the formation, in March 1914, of the East African Indian National Congress at a meeting in Mombasa attended by delegates from all over East Africa. T. M. Jeevanjee, brother of A. M. Jeevanjee, was elected President, and the Congress adopted as 'its fundamental principle the right of the Indians . . . to complete and full equality of treatment in the eyes of the law'.[2] One of its first tasks was to press for the appointment of an Indian member to the Legislative Council; but the Governor, Sir Henry Belfield, was opposed to such Indian representation as he also was to other Indian demands generally. The Indian community, he felt, had 'for good and sufficient reasons been prohibited from acquiring land in the highlands'; while 'the definition of Indian locations in townships' was 'essential to the maintenance of health and sanitation'. Similarly, the Governor explained that the grant of equal status to the Indians with the Europeans as regards trial by jury or judicial appointments was 'for obvious reasons . . . neither necessary nor desirable'.[3] The Government of India, however, supported the

[1] A. M. Jeevanjee, *An Appeal on Behalf of Indians in East Africa* (Bombay, 1912), pp. 6–7, 9–10, and *passim*.

[2] I.O. Emigration—Aug. 1914, Pros. 22, file 34, part A, I.O. to Govt. of India, 31 July 1914, and enclosures—including the report of the first session of the E.A.I.N.C., Mombasa, Mar. 1914 (this report is also in the E.A.I.N.C. records, Nairobi). At first the Congress adopted the name of B.E.A. Indian Congress, which was later changed to the E.A. Indian National Congress.

[3] I.O. Emigration—Aug. 1914, Pros. 22, file 34, part A, Belfield to Harcourt, 1 May 1914. The Governor was also hostile to the formation of the Congress: 'I venture to suggest that it would be well that the aspirations of its members

Indian case, pointing out that there was 'no justification for assigning in the Crown Colonies or Protectorates to British Indians who are not indentured labourers a status in any way inferior to that of any other class of His Majesty's subjects resident in the Colony'.[1] But the generally hostile attitude of the local Europeans—settlers, missionaries, and officials—supplemented as it was by an equally exaggerated account in 1913 of the insanitary conditions of Indian bazaars,[2] presented a picture in London best calculated to prejudice Indian claims to equal treatment. The Imperial Government's response to the resolutions of the Indian Congress in March 1914, therefore, did not differ in any essential detail from the earlier replies to Indian representations, and the Colonial Secretary was 'unable to admit that any injustice is involved in the present position of British Indians in the East Africa Protectorate'.[3] It was left for the Indians to take up their political campaign after the war, and to seek to expose the essential weakness of the various arguments that had been used against them.

The growth of European hostility towards the Indians was, however, not restricted to Kenya alone, for elsewhere in East Africa there was also a steady reversal of the earlier attitudes sympathetic to Indian enterprise. In German East Africa, as in Kenya, the earlier considerations favouring increased Indian immigration gave way to adverse remarks about the Indian role in the country. The factor underlying such a change of attitude lay largely in the growth of economic rivalry; and it found expression chiefly in mounting criticism of the Indians generally and demands for the restriction of their immigration. As in Kenya, so in German East Africa, the European campaign against the Indians revolved largely around the much-exaggerated picture of the Indian as a 'crafty' trader, as an undesirable neighbour owing to his insanitary habits, as well as the

should be checked at the outset by an intimation from yourself which will leave them in no doubt that further agitation on the same or similar subjects will not be sympathetically received.'

[1] I.O. Emigration—Aug. 1914, Pros. 22, file 34, part A, Crewe to Harcourt, 29 July 1914.

[2] W. J. Simpson, *Report on Sanitary Matters in the E.A.P., Uganda and Zanzibar* (submitted in 1913 and published in 1915), C.O. 879/115/1025. In a subsequent criticism of this Report, the Revd. C. F. Andrews described it as politically biased. See I.O. Emigration—Nov. 1920, Pros. 1–116, pp. 39–40, semi-official letter from Andrews, 27 July 1920.

[3] I.O. Emigration—Aug. 1914, Pros. 22, file 34, part A, Harcourt to Crewe, 15 June 1914.

equally abused argument that the Indians showed no interest in becoming permanent settlers but only thought of returning to India with their savings.[1] Apart from being 'racial antagonists', the Indians also appeared to the Germans as 'to a certain extent a national danger' since they were British subjects.[2] The 'Inder Frage' in German East Africa was also intensified by reports implicating a number of Indian traders with 'gun-running' and provision of supplies intended for the Maji Maji 'rebels'. Some Indian merchants were in fact convicted at Kilwa in 1906 for smuggling arms and supplies to the 'rebels'.[3] Armed with such ammunition against the Indians, the Europeans demanded in 1906 the restriction of Indian immigration and objected to the fact that they kept their accounts in a language which the government officials could not understand.[4] The Indians in turn protested against the 'native status' to which they were generally subject, whereby they (excluding the Parsees and Goans) were tried before the 'native judge', who was a second-class official without any legal training. This matter was to remain 'a long-standing grievance of the Indians' throughout the period of German rule.[5] Meanwhile, however, the European demands of 1906 found little favour in official circles. The Governor, von Rechenburg, supported the Indians in the country, pointing out that they were essential intermediaries for the extension of trade into the country-side and along the railway, and also that racial discrimination against them would be a contravention of the Berlin Act.[6] But the Governor's support of their enterprise hardly checked European antipathy towards the Indians. By 1911 the Europeans were able to secure the passage of a 'comprehensive anti-Indian resolution' in the Legislative Assembly—which sought to deny Indians the right to own land and urged the implementation of a policy of segregation and restriction of immigration against them.[7] In fact in 1912 the Colony's annual estimates included a reference to the question of a possible expulsion

---

[1] See article by H. Schnee in *Deutsches Koloniale Lexicon*, vol. ii, quoted in India Archives, Emigration—Sept. 1925, Pros. 1–92, part A, memo. on the Indians in East Africa by Mr. Ewbank; J. D. Karstedt, 'Beiträge zur Inderfrage in Deutsch-Ostafrika', *Koloniale Monatsblatter*, pp. 337–55; and W. R. Louis, *Ruanda-Urundi 1884–1919*, pp. 168–70.

[2] J. Iliffe, 'The German Administration in Tanganyika, 1906–1911' (Cambridge Ph.D. thesis 1965), p. 189.

[3] *E.A.S.*, 13 Jan. and 17 Feb. 1906.   [4] Iliffe, op. cit., p. 189.

[5] Kenya Archives, file no. Mombasa 12/204, H.M. Consul, Dar es Salaam, to P.C., Mombasa; 9 July 1914; and Iliffe, op. cit., p. 187.

[6] Iliffe, op. cit., pp. 149, 191.   [7] Iliffe, op. cit., p. 192.

of some Indians from the territory.[1] Immigration restrictions against the Indians were later enforced in German East Africa, and the policy of segregation more widely applied following the grant of municipal rule to the Europeans on the eve of the war. Indian political opposition to such policies was spearheaded by the Tanga Indian Association formed in 1914, which petitioned the Government to redress the racial disabilities imposed upon them, but with little success.[2]

In contrast to Kenya and German East Africa, there was no parallel campaign against the Indians in Zanzibar and Uganda, although there was a marked change in official policy from the earlier encouragement of the Indian role to measures for its restriction. The arguments used against the Indians generally, however, did not differ much from one territory to another. In Uganda the Indian question was precipitated by administrative measures that introduced restrictions in trade and segregation in the towns. Professor Simpson's report in 1913, which strongly recommended segregation against the Indians in East Africa generally—on the basis of the congested and insanitary conditions of the Indian bazaars[3]— found ready support among the Europeans and encouraged wider application of the existing practice of segregation in Kenya and Uganda. Later, after the war, the report, having already been accepted by the Governments, was to form the basis for the legal enforcement of racial segregation in the towns.[4] Similarly, there was mounting criticism of the Indian traders and middlemen in Uganda; and, under the argument that the African needed protection from the 'sharp practices' and 'craftiness' of the Indian traders, restrictions were imposed upon their enterprise. In 1913 the Uganda Cotton Rules were promulgated and these provided for the purchase of cotton directly by the ginners—since this would ensure European supervision—rather than through the medium of Indian middlemen in the country.[5] As they owned no ginneries in the country at that time, the Indians felt that these Rules would give a virtual monopoly of the cotton industry to the European ginners, and protested to the

[1] I.O. Emigration—June 1912, Pros. 25, file 77, part B.
[2] Iliffe, op. cit., pp. 187–8, 306.   [3] W. J. Simpson, op. cit.
[4] Entebbe Archives, file no. 1016, Attorney-General to Lands Officer, 17 Oct. 1917; and E.A.P. *Minutes of the Proceedings of the Legislative Council*, 10 Feb. 1921, pp. 85–6.
[5] Entebbe Archives, file no. 661, Director of Agriculture to Chief Secretary, 14 Feb. 1913.

Colonial Office in January 1914.[1] At the same time, Allidina Visram, pressed on by the other Indian traders, built a ginnery in Kampala to meet the new conditions of trade.[2] Commercial rivalry between the Europeans and the Indians was intensified during the war, when the Bombay market—and consequently Indian ginners—made rapid gains in the Uganda cotton industry. By 1918 the day of the middle-man was fast passing, and the new Cotton Rules issued in that year restricted cotton buying to ginneries and at specific cotton markets in the country. Similarly a policy of control and regulation of trade generally was initiated—since, as one official pointed out, there was 'grave objection to having too many Indian centres, scattered in-discriminately' over the districts.[3] The small Indian traders protested against the new Cotton Rules on the ground that these gave a monopoly of cotton trade to European and Indian ginners, and asked for the 'liberal policy of free trade' to be continued.[4] On the other hand, the leading Indian firm in the cotton business, Narandas Rajaram, also complained that the new Rules tended to discriminate against the Indians; and pointed out that the whole policy of control was based on 'one side of the tale of the Cotton trade' whereby the entire Indian commercial community was blamed for unfair business methods.[5] On the whole, however, as the Acting Governor of Uganda pointed out in February 1920, relations between the Government and the Indians in Uganda had 'always been good, Indians need apprehend no change in the policy of the Uganda Government to their detriment'.[6] But he also underlined official acceptance of the various arguments used against the Indians—especially their lack of business morality and sanitary standards—which led the Kampala Indian Association to retort that the entire community could not be

---

[1] C.O. 536/74, Jeevanjee to Harcourt, telegram, 14 Jan. 1914, and minutes thereon.

[2] C.O. 536/79, see confidential report on the Uganda cotton industry by S. Simpson, Director of Agriculture, and memo. of J. A. Hutton, chairman of the British Cotton Growing Association.

[3] Entebbe Archives, file no. 5426, Part I, P.C., Eastern Province, to Chief Secretary, 19 July 1918.

[4] Entebbe Archives, file no. 5387, Indian Association to Chief Secretary, June 1918.

[5] I.O. Emigration—June 1919, Pros. 35–40, pp. 231–44, N. Rajaram to Govt. of India, 11 Mar. 1919, enclosing N. Rajaram to Chief Secretary, 23 Dec. 1918. See also I.O. Emigration—Aug. 1920, Pros. 7, file 35, part A, for further representations by N. Rajaram.

[6] Entebbe Archives, file no. 6024, Ag. Governor W. M. Carter to E.A.I.N.C., 18 Feb. 1920.

I

blamed for the conduct of a few individuals, and that insufficient alienation of land and financial expenditure by the Government, rather than any inherent inability of the Indians, accounted for the congested and insanitary conditions of their 'localities' in the towns.[1] The general official attitude towards the Indians in Uganda, however, presented a marked contrast to that in Kenya. And it was perhaps best expressed in the report of the Uganda Development Commission, published in 1920: 'The country owes much to the Indian trader and we consider that a broad policy of toleration should be adopted towards him. He has shown energy and enterprise, and has assisted in the opening up of the more remote districts. He is also of value as an agriculturist. . . .'[2]

The Indian position in Zanzibar was similarly affected during this period by a number of measures in the Protectorate which aroused strong Indian opposition. In a 'mass' meeting in Zanzibar in September 1909, the Indians, led by two prominent businessmen, Y. A. Karimjee and Y. E. Jivanjee, protested against a series of decrees that had been promulgated. These included, inter alia, the Magistrates Jurisdiction Decree of 1908 which deprived the Indians of their existing right to trial by jury and of appeal to the Bombay High Court; the Building Regulations Decree of 1909, which required prior approval of detailed plans for the construction of any building and, as the Indians complained, of mud huts and similar buildings also; the Ngoma Regulations Decree of 1909, which prohibited African and Indian music between sunset and sunrise except by special permission; and the deportation provisions of the Zanzibar Order in Council of 1906. Later, in a memorial in February 1910, the Indians also complained against the hostile attitude of the British Consul, who had refused to entertain an earlier Indian petition in March 1909 and the subsequent representations of the 'mass' meeting in September 1909. Perhaps more important, the memorial complained of the general economic decline of Zanzibar, the fall in the values of buildings and plantations, and the removal of trade to the mainland. In addition, the Indians requested the establishment of a legislative council to oversee future legislation.[3] But the attempts of

[1] Entebbe Archives, file no. 6024, Indian Association to Ag. Governor, 27 May 1920.
[2] Quoted in Govt. of India dispatch of 21 Oct. 1920 in *Correspondence regarding the Position of Indians in East Africa*, Cmd. 1311 (1921), p. 9.
[3] I.O. Emigration—June 1910, Pros. 6–8, file 52, pp. 319–35; Feb. 1911, Pros. 6–7, file 52, pp. 73–93; and Jan. 1911, Pros. 19, file 126 of 1910, part B.

the traditionally commercial Indian population in Zanzibar to turn to politics were speedily thwarted by the Consul. In a dispatch to the Foreign Office in April 1910, he denounced the Indian community with the much-exaggerated arguments that had by now become common stock in East Africa—the Indians remitted their savings to India and had no permanent commitment to the country; they were dishonest traders who cheated the 'innocent' local population and lived in extremely unhygienic conditions:

if Zanzibar is to be grateful for the prosperity which the Indians have brought in their train, they on their side should . . . be equally grateful to a country in which they have been able to do so much better. . . . But . . . the balance is against the Indians . . . and [they] must be compared . . . to the small Jew traders in Russia who, if necessary to the life of the countryside, are at best a necessary evil. There are, of course, a certain number here of respectable old established Indian firms. . . .[1]

The tendency thus deliberately to denigrate the Indian community, by exaggerating its vices and ignoring its virtues, in order to make political capital against the Indians had become popular among the European officials and non-officials throughout East Africa. In the circumstances, the Foreign Secretary, Sir Edward Grey, was unable to entertain the Indian complaints. The Government of India, however, felt that some of the decrees were evidently discriminatory, and assurances were given by the Foreign Office that these would be revised. But on the main Indian demand for the repeal of the Magistrates Jurisdiction Decree, no concessions were made.[2]

The increasing European official and unofficial hostility towards the Indian role in East Africa and the series of rebuffs to their petitions for redress of grievances during this period were to form the background for the dramatic growth of Indian political agitation in East Africa in the immediate post-war years. And it was in Kenya that the simmering discontent was to erupt into a major political controversy, following the passage of additional measures that aggravated Indian disabilities and asserted European paramountcy in the country.[3] These measures included the Crown Lands Ordinance

[1] I.O. Emigration—Feb. 1911, Pros. 6–7, file 52, pp. 73–93, Clark to Grey, 13 Apr. 1910.
[2] I.O. Emigration—Feb. 1911, Pros. 6–7, file 52, pp. 73–93, Grey to Clark, 25 Aug. 1910, and Clark to Grey, 8 Oct. 1910, with enclosures. See also I.O. Emigration—Aug. 1911, Pros. 1, file 76, part A.
[3] The Indian Question in Kenya has been frequently written about; see, inter alia, W. K. Hancock, *Survey of British Commonwealth Affairs*, vol. i; G. Bennett, *Kenya, A Political History*; M. R. Dilley, *British Policy in Kenya*

of 1915, which sought to legalize the reservation of the Highlands for European settlement; the introduction of legal as against administrative segregation—both residential and commercial—in the towns in 1918; the implementation of the European Soldier Settlement Scheme and the grant of elective representation to the Europeans in 1919, which confirmed their predominance in the legislative and municipal councils. Similarly, the change of status of Kenya in 1920 to a Crown Colony and the abolition of the rupee currency during 1920–1 were obvious gains for the Europeans. More important perhaps was the growth of a sustained anti-Indian campaign among the Europeans immediately after the war. The occasion for this was provided by a suggestion by Sir Theodore Morrison that German East Africa should be mandated to the Government of India after the war—partly as an 'olive branch' to Indian public opinion, restive over discrimination in various parts of the Empire.[1] The proposal received scant support from the Indians generally; but the very suggestion was anathema to the Europeans in Kenya and precipitated a campaign by them against the Indian presence in East Africa. Both the suggestion by Morrison and the Indian community generally were strongly condemned in the Legislative Council in December 1918.[2] The campaign was later intensified under the leadership of Lord Delamere and Colonel Grogan, and dominated the proceedings of the Convention of Associations in January 1919. Later it seemed to reach its culmination in the report of the Economic Commission published in 1919, which included a bitter tirade against the presence of the Indians in the country—and caused Lord Milner to dissociate himself from

Colony (New York, 1937); R. Oliver, The Missionary Factor in East Africa (London, 1952); W. M. Ross, op. cit.; Lord Hailey, An African Survey (London, 1957); and R. L. Buell, The Native Problem in Africa (New York, 1928), vol. i. The attempt here, therefore, is to present the political controversy in general outlines and with limited claim to originality.

[1] I.O. Emigration—Mar. 1921, Pros. 48–51, part A, Govt. of India to I.O., 10 Feb. 1921. See also I.O. Emigration—Oct. 1919, Pros. 3, part A.

[2] E.A.P. Minutes of the Proceedings of the Legislative Council, 9 Dec. 1918, pp. 44–8. Characteristically, the European opposition to the Indians was justified by the need to protect African interests—for the motion passed by the Council read: 'that the interests of the African demand that he should be given the opportunity which Indian competition denies, of filling the subordinate posts under European supervision which technical education and contact with European civilisation qualify him to fill.' See also copy of the European petition to the Governor, Dec. 1918, in I.O. Emigration—Oct. 1919, Pros. 1–8, pp. 281–312.

some of the abusive and defamatory remarks made about the Indians by the Commission.[1] Meanwhile the European campaign against the Indians drew some support from official quarters. The Governor, Sir Edward Northey, informed the Legislative Council in February 1919 that 'British European preponderance in the Government is essential'; and in March he pointed out to the Indian Association in Nairobi that 'The principle has been accepted at home that this country was primarily for European development, and whereas the interests of the Indians would not be lost sight of, in all respects the European must predominate.' This was later confirmed in writing in June 1919: 'His Excellency believes that though Indian interests should not be lost sight of, European interests must be paramount throughout the Protectorate.'[2]

Such developments in Kenya led to vociferous Indian protests and to the intensification of their political agitation in the country. This followed a number of unsuccessful representations made by them against the introduction of discriminatory legislation. During 1916 and 1917, the Indian Associations at Nairobi and Mombasa pressed for increased Indian representation in view of the proposals for eleven European elected members on the Legislative Council and two nominated Indian members. The Indian Association in Nairobi also raised for the first time the question of elective representation for the Indians.[3] Similarly the restrictions on the sale of certain plots of

[1] See Milner's dispatch to Bowring, 21 May 1920, in Kenya, *Official Gazette*, 18 Aug. 1920, pp. 774–6; E.A.P. *Economic Commission Report* (Nairobi, 1919) and 'Lecture on the E.A.P. by Major E. S. Grogan', London, 1919, C.O. pamphlet no. 241, ref. P 10554. In a subsequent semi-official letter, Revd. C. F. Andrews commented on the 'enormous harm' that Morrison's suggestion had done and blamed the Economic Commission's 'baseless and irresponsible and grave charges' on it. See I.O. Emigration—Nov. 1920, Pros. 1–116, part A, pp. 4–5.

[2] Quoted in the Govt. of India dispatch of 21 Oct. 1920 in *Correspondence regarding the Position of Indians in East Africa*, Cmd. 1311 (1921), p. 2. See also E.A.P. *Minutes of the Proceedings of the Legislative Council*, 24 Feb. 1919, p. 3. There was in fact an apparent contradiction in the European claims to paramountcy in the country and the much-emphasized argument that their campaign against the Indians was designed to safeguard the African interests. This argument occurs consistently during this period, and led to Indian counter-accusations of 'grossest hypocrisy' on the part of the Europeans. Indeed, as Prof. Ingham points out: '. . . the manner in which European responsibility for the welfare of the African population was used as an instrument with which to attack Indian claims to political equality gave the campaign an aroma of insincerity which brought little credit to its supporters.' K. Ingham, *A History of East Africa* (London, 1962), p. 272.

[3] E.A.P. *Minutes of the Proceedings of the Legislative Council*, 19 June 1917, p. 19; and Kenya Archives, file no. Mombasa 50/1215.

land in Mombasa in 1918 under the Segregation Rules led to direct protests to the Colonial Office by the Indian Association, Mombasa, in August 1918.[1] In Nairobi the Indian Association made a series of representations during 1918 against the various measures that discriminated against Indians.[2] Later, in March 1919, the various Indian Associations in Kenya sent a deputation to Delhi to present a memorial to the Viceroy—complaining of racial discrimination against the Indians and the European campaign to 'squeeze' the Indians out of the country.[3]

But such haphazard and sporadic political effort was largely unsuccessful. The Indians were politically disorganized and the Congress formed by them in 1914 had become virtually defunct. At this juncture the effective leadership of the Indian community passed from the hands of the old-established merchants to the more recently arrived immigrants, who were more aware of nationalist sentiment in India and were also predominantly Hindu rather than Muslim, as in the past. The most important of these was M. A. Desai, who arrived in Kenya in 1915 as a lawyer's clerk, and quickly assumed the leadership of the Indian Association in Nairobi. From then until his death in 1926[4]

[1] I.O. Emigration—Oct. 1919, Pros. 1–8, part A, pp. 301–4, Bowring to C.O., telegram, 29 Aug. 1918, Polak (Secretary, Indians Overseas Association, London) to C.O., 7 Sept. 1918, enclosed protest note from B.E.A. Indian Association, dated 28 Aug. 1918.

[2] I.O. Emigration—Apr. 1918, Pros. 11, filed, I.O. to Govt. of India, 25 Feb. 1918, and enclosures; *Leader of B.E.A.*, 9 Dec. 1918—for 'mass' Indian protest at the proposed municipal reforms; and E.A.I.N.C. records, Nairobi, file: 'Correspondence and Proceedings of the Indian Association Nairobi 1917–22', Indian Association to Chief Secretary, 12 Feb. and 29 Nov. 1918, complaining against the municipal reforms, Crown Lands Ordinance, segregation, restrictions on the sale of ex-Enemy property, and the lack of Indian representation on the Economic Commission and the Land Settlement Commission—'all schemes of reform in this country are introduced for the sole benefit of the European community and just claims of the Indians are entirely ignored'.

[3] I.O. Emigration—Oct. 1919, Pros. 1–8, part A, pp. 281–312, copy of the memorial dated 22 Mar. 1919 and departmental proceedings thereon; Govt. of India to I.O., 4 June 1919, supported the Indian case and reiterated its earlier stand that there was 'no justification in a Crown Colony or Protectorate for assigning to British Indians who are not indentured labourers, a status in any way inferior to that of any other class of H.M.'s subjects resident in the Colony'. The Indian deputation to Delhi consisted of A. M. Jeevanjee, H. S. Virji, C. J. Amin, and Shamsud-Deen. For further action on the Indian memorial by the I.O., see I.O. Emigration—Nov. 1920, Pros. 1–116, part A, I.O. to Govt. of India, 25 Dec. 1919, enclosing I.O. to C.O., 15 Aug. 1919. Copy of the memorial and related proceedings also in Lands Office, Nairobi, file no. 15993: 'General Question of Policy re Indians in E.A.P.'

[4] See the obituary on Desai in *E.A.S.*, 17 July 1926. For Desai's activities, see

Desai was virtually the leader of the Indian community, and helped to arouse it from political apathy and to launch a concerted campaign that transformed the Indian Question in Kenya into a major political issue of Imperial significance. At first Desai reorganized the Indian Association in Nairobi with the help of other Indian leaders—notably B. S. Varma, Shamsud-Deen, H. S. Virji, C. J. Amin, and Mangal Dass—and this Association was registered in 1919. At the same time, he started the newspaper, the *East African Chronicle*, which, together with the *Democrat* edited by S. Achariar, became the principal spokesman for Indian views and sought to counter the anti-Indian bias of the European press. Later in the year, M. A. Desai was actively involved in organizing in Nairobi a conference of the Indian leaders from Kenya, Uganda, Tanganyika, and Zanzibar with a view to reviving the activities of the E.A. Indian National Congress, and to seeking its direct affiliation with the parent body in India.[1]

Thus reorganized, with H. S. Virji, the Ismailia businessman, as President, and B. S. Varma, a Hindu lawyer in Nairobi, as Secretary, and spurred on by the nationalist leaders in India, the E.A. Indian National Congress launched a vigorous campaign designed to extend the scope of the Indian demands for equal treatment in Kenya to the larger question of the position of the Indians throughout the Empire. Apart from representations to the Government of India, the Congress sent a deputation to London in April 1920 which presented a lengthy petition to Lord Milner. In language reminiscent of Milner's

---

also E.A.I.N.C. records file: 'Correspondence and Proceedings of the Indian Association Nairobi 1917–22.'

[1] *E.A.S.*, 17 July 1926; and E.A.I.N.C. records file: 'Correspondence and Proceedings of the Indian Association Nairobi 1917–22', see especially B. S. Varma to Revd. C. F. Andrews, 12 May, 10 and 20 July 1920. As with the European settlers in the Highlands, so with the Indians in Nairobi, the more extreme political activity seemed to have become a special preserve of the up-country immigrants. Hobley, for example, pointed out: 'The antagonism between the Asiatic and the European, which has so unfortunately developed up-country, is little evident at the Coast...'; while Revd. C. F. Andrews in a semi-official letter, dated 27 July 1920, similarly referred to the more moderate 'Mombasa spirit' among the Indians and the more extreme 'Nairobi spirit', which now increasingly dominated their political activity. See I.O. Emigration—Nov. 1920, Pros. 1–116, part A, pp. 39–40; and Hobley, *Kenya from Chartered Company to Crown Colony*, p. 148. For Indian political organization, see also I.O. Emigration—Dec. 1919, Pros. 10, filed; India Archives, Emigration—Mar. 1923, Pros. 32–3, file 23, part B (this refers to the deportation of Achariar for his press campaign); and Entebbe Archives, file no. 4092, which refers to the Indian newspapers published in East Africa in the immediate post-war years.

'Helots Despatch' of 1899, the petition complained that whereas in Kenya the Indians' 'claims to consideration were historically antecedent and economically vastly superior', 'preferential treatment in every sphere has been given to the white settlers and the Indian community have been more and more relegated to the position of helots, enjoying no important civic rights and placed under numerous humiliating and invidious disabilities'.[1] Apart from Indian grievances over the Highlands policy, representation on the legislative and municipal councils, and segregation, the petition complained of restrictions against them in the sale of ex-Enemy property, the lack of adequate Government support for Indian education as against European education, the restriction of higher appointments in the public services to Europeans only instead of candidates with proper qualifications and merit, and lack of any Indian representation on the government boards or other public bodies—notably the Economic Commission, whose report, the Indians pointed out, 'ignores so deliberately all the essential historical facts . . . and outrageously defies the rights of a community of His Majesty's subjects . . .'. In July 1920 Lord Milner sought a solution of the Indian Question in Kenya by offering the Indians two elected seats on the Legislative Council and upholding the *status quo* as regards the Highlands, racial segregation, and immigration policy.[2]

The Milner 'solution' aroused a storm of protest among the Indians; and the Government of India, conscious of the repercussions Indian disabilities in a Crown Colony would have on a politically turbulent India, actively intervened in support of the Indian demands in Kenya. And its dispatch of 21 October 1920 adequately summed up the views of the Indian community which had been expressed in various representations, and more recently in a direct appeal to the Prime Minister by the E.A. Indian National Congress on 6 October 1920.[3]

---

[1] Copy of the petition in Oldham Papers, Edinburgh House, London, file: 'Kenya Indians'; E.A.I.N.C. records, file: 'E.A. Indian deputation in London 1920'; and in I.O. Emigration—Nov. 1920, Pros. 1–116, part A. See also E.A.I.N.C. records for resolutions of Congress sessions of 1919 and 1920—copy of the 1919 resolutions also in Entebbe Archives, file no. 6024. The Indian deputation to London in Apr. 1920 consisted of A. M. Jeevanjee, S. T. Thakore, and S. Achariar.

[2] Kenya, *Official Gazette*, 18 Aug. 1920, pp. 774–6, Milner's dispatch of 21 May 1920 contained the proposals which were later made public in July 1920. See also I.O. Emigration—Nov. 1920, Pros. 1–116, pp. 713–814, for detailed proceedings in this respect.

[3] *Correspondence regarding the Position of Indians in East Africa*, Cmd. 1311 (1921); and E.A.I.N.C. to Lloyd George, 6 Oct. 1920 in E.A.I.N.C. records,

The Indians countered Milner's contention that his policy was designed 'to mete out even-handed justice between the different races' by pointing to the various examples of evident injustice, apart from Northey's pronouncements on European paramountcy, which Lord Milner's 'solution' seemed to uphold. As the Government of India explained: 'It is not clear to us why the European community should require eleven members to voice its views, while two members are considered to be sufficient for the Indian community.' Similarly, the Indian demands for a common electoral roll based on property and educational qualifications received Government of India support:

> We fear that separate representation for the different communities will perpetuate and intensify racial antagonism . . . if the qualification for a common franchise is properly defined, it follows that the number of Indian voters will be far less than the number of European voters . . . the fear of Indian domination is, we submit, unfounded.

Indian grievances over municipal representation, especially in Nairobi, were, as the Indian Government explained, based on the fact that both on the basis of population and the proportion of rates paid, they had better claims to representation than the Europeans, who enjoyed a majority. The Indian case against segregation was perhaps best summed up in the statement:

> It seems to us, indeed, almost inevitable that compulsory segregation will mean that the best sites will be alloted to the race which is politically most powerful. Further, it can be taken as almost certain that the race which controls the Municipal Council will spend an unfair proportion of the revenue of the Municipality on its own quarter, and will neglect the areas occupied by other races. The practical effect of compulsory segregation on the race which is politically weaker, can be seen in the Asiatic ghettos in the Transvaal.

In fact such Asian ghettos already existed in Kenya, as Norman Leys showed with reference to the effects of segregation in Nairobi.[1]

file: 'Outward 1920–33.' For the original of the Govt. of India dispatch of 21 Oct. 1920, which contains more details than the published version in Cmd. 1311, see I.O. Emigration—Feb. 1921, Pros. 4, file 36, part A. For Indian reactions to the 'Milner solution', see also Kenya, *Proceedings of the Legislative Council*, 29 Nov. 1920, p. 6; and I.O. Emigration—Mar. 1921, Pros. 25–6, filed.

[1] N. Leys, *Kenya* (London, 1924), pp. 271–2. The Revd. C. F. Andrews echoed similar views to those expressed by the Govt. of India against segregation and blamed the local government for the rise of Indian ghettos in the towns, see semi-official letter from Andrews, 27 July 1920 in I.O. Emigration—Nov. 1920, Pros. 1–116, part A, pp. 39–40.

Further, the Government of India dispatch dealt with the Indian opposition to the reservation of the Highlands, which obviously did not comprise a relatively small area suitable for European settlement, as was frequently claimed, considering that 11,000 square miles of land had been alienated to the Europeans as against thirty-two square miles to the Indians. The Milner 'solution' was thus unacceptable to the Indians—and as the Government of India explained, it was 'an impossible position that British Indians in a British Colony should be subjected to disabilities to which they cannot be subjected in an adjoining mandated territory'.[1]

In the circumstances, the Imperial Government laid the whole issue of the political controversy in Kenya before the Joint Parliamentary Committee on Indian Affairs; while in Nairobi a round-table conference of Indian and European delegates was convened by the Governor in May 1921, in an attempt to settle the Indian Question. But the conference ended in deadlock over the 'irreducible minimum' concessions acceptable to the Europeans. While the Indians asked for a common electoral roll and opposed the land policy as well as the legal enforcement of segregation, the Europeans were prepared to concede only the abandonment of commercial segregation while insisting on limited communal franchise for the Indians, reservation of the Highlands, and the restriction of Indian immigration.[2] The report of the Joint Parliamentary Committee in July 1921, however, came out strongly in support of the Indian demands for the removal of the racial disabilities imposed upon them; while the Indian case was also strengthened by the resolution of the Imperial Conference of 1921 that: 'there is an incongruity between the position of India as an equal member of the Empire and the existence of disabilities upon British Indians lawfully domiciled in

---

[1] Cmd. 1311 (1921), op. cit.; and I.O. Emigration—Feb. 1921, Pros. 4, file 36, part A. In the case of the mandated territory of Tanganyika, equal rights for nationals of the member states of the League of Nations (which included India) had been secured by Article 7 of the Mandate.

[2] I.O. Emigration—Oct. 1922, Pros. 5, part A, C.O. to I.O., 8 July 1921, enclosing Northey to Churchill, 14 May 1921. The round-table conference was originally proposed by the Indians in Dec. 1920 and the idea accepted by Northey in Jan. 1921. See E.A.I.N.C. records, file: 'Correspondence with Kenya and Uganda Governments 1921', Congress to Northey, 15 Dec. 1920, and Colonial Secretary to Congress, 19 Jan. 1921. For a copy of the proceedings of the conference, see also E.A.I.N.C. records: 'Indian Association Nairobi, Report for the year 1921'. The Indian delegation to the conference consisted of A. M. Jeevanjee, M. A. Desai, B. S Varma, Mangal Dass, H. S. Virji, and A. J. Dewji.

some other parts of the Empire'.[1] The Europeans countered these gains for the Indians by launching a vigorous campaign against the Indian demands, and sought support for their campaign among European settlers in southern Africa. The old arguments against the Indians were buttressed by new ones—the bogy of Indian domination and the European ideal of trusteeship of the Africans being particularly emphasized. At the same time a series of telegrams to the Colonial Office in July and August 1921 denounced Indian presence in the country—claiming widespread support for the European position among the Africans and Arabs, especially in the form of a 'European and African Trades Organization' which sought to boycott Indian traders.[2] In fact the Governor himself telegraphed to the Colonial Secretary that he had received 'strong protests' from the Europeans, Africans, and Arabs against the grant of the common roll and equal status to the Indians as envisaged by the Joint Parliamentary Committee, and added: 'I sincerely trust that you will not make any decision reversing Milner policy except as to segregation in commercial areas. . . .'[3] But for its seriousness for the future of Kenya, the situation would have been farcical, for the Indians similarly sent a series of telegrams to counter European claims that the Indians were unsympathetic to African advancement.[4] In addition they also sought support abroad, particularly in India, where nationalist opinion tended to regard the Kenya controversy as a test case for the Imperial Conference resolution in 1921 that India was an equal member of the Empire; and Revd. C. F. Andrews, one of the most

---

[1] *Proceedings of the Standing Joint Committee on Indian Affairs from 17 March to 13 July 1921* (London, 1921) and *Indians in Kenya*, Cmd. 1922 (1923), p. 5.

[2] For detailed proceedings in this respect, see I.O. Emigration—Oct. 1922, Pros. 1–55, 101–22, part A. For European charges and Indian counter-charges, see, *inter alia*, *The Indian Problem in Kenya* (*E.A.S.*, Nairobi, 1922); C. F. Andrews, *The Indian Question in East Africa* (Nairobi, 1921); Lord Delamere and K. Archer, *Memorandum on the Case against the claims of Indians in Kenya* (Nairobi, 1921); E.A. Women's League, *The Indian Question in Kenya: The Kenya* (*European*) *Women's Point of View* (Nairobi, 1923), copy in Papers of the British Anti-Slavery Society, Rhodes House Library, Oxford, ref. MSS. Brit. Emp. S. 22/G. 135: 'Indians in B.E.A. 1921–24'; Ross, op. cit., pp. 371–2; F. D. Lugard, *The Dual Mandate in British Tropical Africa* (London, 1922, 5th ed. 1965), pp. 317–21; and Imperial Indian Citizenship Association, Bombay, 'Indians Abroad, Bulletin no. 5, May 1923: Kenya', C.O. pamphlet no. 63, ref. P 10554.

[3] I.O. Emigration—Oct. 1922, Pros. 6, part A, Northey to Churchill, telegram, 9 July 1921.

[4] I.O. Emigration—Oct. 1922, Pros. 13, 39, part A, see especially A. M. Jeevanjee and B. S. Varma to C.O., 11 Aug. 1921.

respected missionaries in India and a close confidant of Mahatma Gandhi, was deputed to East Africa to assist the local Indians. Meanwhile, M. A. Desai wrote to General Smuts and other European leaders in southern Africa to counter the claims of the European delegation and explaining that, contrary to the allegations made by the Europeans, the Indians merely demanded equal treatment and no more. Only General Smuts seems to have replied that he would keep the Indian views in mind.[1] Similarly, an Indian delegation was sent to London later in 1921 following Northey's departure for consultations with the Colonial Office—in view of the Governor's hostility towards the Indians. And, as if to complete the show, European claims of African support were rebutted in a telegram from Harry Thuku, leader of the Young Kikuyu Association:

> Native mass meeting held Sunday 10th July . . . declared Indian presence not prejudicial native advancement as alleged by Convention of Associations. Next to missionaries, Indians our best friends. . . . Give franchise all educated British subjects, submit this Kenya's only solution. Authorized Indian delegation consisting Jeevanjee, Varma, also Colonel Wedgwood represent our cause . . . to authorities concerned.[2]

In fact there is evidence that at this juncture the Indians sought to make common cause with the emerging African political organizations—the Young Kikuyu Association led by Thuku, the Kikuyu Association under chief Kinyanjui, the Young Buganda Association, and the East African Association.[3] The acting Chief Native Commissioner in a circular letter to provincial officials on 16 August 1921 warned: 'There are marked indications that an extensive and well financed Indian propaganda in the Native Reserves has been arranged with a view to make common cause with the Indians in bringing pressure to bear upon the Home Government. . . .' Later, on 9 December 1921, the Native Commissioner wrote that 'There is

[1] E.A.I.N.C. records, file no. 8: 'Miscellaneous Correspondence', Desai to Smuts, 18 Aug. 1921, and Smuts to Desai, 16 Sept. 1921. See also Imperial Indian Citizenship Association, Bombay, 'Indians Abroad, Bulletin no. 5, May 1923: Kenya', C.O. pamphlet no. 63, ref. p. 10554.

[2] I.O. Emigration—Oct. 1922, Pros. 6, part A, C.O. to I.O., 21 July 1921, and enclosures. See also 'Indian Association Nairobi, Report for the year 1921', in E.A.I.N.C. records, for details about the Indian delegation to London in 1921—consisting of Jeevanjee and Varma, who were supported in London by Col. J. C. Wedgwood and Polak.

[3] E.A.I.N.C. records, files marked: 'Correspondence 1922' and 'Correspondence with Kenya and Uganda Govt. 1921'; and Oldham Papers, Edinburgh House, London, file: 'Native Unrest (1922): Harry Thuku', letter from Revd. H. D. Hooper to Oldham, 5 Jan. 1922.

reason to believe that Mr. Desai is using the machinery of the Indian Association, of which he is President and of the "East African Chronicle" to stir up disaffection in the Reserves. . . .'[1] In fact Desai as editor of the *East African Chronicle* publicized in his paper the various African grievances over land, labour, and wages policy; and also helped to print articles and pamphlets in Swahili for Harry Thuku, who distributed these to his followers. Such activities later led to a police raid on Desai's newspaper offices.[2] Similarly, Thuku and the other African leaders were allowed the use of the offices of the Indian Association in Nairobi for their political work, and probably received some financial assistance from the various Indian leaders with whom they came in contact regularly.[3] But there was nothing 'sinister' in these contacts, as was later made out when the Europeans accused the Indians of complicity in the African riot in Nairobi in March 1922 that followed the arrest of Harry Thuku. As the Government of India commented: 'The Indian community is between two fires. If it is sympathetic with native aspirations it is said to be politically dangerous. If it keeps aloof, it is said to be doing nothing for the people of the country.'[4]

In spite, however, of the increasing inter-racial polemics of the time, discussions were continued in London between the Colonial and India Offices in an attempt to implement the recommendations of the Joint Parliamentary Committee. The general basis of policy, as Churchill outlined in a secret dispatch in August 1921, was to be 'Equal rights for all civilized men' but no change was envisaged as regards the Highlands policy.[5] These discussions resulted in an

[1] Copy of the circular letters in Kenya Archives, files no. ELGM/10 and DC/KAJ. 9/1/1/1.

[2] *Leader of B.E.A.*, 18 Mar. 1922. See also n. 4, below.

[3] I.O. Emigration—Oct. 1922, Pros. 1–55, 101–22, part A, semi-official letter from Revd. C. F. Andrews dated 23 Apr. 1922. See also Ross, op. cit., pp. 227–9, 234–5.

[4] I.O. Emigration—Oct. 1922, op. cit., minute on semi-official letter from Andrews dated 23 Apr. 1922. See also *Leader of B.E.A.*, 1 and 8 Apr. 1922; and E.A.I.N.C. records, file: 'Correspondence with Kenya and Uganda Govts. 1921', which contains letters and other papers showing the relations between Thuku and the Indian leaders. Desai, for example, was in communication with Thuku after the latter's restriction at Kismayu and undertook to look after Thuku's interests while he was in detention—the same was true of the relations of other Indian leaders with Thuku—notably Mangal Dass, B. S. Varma, D. D. Puri, and Shamsud-Deen; the former even engaged a firm of European lawyers to represent Thuku.

[5] I.O. Emigration—Oct. 1922, Pros. 15, part A, Churchill to Northey, 26 Aug. 1921.

interim award, which was tentatively accepted by the Indians in January 1922, whereby they were granted four representatives on the Legislative Council as against the Europeans' eleven to be elected on a common franchise restricted to 'civilized men'.[1] But no sooner was this compromise reached than Churchill's speech to the East African Dinner in London on 27 January 1922 reopened the whole issue. His support generally of the European aspirations to Kenya 'becoming a characteristically and distinctively British Colony looking forward in the full fruition of time to complete responsible self-government',[2] aroused a storm of protest among the Indians. Renewed discussions were then held between the Colonial and India Offices and direct representations were made in London by European and Indian delegations from Kenya.[3] The whole issue, however, once again ended in deadlock when the Wood–Winterton proposals of September 1922, which conceded the Indian demand for a common electoral roll on the basis of property and educational qualifications that would restrict the franchise to ten per cent of the Indian population, were accepted by the Indians but rejected by the Kenya Government and the Europeans—the latter threatening a *coup d'état* if the proposals were implemented. As a result, representatives of the rival parties to the conflict were summoned to London in 1923, and following this final phase of discussions the celebrated White Paper, *Indians in Kenya*, Cmd. 1922 (1923), was issued.

The 1923 'solution' of the Indian Question in Kenya represented a major set-back for the Indians—for not only were they denied the ideal of racial equality with the Europeans, but for all practical purposes the existing disabilities were to continue. The White Paper granted five seats to the Indians on the Legislative Council to be elected on a communal as against a common franchise, effected no change as regards the Highlands, while its formal declaration against segregation proved inadequate as segregation could still be imposed by administrative action. It had thus essentially failed to redress Indian grievances, although it ensured the containment of the political controversy in Kenya within certain basic principles of policy. The most important of these was the declaration of the

---

[1] I.O. Emigration—Oct. 1922, Pros. 31–4, 47, part A, I.O. to C.O., 9 Jan. 1922; and Kenya, *Official Gazette*, 11 Feb. 1922, p. 173.

[2] I.O. Emigration—Oct. 1922, Pros. 39, part A; *Leader of B.E.A.*, 25 Feb. and 4 Mar. 1922; and Bennett, *Kenya, A Political History*, p. 48.

[3] I.O. Emigration—Oct. 1922, Pros. 39–55, part A; and *Leader of B.E.A.*, 25 Feb., 4 and 11 Mar. 1922.

paramountcy of African rights in the country—which not only reversed the previous declarations of European paramountcy, but ensured the continuation of Imperial control in the Colony. This implied, as the White Paper made it clear, that the grant of responsible self-government to a European unofficial majority was 'out of the question within any period of time which need now to be taken into consideration'. In the larger context of the political history of Kenya, this was the only positive achievement of the post-war Indian political agitation in Kenya—for their sustained opposition both before and after 1923 was largely responsible for frustrating European aspirations to achieve self-government in the Colony in the same manner as elsewhere in southern Africa. Indeed, in the final phase of discussions, which were held amidst mounting tensions both in Kenya and India, the danger of a 'grave breach' with politically turbulent India—if the resolutions of the Imperial Conference of 1921 were not implemented—posed a major dilemma to the Imperial Government and played a key role in the final declaration in favour of African paramountcy. In fact, the Kenya Indian leader, M. A. Desai, seems to have foreshadowed this solution as early as February 1923:

. . . respectfully submit only satisfactory solution observance and practice [of the] just principle of predomination [of] native interests; adequate, effective representation European and Indian interests . . . no legal restrictions transfer [of] land; Government majority to protect native interests until native sufficiently educated, no predomination European or Indian settlers.

But this telegram does not appear to have made any impact; and it was left to Dr. J. H. Oldham and the Archbishop of Canterbury in May 1923 more effectively to propose the resolution of the Imperial dilemma by a declaration in favour of African interests.[1]

Meanwhile, however, the Indian Question in Kenya had wider repercussions throughout East Africa. From the very start of the E.A. Indian National Congress's political campaign, the Indian

[1] India Archives, Emigration—Mar. 1923, Pros. 29–31, file 23, part B, M. A. Desai to C.O. and I.O., telegram, 7 Feb. 1923. For the role of Dr. J. H. Oldham and the Archbishop of Canterbury, Randall Davidson, see R. Oliver, *The Missionary Factor in East Africa*, pp. 260–1; and Oldham Papers, London, file: 'Kenya Indians: Archbishop of Canterbury.' This also reveals Dr. Oldham's close relations with the Indian delegation consisting of V. S. S. Sastri and Revd. C. F. Andrews and the Kenya Indian delegation consisting of Jeevanjee, Desai, Virji, and Varma. See also Lugard, *The Dual Mandate in British Tropical Africa*, p. 321; and Ross, op. cit., pp. 377–8.

National Association in Zanzibar and the Indian Associations in Uganda and Tanganyika were involved in its activities. The question of Tanganyika becoming a mandate of British India, which had aroused so much anti-Indian feeling among the Europeans, found little favour in Indian or Imperial circles, and Lord Milner in August 1919 dismissed the whole issue as impracticable.[1] But, as the Administrator of Tanganyika had reported earlier, 'One effect of Sir Theodore Morrison's pro-Indian campaign has been to excite political agitation among the Indian communities generally in East Africa, leading them into expressions of demands which might not otherwise have been formulated.'[2] In November 1919, the E.A. Indian National Congress passed a resolution demanding that British India be granted the Mandate over Tanganyika—'in consideration of the services rendered by the Indians in conquering the ex-German East Africa'. This referred to the two special Indian expeditionary forces which were employed between 1914 and 1917 in the campaigns against German East Africa. But by January 1920, following advice from leaders in India, the East African Indians had retreated to a more tenable position, pointing out: 'By asking for special treatment in German East Africa we shall be violating the fundamental principle which we have all along been fighting for, namely, that there shall be no differentiation in the treatment meted out to various sections of His Majesty's subjects.'[3] Accordingly they

---

[1] I.O. Emigration—Mar. 1921, Pros. 16–47, part A, I.O. to Govt. of India, 21 Aug. 1919, and enclosures. See also proceedings relating to the future of German East Africa in I.O. Emigration—Apr. 1919, Pros. 32, filed, and May 1919, Pros. 15, filed.

[2] I.O. Emigration—Mar. 1921, Pros. 16–47, part A, H. A. Byatt to Milner, 21 Dec. 1918. Indeed, it is significant that the British attempts to appease Indian nationalist sentiment by concessions elsewhere in the Empire—as for example in the proposed Indian mandate over German East Africa or the earlier schemes for State-aided Indian immigration to East Africa—aroused vague dreams of a 'Greater India' among certain sections of the Indian population. But statements such as those by Jeevanjee calling for the annexation of East Africa to the British Indian Empire or the subsequent demands for an Indian mandate over Tanganyika, while inspired largely by British initiatives, were in essence as innocuous as the original British proposals, none of which came to fruition. In the case of Morrison's proposal for an Indian mandate over Tanganyika, which aroused such bitter criticism of the Indians by the Europeans, Indian counter-claims represented, as Hancock explains, 'little more than an angry rejoinder to the racialist visions of the Europeans in East Africa. Mr. Gandhi and other responsible leaders in India condemned them from the very beginning, and they soon died a natural death.' See Hancock, *Survey of British Commonwealth Affairs*, i. 211–2.

[3] *Report by Sir Benjamin Robertson, dated 4 August 1920, regarding the*

asked for 'definite safeguards' that Indians would not be subject to disabilities in Tanganyika similar to those in Kenya. Assurances were later given by the Colonial Office that the Indians would be allowed freedom of entry and enterprise in Tanganyika, while a scheme was mooted for their possible settlement as agriculturists in the Territory in view of the Imperial sponsorship of European settlement in Kenya. As the Government of India pointed out: 'In view of her services in the war and on general grounds of Imperial policy, [India] had a claim to consideration in the matter.'[1] Subsequently, Sir Benjamin Robertson was deputed to East Africa to report on a possible Indian agricultural settlement in Tanganyika, but his recommendations led to the abandonment of the scheme[2]— rather in the fashion that similar schemes had earlier remained stillborn elsewhere in East Africa. Indian political activity in Tanganyika was thereafter confined mainly to ensuring that no discrimination would be practised in the sale of ex-Enemy property, as occurred in Kenya. In 1921 the E.A. Indian National Congress deputed one of its leaders to inspect ex-Enemy properties in Tanganyika in order to publicize these among prospective Indian buyers, but the authorities opposed such a fact-finding mission.[3] Further Indian representations, however, led the Government of India to intervene in the matter, and regular press communiqués were thereafter issued announcing the forthcoming sales of ex-Enemy property—with the result that the Indians were able to compete on equal terms with the Europeans in the purchase of such property.[4]

In Zanzibar and Uganda, meanwhile, the Indian Associations were spurred into political action by the campaign of the E.A. Indian

proposed settlement of Indian agriculturists in Tanganyika Territory, Cmd. 1312 (1921), pp. 3–6. See also I.O. Emigration—Jan. 1919, Pros. 1, part B, and July 1921, Pros. 1–8, part A, for copies of resolutions passed by the Congress in 1919 and 1920.

[1] I.O. Emigration—Mar. 1921, Pros. 48–51, part A, Govt. of India to I.O., 10 Feb. 1921.

[2] I.O. Emigration—Mar. 1921, Pros. 48–51, part A; Nov. 1920, Pros. 1–116, part A, pp. 713–814; June 1922, Pros. 32, file 44, part B, I.O. to Govt. of India, 11 May 1922, enclosed I.O. to C.O., 26 Mar. 1920, and C.O. to I.O., 12 Apr. 1920. See also Cmd. 1312 (1921), op. cit., and Ewbank's memo. on Indians in East Africa in India Archives, Emigration—Sept. 1925, Pros. 1–92, part A.

[3] I.O. Emigration—Sept. 1921, Pros. 43–61, filed.

[4] I.O. Emigration—Sept. 1921, Pros. 62–4, 73–4, filed; Nov. 1921, Pros. 19–20, 49, filed; Dec. 1921, Pros. 10, 17–17A, filed; Jan. 1922, Pros. 1, filed; and Mar. 1921, Pros. 48–51, part A, Govt. of India to I.O., 10 Feb. 1921. See also Dar es Salaam Archives, file no. 3033/2 for arrangements regarding sale of ex-Enemy property 1920-2.

National Congress. The Indian National Association in Zanzibar took up its pre-war campaign for the redress of grievances with fresh vigour. In a memorial to the Imperial Government in 1921, it demanded elective as against nominated representation on the Legislative Council, the establishment of a municipal council in Zanzibar, and the right to trial by jury.[1] Similar demands were raised in Uganda, where Indian political agitation was precipitated by the application of the Milner 'solution' in 1920. The two main Indian Associations at Kampala and Jinja took up the campaign against the introduction of legal segregation that followed in the wake of Milner's policy; and, more important, refused to accept the one nominated seat offered them on the Legislative Council as against two for the Europeans—demanding instead, in January 1921, 'if not more, an equal number of seats with the Europeans', for 'on the grounds of revenue derived from them, their large vested interests, and their numbers, Indians deserve more representation than Europeans'.[2] Failing to achieve redress, the Indians in Uganda —with the exception of the Ismailia community—took up the E.A. Indian National Congress campaign for elective representation based on a common roll with property and education qualifications, and against the enforcement of legal segregation.[3] The Uganda controversy thus became intertwined with the Indian Question in Kenya, and was similarly settled by the Devonshire Declaration of 1923.

The Imperial arbitration of the Indian Question in East Africa represented in essence a political settlement that confirmed the final abandonment of the early policy of direct Indian association with the Imperial effort in the territories, and substituted for it a policy of toleration of the Indian role in East Africa. The breach between the European and Indian position in the area, which had steadily widened since the beginning of the century, reached its culmination; and the pattern was provided for the future compartmentalization of East African society generally—and of Kenya in particular. The com-

[1] I.O. Emigration—Oct. 1921, Pros. 16–19, filed.

[2] *Minutes of the Proceedings of the Uganda Legislative Council*, 3 Mar. 1921, Appendix B and 10 June 1921, p. 15, and Appendix A. See also I.O. Emigration— Oct. 1920; Pros. 4–5, filed, for resolutions of the Kampala Indian Association, 1920; and Mar. 1921, Pros. 3, part A, Indian Association, Eastern Province to C.O., telegram, 29 Sept. 1920.

[3] *Minutes of the Proceedings of the Uganda Legislative Council*, 20 Aug. 1921 and I.O. Emigration—Sept. 1922, Pros. 16–45, file 36, pp. 257–316—contain full details of the Indian agitation in Uganda, and Mar. 1921, Pros. 3, part A, op. cit.

munal system of representation, the policy of land reservation and segregation, the provision of separate social services for the different races formed the backbone of the three-tier system that became so characteristic of East Africa during the later colonial period. Within this system the Indians were confined largely to a middle position, their role being restricted to subordinate employment and commercial enterprise—the twin foundations for their presence in East Africa that had been laid down at the beginning of the colonial period. Within these spheres they could expect to build a future that, to the extent that freedom of enterprise was allowed them, had certain compensations despite the political struggle for equality that they had lost. It was to be a measure of Indian perseverance—which owed much, of course, to the economic pressures of their homeland—that within these spheres and the related one of professional enterprise, they were to make major contributions to the general process of the evolution of modern East Africa. Nor in fact did Indian political activity as such cease after 1923—although it was certainly doomed to become ineffective, being largely a rearguard defensive action against increasing pressures from the Europeans. For, on their side, the Europeans too were dissatisfied with the 1923 settlement, especially the failure to obtain an unofficial majority in the Legislative Council; and were consequently only temporarily held in check by it, before they renewed their campaign for European paramountcy, and against the Indian role in East Africa generally and for the restriction of Indian immigration.

CHAPTER V

The Crucial Decades
1923 to 1945

By the early 1920s the general character of the Indian role in East Africa had to a large extent been determined by the policies adopted towards them. These had the combined result both of greatly increasing Indian participation in the development of East Africa and, at the same time, of restricting the Indian role within well-defined limits. In the two decades that followed the Devonshire Declaration of 1923 this process seemed to reach its logical conclusion—for both the Indian economic role in East Africa as well as the institutions of the three-tier system were greatly strengthened during this period. In the event these years were of crucial importance in determining the character of the modern Indian settlement in East Africa. Many of the issues that comprised the Indian Question were settled during this period—much to the discomfiture of the Indians, although the community also made substantial social and economic gains in the East African territories. The dominant feature, however, seemed to be the Indian Question, which the declaration of African paramountcy in 1923 could hardly be expected to resolve; and the political controversy between the Europeans and Indians in Kenya, with its widespread repercussions elsewhere in East Africa, continued virtually unabated after 1923.

The various Indian political and racial disabilities in East Africa, however, provided a significant contrast to their social and economic progress during this period. The twin prospects for middle-grade employment and commercial enterprise continued to form the basis for Indian immigration and employment in East Africa; while a growing number of them were able to take advantage of openings in the professions, the secondary industries, and, where possible, as in Uganda and Tanganyika, in agriculture. The general process of Indian adaptation to the British institutions and the East African environment—a process aided by the establishment of comprehensive educational facilities for the community—initiated far-reaching changes within their society. On the other hand, the weakness of their political position—for they neither enjoyed equality with the Europeans nor the long-term political security of the African majority —contributed to the general isolation of the Indians in East Africa. This also owed its origins to the stratification of East African society on racial lines, and to the cultural differences of the Indians. But within the three-tier system the Indians made important social and economic gains during this period—largely on account of the increasing economic opportunities in the territories and the improvements in Indian education.

In 1928, during the heat of the political controversy in Kenya, Sir Edward Grigg had remarked that nowhere else in Africa was there so much evidence of official 'goodwill towards Indian education . . . and Indian welfare generally' as in Kenya.[1] This comment can be taken as indicating the general official attitude in the other East African territories also—although progress in this respect was certainly more marked in Kenya, where, ironically enough, racial antagonisms and hostility towards the Indians were equally more noticeable. During the late 1920s, the question of Indian education, which had been a long-standing political grievance of the Indian community, received official attention in a manner that was reminiscent of the policy advocated by Sir John Kirk in Zanzibar over fifty years before. In a dispatch to the Government of India in January 1877, Kirk had regretted the 'lamentable fact' that while Indian traders in Zanzibar 'are allowed British protection and other privileges . . . yet their sons are not offered any opportunity to learn anything save simply to read and write the vernacular whilst in India liberal education is given. . . . I am therefore anxious . . . to aid in sowing the seeds of education in Zanzibar.'[2] It was, however, not until 1891 that the first school was established in Zanzibar following the efforts of the British Consul, Sir Charles Euan Smith, in this direction and the substantial financial contributions made for the purpose by the leading Indian traders in the island.[3] Later at the various Indian settlements in the interior, private schools were established largely on a self-help basis and with a view to providing elementary education. Most of these schools were built on a communal basis by the various Indian

[1] *Speeches by H.E. Sir Edward Grigg 1925–30*, p. 179.

[2] Kirk to Govt. of India, 15 Jan. 1877, in Bombay Archives, P.D. vol. 281 of 1877, Comp. 62.

[3] F.O. 84/2062, Euan Smith to Salisbury, 30 July 1890; and *Zanzibar Gazette*, 24 Aug. 1892.

religious sects, but among them were larger inter-communal schools at Mombasa, Tanga, Dar es Salaam, Kampala, and Nairobi. In addition, the Uganda Railway established a school in Nairobi in 1906 for the children of its Indian employees, and this was the first to be taken over by the Government in 1912.[1] The Kenya Education Department reported in 1925:

> In Indian education, great credit is due to the various religious sects which have founded schools throughout the country . . . the Indians are voluntarily surrendering their schools to Government, and a policy of absorption is being pursued. Indian education has long needed attention and the Department is glad to be able to record that this attention is now being received.[2]

Similar developments occurred in the other East African territories at about the same time.[3]

Government support for Indian education initiated in the late 1920s was to have far-reaching importance for the development of a comprehensive system of Indian education based on English standards. In addition, it stimulated, under official encouragement, the education of girls—which had been traditionally restricted by the community—as well as the higher education overseas, especially as doctors and lawyers, of an increasing number of pupils.[4] A scheme for government grants-in-aid to Indian schools was instituted in Zanzibar in 1924, in Kenya and Uganda in 1925, and in Tanganyika in 1929; while a little later a special Indian education tax was levied in the various East African countries to finance Indian education.[5] Similarly, advisory committees on Indian education—consisting of government officials and Indian nominees—were set up by the East African Governments; while at a lower level control and supervision was exercised through a series of school management committees. With the Government contributing half the capital costs and

---

[1] Kenya Archives, file no. ARC(GH)—103: Indian Education 1928–48; *Report on Tanganyika Territory for 1924*, pp. 59–60; and *Report on Tanganyika Territory for 1925*, p. 72. See also A. A. Kazimi, *An Inquiry into Indian Education in East Africa* (Nairobi, 1948).

[2] Kenya, *Annual Report of the Education Department for 1925*, pp. 4, 10.

[3] Dar es Salaam Archives, file no. 7017 (1925): Indian Education; Zanzibar, *Report of a Sub-Committee of Zanzibar Advisory Council on Education on Grants-in-Aid and on the Reorganization of Indian Education* (Zanzibar, 1935), p. 5; Uganda, *Annual Report of the Education Department for 1937*, p. 4; and Kazimi, op. cit.

[4] See, for example, Kenya, *Annual Report of the Education Department for 1925*, p. 11; and *Annual Report of the Education Department for 1929*, p. 6.

[5] Kazimi, op. cit. See also n. 3, above.

the Indian community raising the other half, modern government schools were successively built in the major East African towns. Apart from the existing Indian school in Mombasa, which was now brought under government control, a new government school opened in Nairobi in 1929. In Uganda, the modern Indian schools at Jinja and Kampala were completed during 1932–3; while similar progress was made by the Indian schools at Tanga and Dar es Salaam —which had been administered by the Government since 1929.[1] Greater progress was, however, made in Kenya, where, as Sir Alan Pim later pointed out, development had been 'so rapid and continuous as to be embarrassing to a small country, but it has been helped by the traditional zeal and generosity of the Indian Community in the education of their children'.[2] Equally important was the introduction in the government schools of the London Matriculation and the Cambridge School Certificate syllabuses. And the resulting improvement in the standard of education and of the facilities in the government schools presented a marked contrast to the conditions in the large number of private or 'provincial' Indian schools, which merely received grants-in-aid from the Governments.[3] By the end of this period, the basis of modern Indian education had been laid all over East Africa—Kenya leading the way with the introduction in 1941 of compulsory primary education for Indian children resident in Nairobi, Mombasa, and Kisumu. But it was essentially in the post-war period that more substantial progress was made following an inquiry into Indian education in East Africa.[4] However, the extension of government control and supervision of Indian education during this period, the establishment of modern schools, and the introduction of the English system of education foreshadowed the crucial role that education was to play in the social and economic improvement of the new generation of the

[1] Kazimi, ibid., and Kenya, *Annual Report of the Education Department for 1929*, p. 5; Dar es Salaam Archives, file no. 7017 (1925), and *Report on the Tanganyika Territory for 1926*.

[2] *Report of the Commission . . . on the Financial Position and System of Taxation of Kenya*, Colonial no. 116 (1936), p. 163.

[3] See, for example, Uganda, *Annual Report of the Education Department for 1937*, p. 12.

[4] Kazimi, op. cit.; Kenya, *Report of Committee on Education Expenditure (European and Asian)* (Nairobi, 1948), and *Report of the Select Committee on Indian Education* (Nairobi, 1949) reflect upon similar developments elsewhere, as later reports for Uganda and Tanganyika indicate—see, for example, Tanganyika, *Department of Education, Triennial Survey for 1955–7* (Dar es Salaam, 1958).

Indians born and/or brought up in East Africa. The more obvious gains lay in the opportunities for the educated Indian to enter the professions or, more frequently, to qualify for better administrative posts in public or private employment. As Sir Alan Pim pointed out in 1936 with regard to the civil service in Kenya:

Many Asian officers have in the past rendered valuable service to the Government, and the local Asian Community have strong claims to a fair share of Government employment in the future. . . . Recruitment has been recently confined to local candidates, both Indian and Goan. The number of their children and the praise worthy efforts of the community to give them an adequate education, as well as the actual examination results, show that there should be no want of suitable candidates.[1]

Meanwhile, the Indian economic role in East Africa steadily expanded during this period; and both population and enterprise was to increase greatly. In a sense this represented a logical development from the early colonial period, when Indian enterprise as traders, artisans, and as subordinate staff had acquired increasing importance, and in these capacities the Indians continued to play a growing role in East Africa. But more significant during this period was the gradual transition in their economic activities from the small-scale enterprise of the early years to larger business undertakings. From their beginnings in East Africa as petty traders and middle-grade employees, an increasing number of the Indians, with the help of a steady accumulation of capital, were able to invest in large-scale enterprise in cotton, sugar, sisal, and other secondary manufacturing industries, or to operate as builders, contractors, and saw-millers. Moreover, others who availed themselves of the opportunities for education were able to enter the professions. This process was also accelerated, interestingly enough, by the introduction of marketing restrictions in the 1930s, the lack of opportunities for Indian advancement to superior administrative posts, and the gradual growth of African competition as small traders and skilled workers.[2] But it owed more, obviously, to the enterprise with which

---

[1] Colonial no. 116 (1936), op. cit., p. 54.

[2] In the long run, the advantages arising out of an ability to survive on meagre profits and generally from a lower standard of living, which enabled the Indians to compete successfully against the Europeans as small traders and artisans, were to be more marked in the case of the Africans. So that, as one writer noted: 'the Asian artisan who replaced the European artisan is now finding that the African artisan is beginning to take his place.' See C. Leubscher, *Tangnayika Territory* (London, 1944), pp. 57, 79–80. The Hilton Young Commission had

the Indians exploited fresh avenues for economic activity and to their general economic resilience. The economic slump of the early 1930s, for example, caused considerable hardships,[1] with its much-dreaded retrenchment of Indian staff from public and private employment and the general depression in trade. And it was only with an abundance of fortitude and perseverance, comparable to that which had enabled an earlier generation of Indian traders to penetrate the interior in search of trade, that the community was able to face these difficult years. Moreover, the economic resilience of the Indians generally owed much to the traditional organization of their enterprises on the basis of the joint-family. This allowed for the pooling of capital resources and the entrepreneurial skills of a number of related

earlier foreshadowed similar developments: 'As the education of the natives progresses, African competition may be expected to become more and more effective. . . .' See *Report of the Commission on Closer Union . . .*, Cmd. 3234 (1929), p. 30. The growth of African competition as small traders had also become noticeable during this period. In fact, this also arose out of 'a tendency for Indian Traders to put natives in charge of their shops at Trading Centres', or to appoint Africans as agents of their firms in the Reserves—see, for example, Annual Report on the Ukamba Province for 1929, pp. 15–16, 47, and for 1930, p.27, in Kenya Archives, file no. PC/CP. 4/2/3. The Annual Report on the Eastern Province, Uganda for 1926, p. 15, showed that the number of African shops in the country was rapidly increasing—Entebbe Archives, file no. 703; while the Annual Report on the Kikuyu Province for 1928, p. 2, showed: 'There is little doubt that the native is now competing with the Indian traders in a manner that is bound to make itself felt.' See Kenya Archives, file no. PC/CP. 4/1/2. Later reports indicate that African competition tended to become more marked: 'In some districts it is apparent that much of the trade formerly in the hands of the Indian trader has passed into African hands'—Annual Report on the Central Province for 1936, p. 84, Kenya Archives, file no. PC/CP. 4/3/1—or 'The African is today entering into very determined competition with the Indian traders, both in the purchase of produce and the retail shop trade'—Annual Report on Nyanza Province for 1945 in Kenya Archives. See also Annual Report on the Uasin Gishu District for 1944: 'The Kikuyu petty trader is trying everywhere to "get his foot in". . . .'

[1] Local Indian tradition contains frequent references to the sufferings caused by the economic depression of the 1930s, while a number of reports bear this out. The Kikuyu Province Annual Report for 1930 (Kenya Archives, file no. PC/CP. 4/1/2), pp. 32, 36, refers to the bankruptcy of the leading Indian firm in the Province, and loss of money by many other Indian traders. Growing indebtedness and bankruptcies among the Indian traders are also shown by the Annual Reports on the Ukamba Province for 1930, p. 27, and for 1931, p. 14 (Kenya Archives, file no. PC/CP. 4/2/3). The Annual Report on the Kikuyu Province for 1933, p. 54, similarly showed that: 'The shopkeeper population has . . . been passing through a very difficult time . . . the smaller Indian traders in many cases, at the close of the year under review, found their affairs in a very embarrassed state.' Indian trading activity continued to be at a 'low ebb' during 1934–5—Annual Reports on the Central Province for 1934, p. 88, and for 1935, p. 58 (Kenya Archives, file no. PC/CP. 4/3/1).

individuals, and provided security for new business ventures as well as for the expansion of the existing enterprises. Later, when opportunities allowed, such original partnerships were to disintegrate into a number of smaller firms—although the family continued to be the basis for much of the Indian economic activity in East Africa. This pattern of development applies to numerous Indian firms in East Africa, both large and small, and can be taken as the standard for Indian business operations. Many Indian firms in East Africa developed a variety of commercial and other interests during this period, largely on the basis of such original partnerships, while the more skilful among them expanded into new fields of secondary industry, motor transport, and agriculture. The introduction of motor transport in the mid 1920s by the otherwise much-maligned Indian country trader is particularly significant, for it opened up areas which he had previously penetrated by carts and wagons to more speedy economic development. As Sir Edward Grigg later commented: 'I have been deeply struck by the enterprise and spirit and the disregard of risk with which Indians in many places make themselves the pioneers of road transport . . .', and referred to the Indian lorry driver 'whom I have frequently seen without lights, without brakes, apparently without tyres, and with an engine which looked like conking out at any moment, pushing trade through the most inaccessible places. . . .'[1] In fact, in their various capacities as *fundis* and *dukawallas*, cotton ginners and building contractors, wholesalers and retailers, lorry drivers and clerks, and indeed in every conceivable business activity, the Indians played a crucial role in the overall economic development of the East African territories.

In addition a number of Indian firms developed their enterprise on an East African basis during this period—a process encouraged by the common factor of British rule in the various territories. The opportunities for expansion of which some of the larger firms availed themselves reflected in part the wide variety of openings in the

[1] *Speeches by H.E. Sir Edward Grigg 1925–30*, pp. 235, 381. Similar references to the Indian role in introducing motor transport are found in the Annual Reports on the Ukamba Province for 1926, p. 23, and for 1930, p. 28—Kenya Archives, file no. PC/CP. 4/2/3—the latter indicating: 'There is still a considerable traffic by lorries from the Coast to Nairobi, Eldoret and beyond, competing with the Railway. These are often 6-wheelers, doing 10 miles or so to the gallon of petrol, and spending a week or more on the journey. One would imagine that there could be but little profit left at the end of their trip which as often as not is run practically empty.'

economic life of East Africa available to the lesser Indian traders. The number of Indian firms that developed extensive inter-territorial business interests was essentially limited, but among them were some that came to particular prominence in the post-war years. Of special significance, for example, was the expansion of the enterprise of Nanji Kalidas Mehta, who had earlier made important beginnings in the Uganda cotton industry. In the 1920s, he branched out into the sugar industry, having acquired 5,000 acres of derelict plantation land from the Government, and opened a sugar factory at Lugazi, near Jinja, in 1924—with a reputed investment of £25,000. Similarly, his family acquired additional cotton-ginning interests in Tanganyika, as well as sisal estates, following the sale of ex-Enemy property in that territory. Such interests, coupled with the extension of his business operations into Kenya and Bombay, were to form the basis for the extensive present-day Mehta enterprises in East Africa. In similar fashion Muljibhai Madhvani and the related Hindocha families diversified their business activities from the cotton interests they had earlier acquired in Uganda.[1] In 1929, Madhvani built the second sugar factory in Uganda at Kakira, near Jinja—having earlier acquired plantation land, reputed to be just as derelict and 'infested by the Umba and Tsetse fly' as that purchased by Mehta. Later the family also branched out into sugar and cotton enterprise in Kenya and Tanganyika; and its modern industrial and business network in East Africa traces its origins to the diverse inter-territorial interests acquired during this period. Equally significant was the expansion of the enterprise of the old-established Karimjee–Jivanjee family, which held considerable commercial interests in Zanzibar and along the Coast. Its operations, based on Zanzibar, Dar es Salaam, and Mombasa, were substantially diversified during this period, following the family's acquisition of sisal, coffee, and cotton interests in Tanganyika, and its expansion into secondary industry. Both Tyabali Karimjee and Yusufali Jivanjee, who were later knighted, were leading traders in East Africa at this time; while the career of the latter's successor, A. Y. A. Karimjee, as a future mayor of Dar es

[1] Oral information about the Mehta, Madhvani, and Karimjee–Jivanjee families. See also Entebbe Archives, file no. 7401, minute by Land Officer, 9 June 1922, regarding lease of agricultural land by Mehta at Lugazi; file no. 1138 P: Annual Report on Buganda for 1924, p. 12; and *Annual Report on Uganda for 1933*, p. 26. *Saben's Commercial Directory and Handbook of Uganda 1947–48* (Kampala, 1948) and G. F. Sayers, *Handbook of Tanganyika Territory* (London, 1930), give popular accounts relating to the activities of these firms.

Salaam and as a prominent political leader provides an interesting parallel with that of A. N. (later Sir Amar) Maini in Uganda—who similarly succeeded to the business and cotton-ginning interests acquired by his family in Kenya and Uganda during this period, and later became the first Asian mayor of Kampala.

On the whole, however, apart from the number of Indian business-men who developed large-scale enterprises during this period, Indian economic activity was confined largely to the middle roles in commerce and industry; and an overwhelming majority of the community was engaged in a wide variety of small-scale enterprise or employed as subordinate staff. But their numbers had greatly in-creased, both by a free flow of immigrants attracted to East Africa by the prospects of economic betterment, and by natural growth estimated at two to three per cent per annum. By 1948, Kenya had a population of about 97,000 Indians, Uganda 35,000, Tanganyika 46,000, and Zanzibar 16,000—the greatest proportionate increase since 1921 having occurred in Uganda. Of the Indian working population, the census report for Kenya in 1948 showed that 82·2 per cent were engaged in private industry, commerce, finance, insurance, building, and contracting—about half of this percentage being directly involved in wholesale and retail trade, while the balance of the working population were employed in public transport and the civil service. The picture did not vary noticeably from one territory to another, as the corresponding census reports for Tanganyika and Uganda indicated in 1948. In the latter territory, the figures revealed that 5,065 Indians were engaged in commerce, 2,878 in manufacturing industry, 716 in public services, 452 in transport and communications, 330 in building and construction, and 221 in agriculture.[1] The pattern of Indian employment also contributed to their greater concentration in the urban areas—the major East African towns of Dar es Salaam, Zanzibar, Tanga, Mombasa, Nairobi, and Kampala being the principal centres of Indian popula-tion and economic activity. Meanwhile, the average earnings of the Indian working population also steadily increased during this period—as the Indian leader, A. B. Patel, commented in 1946: 'I can say that, within my experience of the last twenty years in this country, the average standard of living of the Indian has risen much higher

---

[1] Sources: Non-Native Census Reports for Kenya, Uganda, and Tanganyika, 1948. See also *E.A. Royal Commission 1953–55 Report*, Cmd. 9475 (1955), pp. 204, 457.

than it was when I came to this country. . . .'[1] Figures available for Asian earnings in Kenya in 1948 reveal what was roughly the pattern elsewhere in East Africa: approximately a quarter of the Indian working population had an income of up to £15 per month, about sixty per cent earned between £15 and £30, and the balance up to £50 per month, including about 2 per cent with an income of from £50 to £100. It was, however, in the post-war period that the rise in incomes generally became more marked, as also did Indian investment in the territories.

The overall improvement during this period in the Indian economic status in East Africa and in Indian education contributed to the social progress of the community. This was essentially a gradual process, and like their economic progress in the territories, it spanned the full extent of the colonial period. But the process of settling down, of adaptation to the East African environment and to British institutions, the extensive urbanization of a community emigrating from Indian villages, the rise of a new generation exposed to the influences of Western education and to better economic standards—all these factors foreshadowed far-reaching changes within the Indian society. In essence, they initiated a process of greater East Africanization of the Indian immigrants, and the gradual decline of their initially strong links with India—this was to be particularly true for the younger generation born or brought up in East Africa. Similarly, the older immigrants, reacting in part to the European criticisms of their lack of any permanent commitment to the country, tended, with the passage of time, to become less temporary visitors, attracted to East Africa by the prospects of employment and economic improvement, and more settlers with an increasing stake in the territories. Such developments were, however, partly checked by the growing isolation of the Indians as a distinct racial and cultural minority in East Africa.

In part, the isolation of the Indian community was the product of its rigid communal and caste traditions. While the caste system as such could not operate in East Africa, the social mobility of the individual and frequently his choice of employment continued to be influenced by considerations of caste and creed. This was true, for example, of much of Indian commercial enterprise in East Africa where the traditional trading groups—Bhattias, Khojas, Lohanas, Bohras, and Vanias—continued to play the dominant role; while

---

[1] Kenya, *Legislative Council Debates*, 29 Nov. 1946, p. 479.

Indian immigrants belonging to the artisan castes similarly took to employment as *fundis*, masons, carpenters, tailors, etc. The most notable exception to this rule was the large number of immigrants belonging to the agricultural castes—for example, the Patels (Patidars) from Gujerat—who took to a variety of business and other activity, but hardly ever to agriculture. In addition, the various Indian communal and caste groups sought, with the growth of their population, to assert their separate identities by organizing a series of social and cultural facilities for their adherents in East Africa—so that Indian society represented essentially a conglomeration of a series of close-knit castes and sects, the diversity of the old-established Zanzibar communities having been accentuated by the new immigrant groups from Gujerat and Punjab. Apart from the numerous sects and castes that comprised the Indian population, the broader distinctions within the community were mainly religious. Up until the eve of the First World War, the Muslims formed a majority of the Indian population, largely as a continuation of the late nineteenth-century pattern in Zanzibar and also as a result of the predominantly Muslim character of the coolies imported for the construction of the Uganda Railway. But later, as the Indian immigrants began to settle down in East Africa, and the Hindus, like the Muslims before them, were joined by their families, the Hindu population rapidly increased, especially in Uganda and Kenya. By 1948, for example, there were 45,238 Hindus and 27,583 Muslims in Kenya, the corresponding figures available for Uganda being 20,441 and 11,172 respectively. There were, in addition, 6,146 Jains, 10,621 Sikhs, and 7,145 Goans in Kenya; and in Uganda 397, 1,549, and 1,448 respectively.[1] But the general compartmentalization of the Indian community into religious, communal, sectional, and caste groups largely reinforced rather than created their isolation in East Africa. For this, in essence, was the product of the 'historical process' in East Africa, which had tended to be 'one of communities for the most part living separately and not one of partnership in development'.[2] In the circumstances, while the social and economic progress of the community underlined its racial and cultural dis-

---

[1] Some indication of the earlier pattern of Indian population in Tanganyika is provided by the figures available for 1957, which showed that there were: 29,048 Hindus, 36,361 Muslims, 4,232 Sikhs, 913 Jains, and 4,732 Goans. In Zanzibar, the 1931 census revealed that the Indian population was comprised of approximately 7,000 Muslims, 5,000 Hindus, and about 900 Goans.

[2] *E.A. Royal Commission 1953–55 Report*, Cmd. 9475 (1955), p. 350.

tinctiveness, the limitation of their role, on account of restrictions, to the urban areas and to middle-grade employment—especially as shopkeepers and traders—exposed the Indians to continuing criticism for exclusiveness and economic 'exploitation'. The position of the Indian settlement in East Africa, as it had emerged by the end of this period, presented in fact a marked parallel to that of Jewish communities elsewhere—for, like them, the Indians, though constantly under scrutiny, had played a crucial role in the general process of development.

Much of the Indian political activity in East Africa, and particularly in Kenya, consequently continued to be based on the ideal of racial equality with the Europeans, and took the form of a sustained opposition to European demands for political advancement. In fact the settlement of 1923, the Indians felt, tended to ensure the continuation of European paramountcy notwithstanding the declaration in favour of African interests; and after protests that the Imperial Government had been influenced by the European threats of violence and that the Governor, Sir Robert Coryndon, had shown partiality towards the Europeans, they took recourse to a policy of non-co-operation.[1] The boycott of the legislative and municipal councils, begun in Kenya in 1919, was continued, and, apart from brief periods of co-operation, this was to last until 1933. In addition, during 1923–4, Indian non-co-operation took the extreme form of a refusal to pay taxes. This was partly due to fresh pressures from the Europeans—especially the introduction in 1924 of a bill in the Legislative Council for the restriction of Indian immigration.[2] The Europeans had long demanded such a measure, believing that unrestricted Indian immigration presented the threat of their 'swamping' the country and forming a barrier to African advancement, for while the interests of the Europeans and Africans were regarded as being in many respects complementary to each other, those of the Indians were not. Such arguments were, however, not entirely tenable,

[1] E.A.I.N.C. records: Presidential Address by Sarojini Naidu and resolutions of the 5th session, Jan. 1924. See also India Archives, Emigration—Nov. 1923, Pros. 73–157, part B, for Indian protests at the 1923 'solution'; June 1923, Pros. 26–73, part A, semi-official letter from Revd. C. F. Andrews dated 24 Mar. 1923; and N. V. Rajkumar, *Indians Outside India* (New Delhi, 1951), p. 64.

[2] E.A.I.N.C. records, files: '1923–24 Notices of Meetings and Agenda' and 'Correspondence with Kenya Government re Poll Tax'. Apart from the immigration bill, the Territorial Defence Force Bill of 1923 also aroused Indian opposition.

and the bill was later vetoed by the Imperial Government upon the recommendation of a committee appointed by the Colonial Office to deal with the issue.[1] The committee discounted European fears of a 'serious Indian invasion', for there was 'nothing in the economic condition of the Colony which would suggest that there will be a greater opening in the near future for Indians than in the past'. Further, the argument against Indian competition could apply equally to the European settlers, considering that the Africans were predominantly agriculturists. But more important the services of the Indian country trader and artisan contributed to African advancement to similar occupations, while the former played a crucial part in stimulating local production:

> The Indian trader or dukawalla is of great value to the African native, firstly, because he is willing to buy and sell commodities in very small lots such as no European would care to deal in, and secondly, because by bringing new and desirable articles to the notice of the natives he creates in the latter a desire to possess such commodities and gives them a stimulus to work harder. . . . In a new country such as Kenya every extension of trade creates new openings and leads to more work all round.

For the moment, therefore, the 1923 White Paper's support of unrestricted immigration, which the Indians regarded as virtually the only concession they had obtained from the Imperial arbitration of the Indian Question, was upheld; but the issue was never quite closed. Following the withdrawal of the immigration bill, prospects of the Indians abandoning non-co-operation were somewhat improved. The Kenya Government offered to nominate Indian representatives on the Legislative Council so as to ensure Indian co-operation, without prejudice to their demands for a common electoral roll. Later, in 1924, the Local Government Commission similarly recommended nominated representation on the municipal councils; and in view of their larger urban population and the proportion of rates paid, the Indians were given greater representation than

---

[1] India Archives, Emigration—Sept. 1925, Pros. 1–92, part A, copy of the minutes of the proceedings of the E.A. Enquiry Committee under the chairmanship of Lord Southborough and memo. by the Committee, dated 14 May 1924. For the controversy over immigration restriction, see also semi-official letter from Revd. C. F. Andrews dated 24 Mar. 1923 in India Archives, Emigration—June 1923, Pros. 26–73, part A, and petition of the E.A.I.N.C. to the Viceroy, 27 Jan. 1923, Emigration—Mar. 1923, Pros. 29–31, part B. The Hilton Young Commission later echoed views similar to those of the E.A. Inquiry Committee—that economic forces were already operating as a check to Indian immigration, see *Report of the Commission on Closer Union . . .* , Cmd. 3234 (1929), p. 30.

they had previously enjoyed. Such developments formed the background to a special session of the E.A. Indian National Congress in December 1924, when Abdul Wahid, a wealthy building contractor, successfully moved that the policy of non-co-operation be abandoned in favour of the compromise arrangements, and on the basis of a three-year 'trial' period.[1]

Political developments after 1925, however, rendered such a compromise essentially untenable. The sale of certain township plots in 1924 and at subsequent dates under restrictive covenants aroused Indian fears that segregation could still be imposed by administrative action—indeed the right of the Kenya Government to impose such restrictions was later upheld following legal action against it by A. H. Kaderbhoy, a leading Indian businessman in Mombasa.[2] Meanwhile, the renewed European demands for political advancement, the proposals for the Closer Union of the East African territories, and the pursuance of the Dual Policy aroused fresh political controversy. By 1927 the political position in Kenya had become as tense as it had been in the immediate post-war years. The promulgation of the new Constitution of Kenya in that year, and the subsequent acceptance of the Feetham Commission's report on local government, which had recommended European unofficial majorities in the municipal councils, led to the abandonment of the 1924-5 compromise—whereby the Indians had participated in the legislative and municipal councils. Further, the support by the Governor, Sir Edward Grigg, of the Europeans' demands for constitutional advancement, which formed part of the terms of reference of the Hilton Young Commission on Closer Union, as well as his generally hostile attitude towards the Indian demands for a common roll and equal consideration with the Europeans, aroused Indian fears that both the Closer Union of the East African territories and the Dual Policy would work in favour of the Europeans. This was evident from Grigg's conception of the Dual Policy, as he later pointed out: 'The interests of the white and black in Kenya are, in

---

[1] Kenya, *Report of the Local Government Commission* (Nairobi, 1927), pp. 6, 177-9; Cmd. 3234 (1929), op. cit., pp. 205-6; The *Hindu* (Madras), 30 Dec. 1924; and *Joint Select Committee on Closer Union, Minutes of Evidence* (London, 1931), ii. 769.

[2] India Archives, Emigration—Oct. 1929, Pros. 148, part B, contains full details of the controversy over segregation. See also Sidney Webb (Lord Passfield) Papers, London, vol. ii, file C, item 41; the *Guardian* (Manchester), 4 Feb. 1931; P. D. Master, *Segregation of Indians in Kenya* (Mombasa, 1931); and India Archives, Emigration—1932, file 289, L and O.

truth, not antagonistic but complementary, not mutually exclusive but naturally necessary and beneficial'; whereas 'the main services rendered by the Indian to the Colony are just those which bring him into competition with the native, as the latter gains a wider outlook, education, and technical skill'.[1] In fact the main Indian grievance against the Dual Policy, which was initially advocated by Sir Robert Coryndon and later defined in two White Papers,[2] was not merely that it tended to dilute the declaration of African paramountcy, but the official references to it as 'the complementary development of non-native and native production' and the association of the 'immigrant races' with the trusteeship of the Africans gave the impression of equal consideration for the Indians, when in practice this was not the case.[3]

In the circumstances, Indian political agitation in Kenya was renewed in 1927 with the demand for a common roll; and the policy of non-co-operation was particularly emphasized. This was partly due to the influence of the more radical leaders—notably Isher Dass and U. K. Oza[4]—who came to prominence in the affairs of the E.A. Indian National Congress at this time. In March 1927, when elections for Indian representatives to the Legislative Council were held under the newly promulgated Kenya Constitution, only one candidate presented himself for election—and was duly returned by the small number of voters (360) who had registered on the communal roll.[5] At the same time an Indian delegation made direct

[1] Grigg to Lord Passfield, 11 Sept. 1930, in *Papers Relating to the Question of the Closer Union of Kenya, Uganda and the Tanganyika Territory*, Colonial no. 57 (1931), p. 12, *passim*; *Speech by H.E. the Governor Sir Edward Grigg, 10 July 1930* (Govt. Printer, Nairobi, 1930); and Cmd. 3234 (1929), op. cit., p. 36.

[2] *Report of the East Africa Commission*, Cmd. 2387 (1925), and *Future Policy in regard to Eastern Africa*, Cmd. 2904 (1927), p. 3.

[3] See, for example, the evidence of the Govt. of India representative, V. S. Srinivasa Sastri, in *Joint Select Committee on Closer Union, Minutes of Evidence*, ii. 729–30.

[4] E.A.I.N.C. records: report of the 7th session, Dec. 1927. See also K. Robinson and F. Madden (eds.), *Essays in Imperial Government Presented to Margery Perham* (Oxford, 1963), p. 157, n. 4. Isher Dass, a Punjabi Hindu, and Oza, a Gujerati Hindu, were both privately employed.

[5] This was A. H. Malik, a Muslim, although he can hardly be regarded as a representative of the Muslim opinion of the time, considering that the other Muslim leaders—Jeevanjee and Abdul Wahid, who participated in the Legislative Council under the 1925 compromise—joined the other Indian members of the Council—Desai, Varma, and Pandya—in boycotting the elections and withdrawing from the Legislative Council. See, Kenya, *Legislative Council Debates*, 8 Mar. 1927, p. 7, report by the Ag. Governor, and India Archives, Emigration —Oct. 1931, Pros. 1–11, part A.

representations in London. In a lengthy memorandum complaining of the continuing racial disabilities of the community, the Indians opposed the European claims for constitutional progress as being 'absolutely in contravention to the letter and spirit' of the 1923 Declaration. Further, they accused the Governor of endeavouring to 'coerce' the community into accepting communal franchise by abandoning the practice of nominated representation for the Indians.[1] Similar views were later expressed, following Sir Edward Grigg's address to the E.A. Indian National Congress in December 1927, when he announced the Government's acceptance of the recommendations of the Feetham Commission, supported the communal franchise, and questioned Indian fitness to be associated with the Dual Policy—which had the effect of drowning his other, more conciliatory, remarks. The Indians retorted by expressing their 'emphatic protest' at the Governor's 'generally hostile attitude' and the lack of a 'fair deal' for them in the country. The President of the Congress, Tyeb Ali, in tracing at length the various racial restrictions against the Indians, expressed the community's growing restiveness at the recent political developments.[2] However, Sir Edward Grigg's ready support for the European position in Kenya was tempered by efforts to end Indian non-co-operation. Earlier in the year, he had appealed to the community to accept communal representation as it had 'in truth given security to Indians no less than to Europeans'; while it was time that 'any fear or bitterness left by the controversy of four years ago should disappear. Some extreme things were then said, no doubt, upon both sides, but they were spoken in the heat of the controversy.'[3] But the Indian Question was destined to become 'more difficult and more controversial' later in the year, following the report of the Feetham Commission, the appointment of the Hilton Young Commission on Closer Union, and the Indian insistence

[1] Copy of the memo. in Kenya Archives, file no. ARC(GH)—77 and India Archives, Emigration—July 1927, Pros. 13–17, part A.

[2] For fuller details of Indian protests at Grigg's policy, see India Archives, Emigration—Feb. 1929, Pros. 1–31, part A; and Indians Abroad, Bulletin no. 19, *East Africa: Royal Commission on the Union of East Africa* (Imperial Indian Citizenship Association, Bombay, 1927). Grigg repeated similar views in his farewell speech of 23 Sept. 1930 and aroused similar Indian protests—see India Archives, Emigration—Jan. 1931, Pros. 41–3, part B, E.A.I.N.C. to Govt. of India, 1 Sept. 1930, and Viceroy to I.O., 6 Nov. 1930. See also E.A.I.N.C. records: Presidential Address by Tyeb Ali, Dec. 1927; *Speeches by H.E. Sir Edward Grigg 1925–30*, pp. 211, 381; and *E.A.S.*, 31 Dec. 1927.

[3] *Speeches by H.E. Sir Edward Grigg 1925–30*, p. 179; and Kenya, *Legislative Council Debates*, 30 Aug. 1927, pp. 300–1.

on a common as against communal franchise. Eventually, the compromise arrangements of 1925 were revived in 1928 for one more year and Indian participation on the legislative and municipal councils was secured by nomination.[1] In Mombasa, on the other hand, the Indian Association, led by A. B. Patel and J. B. Pandya, was able to abandon non-co-operation as regards the Mombasa Municipal Council—following an undertaking by the Government in 1929 that one of the official members on the Council would be a senior Indian civil servant.[2]

Meanwhile, the Indian Question in Kenya once again had wider repercussions. The Government of India deputed two representatives to East Africa to assist the local Indian community in presenting evidence to the Hilton Young Commission. This took the form of a lengthy memorandum, together with a supplement to it, in which the E.A. Indian National Congress opposed the proposals for the Closer Union of the East African territories for fear of the 'Kenyanization' of East Africa, and also the grant of an unofficial majority in the Kenya Legislative Council. The memorandum also emphasized the Indian case for a common roll as against the communal system of representation, recounted the long list of the racial disabilities imposed upon the Indians, and defended the community's contribution in commerce and skilled employment to the general advancement 'both of the Colony as a whole and of the African Native'.[3] The crucial question, from the Indian point of view, was that of a common roll—for in that lay 'the recognition of their rights as British subjects to equality of treatment'. The report of the majority of the Hilton Young Commission, with the chairman dissenting, in favour of 'a common roll for Europeans and Indians, with a franchise

---

[1] *Speeches by H.E. Sir Edward Grigg 1925–30*, p. 250; India Archives, Emigration—July 1929, Pros. 15–16, part B; Kenya, *Legislative Council Debates*, 12 Nov. 1936, p. 549, comments by Isher Dass; and Kenya Archives, file no. ARC(GH)—40, copy of Polak to Passfield, 20 Sept. 1929.

[2] Kenya, *Legislative Council Debates*, 29 Nov. 1946, pp. 487–8, comments by A. B. Patel; and India Archives, Emigration—Feb. 1929, Pros. 1–31, part A. These proceedings also show that the compromise measures of 1928–9 were opposed by the Radicals, Isher Dass and U. K. Oza, and supported by the more moderate Indian leaders, Pandya, Phadke, Malik, and Kaderbhoy.

[3] E.A.I.N.C. records: offprints of the 'Memorandum submitted by the E.A.I.N.C. to the Hilton Young Commission' and 'Supplement to the Memorandum submitted by the E.A.I.N.C. to the H.Y. Commission'. See also Indian Archives, Emigration—Oct. 1929, Pros. 1–12, part A, for proceedings connected with the representations made by an Indian deputation, led by J. B. Pandya, to Govt. of India in Sept. 1929.

based on a high education and property test' greatly aroused Indian expectations in this respect. But the Europeans were strongly opposed to the common roll for fear that 'the admission of the [Asian] vote on the same terms as the Europeans might lead in the end through superiority of numbers to the control of their interests and institutions passing into the hands of another race'.[1] In the event, the Indians tried to convince Sir Samuel Wilson, during his mission to East Africa, that they did not seek political domination in Kenya and would be prepared to accept necessary safeguards within a common electoral roll. These views received the strong support of the Government of India.[2] But Sir Samuel Wilson, while recognizing like the Hilton Young Commission that the fear of Indian domination was unrealistic, emphasized that the Hilton Young Commission had made the adoption of a common roll dependent on local agreement. Moreover, he supported the European demands for an unofficial majority in the Kenya Legislative Council—with the result that the Indians denounced his report as 'one-sided and reactionary'.[3] The subsequent reiteration by the Imperial Government in 1930 of the principle of African paramountcy and the declaration that a common roll, with a franchise based on a 'civilisation test', was 'an object to be aimed at and attained'[4] greatly dampened Indian political agitation in the country. But it was not until the report of the Joint Select Committee on Closer Union in 1931 that the issues of Closer Union, constitutional change, common roll, and the Dual Policy—which had aroused so much Indian political agitation since 1923—were finally put to rest. Both the European and Indian communities once again took the opportunity to make a series of representations to the Imperial Government, voicing their claims and counter-claims. In a dispatch of September 1930, Sir Edward Grigg reiterated his support for the European demands in Kenya and

[1] Cmd. 3234 (1929), op. cit., pp. 205–7.
[2] *Report by Sir Samuel Wilson on his visit to East Africa*, Cmd. 3378 (1929), pp. 24–5 and Appendix I. See also *Report by the Rt. Hon. V. S. Srinivasa Sastri, P.C. regarding his mission to East Africa* (Delhi, 1930), p. 9. The Hilton Young Commission in its Report also pointed out that the Indians sought 'not political domination, but the recognition of their rights as British subjects to equality of treatment . . .'. See Cmd. 3234 (1929), op. cit., p. 206.
[3] Cmd. 3378 (1929), op. cit.; and E.A.I.N.C. records: resolutions of the 9th session, 1930.
[4] *Memorandum on Native Policy in East Africa*, Cmd. 3573 (1930), and *Statement of the Conclusions of H.M. Government in the United Kingdom as regards Closer Union in East Africa*, Cmd. 3574 (1930), pp. 8, 19.

opposition to the Indian claims. He pointed out, *inter alia*, that the argument that a common franchise based on high education and property qualifications would remove 'the discrimination against educated Indians . . . without in any way endangering the predominance of British methods, British tradition, and in all respects, of British Civilization', was essentially untenable. For, 'in practice the limitations imposed upon the number of Indian voters would either be found illusory', or else would lead to further Indian 'agitation which would certainly be promoted from India, like the present one'.[1] The Government of India in turn in a dispatch of November 1930 similarly voiced the views of the Indian community. The federation of the East African territories was 'bound to be affected by the political ideals of the European settlers in Kenya on account of their number and influence, and that, as these ideals in the past can only be described as complete political domination by the European community, Indian interests must necessarily be endangered by Closer Union'. Further, while the Indians welcomed the reiteration of the paramountcy of African interests, they feared that the doctrine might be 'interpreted and applied to discriminate against the immigrants of a particular race'. Therefore qualified Indians should also be considered for appointment to the Legislative Council as representatives of African interests. But, above all, the question of a common electoral roll was 'of primary and vital importance, as on it depends a satisfactory solution of the East African problem from the Indian standpoint'.[2] As the Government of India representative later pointed out to the Joint Select Committee, the Indian demand for a common roll derived its 'strength from a firm belief that the general progress and welfare of the Colony as a whole can be secured only by a system of representation based on common electorates'.[3] But in spite of strong support from the Government of India, the Joint Committee concluded, in view of the equally strong European opposition, that the common roll was not immediately practicable—although the question could later be 're-examined without prejudice'.

[1] Grigg to Passfield, 11 Sept. 1930 in *Papers Relating to the Question of the Closer Union of Kenya, Uganda and the Tanganyika Territory*, Colonial no. 57 (1931), p. 11. See also Cmd. 3574 (1930), op. cit., p. 19.

[2] Colonial no. 57 (1931), op. cit., Govt. of India to I.O., 24 Nov. 1930, pp. 126–9; Cmd. 3574 (1930), op. cit., pp. 18–19; *Joint Select Committee on Closer Union*, vol. ii, *Minutes of Evidence*, pp. 758–78 and vol. iii, *Appendices*, Appendices 22, 23, for views expressed by A. B. Patel and V. V. Phadke.

[3] *Joint Select Committee on Closer Union*, vol. ii, *Minutes of Evidence*, pp. 728–49.

The Committee, however, decided against the political union of the East African countries and the grant of an unofficial majority in the Kenya Legislative Council.[1]

Indian political agitation in Kenya based on the policy of non-co-operation and the insistence on a common roll was, however, already considerably diluted as a result of internal dissensions within the community. The Congress itself was able to contain the separatist tendencies within the community only by direct support from the parent body in India—in 1924 and again in 1930 Mrs. Sarojini Naidu and in 1929 H. N. Kunzru were 'drafted' from India to act as President of the E.A. Indian National Congress.[2] Later in 1930, the conflict between the moderate and extreme groups within the Congress came into the open. The moderates, mainly the 'Mombasa group', led by J. B. Pandya, A. B. Patel, and A. H. Kaderbhoy,[3] were prepared to abandon non-co-operation on the basis of the 1929 compromise and the Imperial declarations contained in the White Papers of 1930. But the more radical 'Nairobi group' led by Isher Dass, U. K. Oza, B. S. Varma, and Shamsud-Deen[4] campaigned for an extreme policy of non-co-operation until the common roll was granted. The situation was further complicated by a struggle for power within the Congress between Isher Dass and Shamsud-Deen, when both of them sought election as Secretary in January 1931— with the result that the Congress session broke up in disorder, leaving the more moderate group in virtual control of the organization. They, in turn, were recognized by the Government as the representative Indian political group and accepted nomination as Indian members to the Mombasa and Nairobi Municipal Councils; while A. B. Patel and V. V. Phadke were selected as Indian delegates to appear before the Joint Select Committee in London. In spite, however, of government refusal to entertain the claims of the radicals, who controlled the Indian Associations at Nairobi and Mombasa under Isher Dass and A. D. Sheth, that they were in fact more representative of Indian opinion, the dissensions within the Congress

[1] *Joint Select Committee on Closer Union*, vol. i, *Report*, pp. 39–42, *passim*.
[2] E.A.I.N.C. records: Presidential Addresses by Naidu and Kunzru in 1924, 1929, 1930.
[3] *Joint Select Committee on Closer Union*, vol. ii, *Minutes of Evidence*, evidence of A. B. Patel, p. 769. Pandya (Hindu) and Kaderbhoy (Muslim) were leading businessmen at Mombasa, while Patel (Hindu) was a lawyer.
[4] Sidney Webb (Lord Passfield) Papers, London, vol. v, file F, items 123 and 128, notes and pamphlets from Isher Dass. Shamsud-Deen (Muslim), like Oza and Dass, was self-employed, while Varma (Hindu) was a lawyer in Nairobi.

were quickly repaired. In May 1931, Indian candidates participated in the elections to the Legislative Council, and all the five members elected were pledged to support the policy of non-co-operation. Later, in August 1931, another session of the Indian Congress ended the split that had occurred in January; and the policy of non-co-operation was continued for the next two years. Moreover, apart from A. B. Patel, the other Indian delegates before the Joint Select Committee were disowned by the Congress.[1] Eventually, however, the Joint Committee's conclusions against the European demands for responsible self-government and the Indian demands for the immediate adoption of the common roll largely endorsed the views expressed in the White Papers issued in 1930. The E.A. Indian National Congress was thus obliged to take recourse in 1933 to the policy of co-operation which the moderates had advocated in 1931. In fact after 1933, the effective leadership of the Indian Congress passed largely into the hands of the more moderate Indian leaders, although the radicals were able to take comfort from the Joint Committee's rejection of the proposals for a political federation of the East African territories.[2]

But no sooner was the policy of non-co-operation abandoned in 1933 than the separatist tendencies within the Indian community became apparent. The various Indian communities were able to co-operate in the elections to the Legislative Council in 1933, and the candidates elected represented a fair cross-section of the various communal interests: J. B. Pandya (Gujerati Hindu), Shamsud-Deen (Muslim), Dr. A. C. L. De Souza (Goan), N. S. Mangat (Sikh), and Isher Dass (Punjabi Hindu)—the last being described by the Con-

[1] Sidney Webb (Passfield) Papers, vol. iv, file E, item 108 d and vol. v, file F, item 134 i; E.A.I.N.C. records: Presidential Address by A. D. Sheth, 11th session 1932; India Archives, Emigration—Oct. 1931, Pros. 1–11, part A, contains details of correspondence from the moderates and extremists, see especially E.A.I.N.C. to Govt. of India, 17 Feb. 1931, and Governor to C.O., 22 Mar. 1931; and Emigration 1934, file 130, L and O, note on position of Indians in Kenya prepared for the Viceroy.

[2] The radicals in fact hailed the decision as a 'decent burial' of 'that idol of Sir Edward Grigg's [which] passes away from our midst, unwept and unsung'. See Presidential Address by A. D. Sheth, 11th session, 1932, in E.A.I.N.C. records. The moderates, however, came to dominate the Congress: Pandya was President from 1934–8 and Patel from 1939–42, Kaderbhoy in 1938–9, while T. M. Jeevanjee, the first President of the body in 1914, presided again during 1933–4. The radicals controlled the Congress during 1931–3, when Varma and Sheth acted as Presidents—but it was not until 1944 that one of their ranks again achieved a similar status in the body, when Shamsud-Deen was elected President.

gress secretary as a socialist, 'still a great popular favourite (who) will be a good addition as one extreme fellow in the team is often an advantage in a Country like this'.[1] But as regards representation on the Municipal Council in Nairobi, the various Indian communities failed to co-operate. This was in marked contrast to the position in Mombasa, where the principle of nominated representation had been accepted by both the Europeans and Indians in 1929. During 1932–3, the Muslim community in Nairobi opposed the holding of elections for the Municipal Council and sought the reservation of seats for fear of Hindu predominance. Consequently, Indian representatives were nominated to the Nairobi Municipal Council by the Government; and it was not until 1936, after repeated Indian allegations that the Government was encouraging the minority groups in their demands, that the elective principle was finally implemented. But even then, elections were held only after two of the seven Indian seats were specifically reserved for the Goan and Muslim communities.[2] Communal differences among the Indians in Kenya—like their demand for the common roll—represented in effect the influence of developments in India on Indians abroad. The growing rift between the Hindus and the Muslims in that country inevitably affected relations between the two communities in Kenya— culminating in the grant of separate religious representation to the Muslims in 1951, amidst Indian and African protests.[3]

On the whole, however, the various Indian communities were largely in agreement in their attitude towards political developments after 1933 which adversely affected their interests in the Colony. These included the renewed European demands for constitutional advancement and for unofficial financial control, the implementation of the recommendations of the Carter Land Commission, the introduction of marketing legislation, and the control of Indian

[1] E.A.I.N.C. records, file: 'Outward 1933', S. D. Karve to H. S. L. Polak (the Jewish lawyer in London who had been Secretary of the Indians Overseas Association in London since its inception in 1919), 30 Apr. 1934.
[2] Kenya, *Legislative Council Debates*, 12 Nov. 1936, p. 549, and 16 Nov. 1936, pp. 610–1, comments by Isher Dass and N. S. Mangat, respectively. See also memo. presented to the Govt. of India by J. B. Pandya in Sept. 1935 in India Archives, Emigration—Sept. 1935, file 62—44/1935, L and O.
[3] E.A.I.N.C. records, file: 'Constitutional Developments 1950–51', contains information about a joint Congress—Kenya African Union meeting on 13 May 1951 and offprint of the 'Petition of the E.A.I.N.C., to the King to Disallow Religious Separate Electorates, 10 Jan. 1952', which refers to joint Congress—K.A.U. protest at a meeting on 7 Dec. 1951.

immigration. In addition, much of the Indian political activity was dominated by opposition to racial discrimination against them, as the proceedings of the Legislative Council make amply clear. The effectiveness of such Indian opposition was dependent largely, as previously, upon the continued support of their demands for equal treatment by the Government of India, and the consideration of their views ensured by Imperial control in the Colony. In fact, while the Indians increasingly felt that the Government of India failed to take sufficiently 'strong action' on their behalf,[1] they were conscious that the Imperial Government was 'more likely to hold the scales of justice even' in view of the partisan attitude of the local Government towards the Europeans.[2] As one Indian leader later commented upon Imperial control in the Colony: 'Thank God that is so, because we don't know where we should have been if that control had not been there.'[3]

After the political issues of the late 1920s, particularly that of the common roll, had been put to rest by the Joint Select Committee, Indian political activity was channelled into more immediate problems of racial inequality. Frequent allegations were made that government expenditure was weighted in favour of the Europeans, and that the fiscal policies—especially the protective customs duties and railway freight rates for agricultural products as well as subsidies to the farmers—directly favoured European agricultural interests, whereas the actual revenue derived from the different races did not justify such measures.[4] The question was evidently highly controversial, for as the Governor, Sir Joseph Byrne, had explained in 1931, it was virtually impossible 'to allocate with precision either expenditure, or indeed indirect taxation, as between races', and the

---

[1] See, for example, Presidential Address by A. B. Patel, Dec. 1938, in E.A.I.N.C. records, and Indians Abroad, Bulletin No. 19, *East Africa: Royal Commission on the Union of East Africa* (Imperial Indian Citizenship Association, Bombay, 1927).

[2] See the memo. presented by the E.A.I.N.C. to K.P.S. Menon for transmission to the Govt. of India in India Archives, Emigration—1934, file 370/34, L and O.

[3] Kenya, *Legislative Council Debates*, 18 Apr. 1939, p. 165, comment by Dr. Karve.

[4] E.A.I.N.C. records, 'Memorandum presented to Lord Moyne . . .' in file: '1931–33 correspondence, Miscellaneous'; *Report by the Financial Commissioner (Lord Moyne) on certain questions in Kenya*, Cmd. 4093 (1932), pp. 19–21, 28; Kenya Archives, file no. Mombasa 2/241, Indian Merchants Chamber, Mombasa, to Lord Moyne, 30 Mar. 1932. See also Kenya, *Legislative Council Debates*, 26 Nov. 1946, p. 371, for similar allegations by A. Pritam, and 20 May 1936, pp. 57–67, 74, comments by Isher Dass and Shamsud-Deen.

result derived 'must be very largely conjectural'.[1] But in 1932 Lord Moyne, the Financial Commissioner appointed to report on the issue, indicated that 'the tariff as at present framed is just in its incidence upon racial communities so far as the main structure is concerned', and recommended that income-tax be introduced in the Colony.[2] The question of introducing income-tax had long been a bone of contention between the Europeans and the Indians since proposals to this effect were first made in 1921. The Indians favoured such taxation, while the Europeans opposed it; and it was not until 1936 that income-tax was finally introduced. Meanwhile the provision of separate social services for the different races aroused similar Indian opposition—especially in view of the wide difference in government expenditure on such important services as European and Indian education.[3] This was appropriately based on the ability of the different communities to pay for the services provided for them; but the question of equal treatment with the Europeans made the principle of common social services an attractive political weapon for the Indians. In the same vein the Indians opposed the establishment in 1934–5 of separate terms of service for the European and Indian staff in the public services. Apart from the wide difference in salary scales—which provided for an Indian maximum of £502 per annum as against the European £2,117—and the 'recent tendency',

[1] Byrne to Passfield, 29 June 1931 in *Joint Committee on Closer Union*, vol. iii, *Appendices*, Appendix 26, pp. 179–80. For the question of taxation and government expenditure see also Cmd. 4093 (1932), op. cit., pp. 22, 63–5, 97, where (p. 97) Lord Moyne provided the following details regarding revenue and expenditure: Direct Taxation: Europeans £42,596, Asians £60,535, and Africans £530,877; Indirect Taxation: Europeans £109,113, Asians £55,704, and Africans £199,181. Expenditure: Europeans £171,247, Asians £46,080, Africans £331,956 —Indivisible: £1,771,180. The Indians were later to question the figures regarding Indirect Taxation and Indivisible Expenditure—see memo. by the E.A.I.N.C. to Govt. of India and to Cunliffe-Lister in India Archives, Emigration—1934, files. 78/34, and 370/34, L and O. See also Kenya, *Legislative Council Debates*, 26 Nov. 1946 p. 371, comments by A. Pritam, and Kenya, *Report of the Taxation Enquiry Committee 1947*—which showed that the Indians paid 27¾ per cent of the Indirect Taxation in 1944 and the Europeans 37 per cent (quoted in Lord Hailey, *An African Survey*, p. 405).

[2] Cmd. 4093 (1932), op. cit., p. 22.

[3] *Report of the Commission appointed to enquire into and report on the Financial Position and System of Taxation of Kenya*, Colonial no. 116 (1936), pp. 23–4, 166–8; memos. submitted by the E.A.I.N.C. to Govt. of India and to Cunliffe-Lister in India Archives, Emigration—1934, files 78/34 and 370/34, L and O—copy of the former also in E.A.I.N.C. records, 'Secretary's Report for the year 1933–34'. See also Kenya, *Legislative Council Debates*, 29 Nov. 1946, p. 491, comments by A. B. Patel.

as Sir Alan Pim explained, 'to replace Asians by Europeans', the Indians were particularly chagrined by the ban on their advancement to superior posts imposed by such racial differentiation.[1] As an Indian leader complained with regard to the police service—a remark that can be taken as indicative of the position in the public service generally—'An Indian, no matter how efficient, how capable and deserving, cannot rise above the rank of a wretched sub-inspector in this Colony.'[2] The position was earlier explained by an Indian memorandum on the subject:

The Civil Service must be open to all British Subjects without distinction of race or colour, provided that the necessary standard of education and other qualifications are possessed, and once a man is engaged, there ought to be no barrier to his advance and all [sic] should have equal opportunities to rise in his particular department to any position that he can attain by reason of his efficiency, qualifications and intelligence.[3]

But as Sir Alan Pim later explained, the new terms held certain compensations for the Indians:

Indian representatives have criticised the provision of separate scales of pay for Europeans and Asians doing similar work, but the new scales are substantially higher than would be paid in India for similar posts, and even allowing for the higher standard of living of Indians resident in Kenya, the terms laid down are not ungenerous.'[4]

Meanwhile the introduction of marketing legislation in Kenya during 1933–4 aroused fresh Indian political agitation. These measures, designed to control and regulate the marketing of African produce by establishing special marketing facilities and providing for exclusive licences for the purchase of certain commodities, represented in essence the Administration's mistrust of the Indian middlemen—who had long been the target of European criticism. As one writer has explained the position:

The idea that 'middlemen' are an incubus on producer and consumer alike is deeply engrained, particularly in the British administrative classes. When, in East Africa, to this cast of mind there was added a fairly wide-

[1] Colonial no. 116 (1936), op. cit., pp. 24, 261–2. See also Kenya, *Legislative Council Debates*, 9 May 1934, pp. 185–210, and 10 May 1934, p. 221, for views expressed by Isher Dass, De Souza, Pandya, Mangat, and Shamsud-Deen.
[2] Comment by Shamsud-Deen in Kenya, *Legislative Council Debates*, 14 Feb. 1939, pp. 360–1.
[3] E.A.I.N.C. records, file: 'Outward 1933', memo. presented by the E.A.I.N.C. on the position of the Indians in the public services of Kenya, 1933—copy also in India Archives, Emigration—1934, file 78/34, L and O.
[4] Colonial no. 116 (1936), op. cit., p. 54.

spread prejudice against Asians, who were naturally the chief middlemen, it was almost inevitable that policies would appear by which government, or a government agency, would buy as directly as possible from the peasant producer and sell on world markets.[1]

Indian opposition to such legislation revolved around the fear that the grant of exclusive licences would lead to a monopoly, while the establishment of separate produce markets would ruin the existing Indian trading centres in the interior—for much of the enterprise of the Indian country trader had been based on local produce since the early days. The question was taken up by the Federation of Indian Chambers of Commerce and Industry of Eastern Africa, which had been formed in 1932 following the introduction of marketing legislation in Tanganyika and Uganda. Its activities, like those of the E.A. Indian National Congress, were, however, dominated by developments in Kenya and most of its leaders—notably J. B. Pandya, D. D. Puri, M. Kassam Lakha, Yusufali Jivanjee, and Premchand Vrajpal Shah—were leading traders in Kenya.[2] The Government of India deputed a representative to East Africa in 1934 to study the situation, and his report largely endorsed Indian criticisms that the marketing legislation, by inhibiting free competition, would work against the interests both of the Indian country trader and the African producer. The Kenya Government, on the other hand, felt that official supervision was necessary to ensure fair prices for the African producers and to avoid 'cheating' by Indian middlemen as well as to encourage exports by maintaining proper standards and preventing adulteration, etc.[3] In a series of representations, the Indian leader, J. B. Pandya, argued against the Government's claims, point by point, and exposed the essential weakness of its arguments. Indeed even the Government of India was moved to comment: 'One has come to be

[1] Guy Hunter, *The New Societies of Tropical Africa* (London, 1962), p. 149.
[2] Kenya Archives, file ARC(GH)—141 I, Proceedings of the Federation of Indian Chambers of Commerce and Industry 1932–3 (copy also in E.A.I.N.C. records: 'Secretary's Report for 1933–34'). Pandya was a leading businessman in Mombasa, while Shah was a leading produce dealer in Kenya—for the latter, see also *E.A.S.*, 25 Apr. 1963. Puri was a leading businessman at Machakos, Lakha at Kisumu, and Jivanjee in Dar es Salaam and Mombasa. See also India Archives, Emigration—1934, file 362/33, L and O, for detailed proceedings regarding the marketing controversy in Kenya.
[3] *Report by K. P. S. Menon on Marketing Legislation in Tanganyika, Uganda and Kenya*, 1935, C.O. pamphlet no. 274, folio P. 10942, includes connected correspondence from the Governments—also published in the *Gazette of India Extraordinary*, 24 June 1935. See also India Archives, Emigration—1934, file 362/33, L and O, dispatch of the Kenya Govt., 18 May 1935.

suspicious of legislation or acts in Kenya designed to help the native. . . .' Apart from its effects on the Africans, the legislation, as Pandya complained, would 'squeeze us out of the country economically'—especially the petty Indian traders, who had rendered 'meritorious service' in stimulating African production, and would now be pushed 'from the position acquired by them after a great deal of personal suffering and sacrifices in men and money'. Further, he compared Indian opposition to the measures with the Elizabethan attacks on monopolies.[1] Eventually, when the marketing legislation was passed in 1935, the Government gave assurances that exclusive licences would be granted only by a motion of the Legislative Council and that marketing of local produce would not be completely separated from the existing trading centres. But Indian allegations that the Europeans were 'manipulating economic forces to oust the Indians' were later repeated when transport licensing legislation was introduced in 1937 in order to protect the Railway from the competition of road transport, in which the Indians had acquired considerable interests since the mid-1920s.[2]

Similar Indian agitation was precipitated by the measures designed to implement the recommendations of the Carter Land Commission regarding the reservation of the Highlands. The promulgation of the Highlands Order-in-Council in 1939 led to a series of Indian representations against the legalization of what had until then been an 'administrative practice', and against the permanent exclusion of the Indians from the Highlands where Europeans of any nationality enjoyed the right of settlement. The Indian leader, A. B. Patel,

[1] Indeed Pandya at this time was described by K. P. S. Menon as the ablest of the Indian leaders and the brain behind the Federation of Indian Chambers of Commerce and Industry—although the Congress itself was dominated by Isher Dass, who had the 'ear of the masses' and was supported by the other Indian elected members, De Souza, Mangat, and Shamsud-Deen. See Menon to Govt. of India, 1 Nov. 1934, in India Archives, Emigration—1934, file. 370/34, L and O. For the Govt. of India minute, see India Archives, Emigration, file 362/33, L and O and for Pandya's 'Marathon effort' against the marketing legislation, see Kenya, *Legislative Council Debates*, 3 July 1935, pp. 188–231; Kenya Archives, file ARC(GH)—141 I, memo. of dissent by J. B. Pandya on the issue of introducing restrictive legislation in Kenya . . . , Dec. 1933, and E.A.I.N.C. records: Presidential Address by J. B. Pandya, 13th session, 1934; address by A. H. Kaderbhoy to the Kenya Indian Conference, Nov. 1935; and Kenya, *Legislative Council Debates*, 3 July 1935, pp. 183–8—for protests by other Indian leaders against the introduction of the marketing legislation.

[2] Kenya, *Legislative Council Debates*, 10 Nov. 1937, p. 189, comment by Isher Dass, and 12 Nov. 1937, p. 261, comment by Pandya. See also E.A.I.N.C. records: address by A. H. Kaderbhoy to the Kenya Indian Conference, Nov. 1935.

introducing a motion in the Legislative Council for the repeal of the Order-in-Council, commented in the course of an impassioned speech that 'no event in the last fifteen years in this country has so much stirred the feelings of the Indians' for the permanent racial stigma it attached to the community.[1] At the same time, A. B. Patel and other Indian leaders sought to organize a multi-racial Kenya Highlands League to campaign against the reservation of the Highlands. The League held a few public meetings of protest and printed pamphlets in English, Swahili, and Gujarati in an effort to win popular support; but the outbreak of war in September 1939 put an end to its activities.[2]

The war years, however, had a greater significance in settling, largely to the satisfaction of the Europeans, the other outstanding issues that had formed the Indian Question in East Africa. The constitutional issue had been continuously raised during the 1930s. In July 1933 the Europeans had launched a campaign for unofficial financial control in the Legislative Council; and later, in September 1935, their demands for responsible self-government and Closer Union were renewed. The Indians in turn had countered by organizing special political conferences—first under Yusufali Jivanjee in 1933 and later under A. H. Kaderbhoy in 1935—to protest against the European demands, and by urging that the adoption of the common roll must be a prerequisite to any constitutional changes.[3] However, during the Second World War the Europeans were able

[1] Kenya, Legislative Council Debates, 21 Apr. 1939, pp. 255 71; E.A.I.N.C. records: 'Memorandum submitted to the Secretary of State for the Colonies on the Reservation of Highlands of Kenya for Europeans', 7 Oct. 1938, and Presidential Address by A. B. Patel, Dec. 1938.

[2] Kenya Archives, file Mombasa 2/283: 'Kenya Highlands League', circular letter from Ag. Chief Secretary, 26 May 1939; E.A.I.N.C. records, file: '1939 Correspondence', and Presidential Address by A. B. Patel, Dec. 1942; and Kenya, Legislative Council Debates, 21 Apr. 1939, pp. 255-71.

[3] E.A.I.N.C. records: address by Y. Jivanjee to the Kenya Indian Conference, July 1933, and resolutions of the Conference; address by A. H. Kaderbhoy to the Indian Conference, Nov. 1935; pamphlet: 'Control of Finances by Unofficial Europeans', by A. B. Patel, Shamsud-Deen, and U. K. Oza. These proceedings are found also in India Archives, Emigration, file no. 214 of 1933, L and O, see especially, E.A.I.N.C. to Govt. of India, 29 May 1933; Emigration—1934, file no. 78/34, L and O for copy of the E.A.I.N.C. memo. to Cunliffe-Lister; and Emigration—1934, file no. 370/34, L and O, P. S. Menon to Govt. of India, 1 Nov. 1934. See also, Kenya, Legislative Council Debates, 5 Nov. 1936, pp. 392–416, 10 Nov. 1936, p. 519, and 12 Nov. 1936, pp. 545–8, for comments by Pandya, De Souza, and Isher Dass respectively; and Lord Francis Scott Papers, Nairobi: file no. D/37, resolutions on constitutional advance July 1933; file no. E/10, and E/25, European constitutional demands Sept.–Oct., 1935.

to make rapid political gains under the Defence Regulations—especially with the appointment of European non-officials to a number of committees and boards set up to enforce wartime controls. In addition, their demands for self-government, Closer Union, and the restriction of Indian immigration were revived—the last leading to a further exchange of inter-racial polemics between the two immigrant communities. While the European charges of the Indians 'swamping' the country and casting a stranglehold on African advancement were apparently much exaggerated, the Indian counter-argument revolved around the fear that the Europeans wished to 'shut the door' for the Indians while keeping it open for themselves as in South Africa.[1] Identical immigration restrictions were, however, duly introduced in the East African territories in 1944. These, together with the European political gains during the period, led to a renewed East Africa-wide Indian political agitation. The E.A. Indian National Congress had largely disintegrated during the 1930s on account of its preoccupation with the racial controversies in Kenya, which had relatively little bearing on the other territories; but towards the close of this period a series of inter-territorial political conferences was held by the Indians to campaign against what A. B. Patel described as the 'active mobilisation' of 'the forces opposed to Indian settlement'.[2] The Indian leader Shamsud-Deen explained the fears of his community in this respect:

History has repeated itself in this Colony. Almost immediately after the last Great War was over, this country was the theatre of an intensive struggle between the European and Indian communities. And so it is today. . . . Then, as now, our opponents thought that the moment was opportune for snatching from the weaker Indian Community whatever rights for fair play and equality they had acquired as common British subjects. Then, as now, our opponents insisted that the Indian population of the Colony and of East Africa generally shall be restricted. . . .[3]

Indeed, in this limited sense history did repeat itself, for the European gains during the war years were confirmed by the immediate post-war developments. The proposals for the reorganization of the Kenya Administration in 1945 provided for the appointment of European

---

[1] Chanan Singh, *The Indian Case Against the Immigration Bill* (Nairobi, 1947); and G. Bennett, *Kenya, A Political History*, p. 95.

[2] E.A.I.N.C. records: Presidential Addresses by A. B. Patel, Dec. 1942 and Oct. 1945, and by S. G. Amin, Sept. 1946; and proceedings of the first inter-territorial conference, Dec. 1943, and the second inter-territorial conference, Apr. 1944.

[3] E.A.I.N.C. records: Presidential Address by Shamsud-Deen, Apr. 1944.

non-officials to ministerial portfolios, while an unofficial majority in the Legislative Council was later granted in 1948.[1] More important, the immigration restrictions introduced in 1944 were later confirmed by legislation—the identical bill submitted to the East African legislatures in 1946 was passed in 1949. The last major issue that had formed the Indian Question in Kenya, and East Africa generally, was thus settled to the satisfaction of the Europeans; and, as with their political agitation against the reservation of the Highlands, the communal system of representation, and racial segregation, so with immigration restriction, Indian opposition was essentially ineffective.

For much of this period, Indian political activity in East Africa was dominated by developments in Kenya, for the racial antagonisms of that Colony had relatively little bearing on the adjoining territories. But the continuing controversy over the Indian Question in Kenya was bound to have certain repercussions in the other East African territories. In Uganda, the Indian boycott of the Legislative Council, started in 1920 after the application of Lord Milner's 'solution' of the Indian Question, was to continue until 1926. But the Government's more sympathetic attitude towards the community was evident when the Governor, Sir William Gowers, welcomed the Indian member, C. J. Amin, to the Council:

> I may say that the role of the Indian Community in Uganda's development has not been merely important, but positively indispensable. I refer not only to the larger commercial enterprise for which it is responsible, but also for its provision of the personnel necessary for many essential functions of government.

Further, the Governor praised 'the initiative and perseverance which has been shown by Indians in penetrating and establishing themselves in the most out-of-the-way places, and thereby bringing about the extension of trade and commerce to a degree that could not have been achieved otherwise'.[2] Meanwhile, however, the Central Council of Indian Associations in Uganda was stirred into political activity by developments in Kenya; and after the publication of the report of

---

[1] *Proposals for the Reorganization of the Administration of Kenya*, sessional paper no. 3 of 1945; and E.A.I.N.C. records: Presidential Address by D. D. Puri, Aug. 1948.

[2] Uganda, *Proceedings of the Legislative Council*, 28 May 1926, Appendix B. The Indians agreed to abandon non-co-operation in 1926 on the understanding that this would not prejudice their demands for a common roll—see *Joint Select Committee on Closer Union*, vol. iii, *Appendices*, Appendix 21, p. 154.

the Hilton Young Commission in 1929, it submitted a lengthy memorandum to Sir Samuel Wilson opposing the proposals for the political, as distinguished from the economic, union of East Africa and the implementation of the Dual Policy. Further, the Council echoed the E.A. Indian National Congress's demand for a common electoral roll and complained of inadequate Indian representation in comparison to the Europeans.[1] But, as Sir Samuel Wilson pointed out, 'The situation as regards the position of Indians in Kenya has no counterpart in Uganda and Tanganyika, where there is no system of elective representation and where the different communities have been accustomed to live amicably side by side and to work together in the closest harmony for the common good.'[2] There was certainly evidence of this when the Local Government Committee recommended in 1930 elective representation on the Kampala Municipal Council, with reservation of seats so as to ensure a European majority—but, as Dr. R. C. Pratt points out, 'Nowhere else in East Africa were Europeans ready to accept at any level of government a common roll on which at some future date they might be outnumbered by either Asians or Africans.'[3] Indian demands for a common roll and equal representation with the Europeans were, however, continually raised at this time,[4] although the White Papers of 1930 greatly dampened their enthusiasm in this respect in view of the reiteration of the paramountcy of African interests, which the Indians welcomed. Moreover, as the Uganda Government reported in 1930:

The claim of the Central Council of the Indian Association [sic] to represent the whole of the Indian community in Uganda is not admitted by all sections of that community. Most of the Indians domiciled in the Protectorate are small traders and shopkeepers whose chief ambition is to

[1] Cmd. 3378 (1929), op. cit., Appendix II, memo. submitted by the Central Council of Indian Associations in Uganda.

[2] Cmd. 3378 (1929), ibid., pp. 23-4.

[3] History of East Africa, ii. 512; Uganda, Report of the Local Government Committee (Entebbe, 1930); and Papers Relating to the Question of Closer Union . . ., Colonial no. 57 (1931), p. 101.

[4] Colonial no. 57 (1931), p. 106, memo. of the Central Council of Indian Associations in Uganda, 28 July 1930—see also pp. 101-2, where the Governor pointed out that 'In Uganda the question of communal franchise versus a common roll is not only a question between Europeans and Asiatics. The admission of Africans to a common roll is already an issue in the case of municipal elections. . . .' For additional Indian representations, see Joint Select Committee on Closer Union, vol. iii, Appendices, Appendix 21 and vol. ii, Evidence, pp. 750-8, evidence of P. V. Mehd.

be allowed to carry on business with the minimum of interference, and so far they have not developed political ambitions.[1]

But the Council evidently enjoyed the support of the majority of the Indians, and as with the first Indian representative on the Legislative Council, the appointment of the second in 1933 was based on the candidate nominated by it.

Indian political agitation in Uganda was particularly aroused by the introduction of cotton-zoning and produce-marketing legislation in 1932–3. This marked in a sense the logical conclusion of the policy of control and regulation of trade initiated in the early years, and was designed, as one official pointed out, 'to eliminate the petty non-native traders scattered all over the country and often living in hovels under insanitary conditions'.[2] The proposals to establish special trading centres and grant exclusive licences for the purchase and export of certain commodities led to Indian protests, which, as in Kenya, were later supported by the report of the Government of India representative, K. P. S. Menon.[3] As Dr. Ehrlich has explained the position, this legislation 'consolidated a rigid framework into which it was virtually impossible for small-scale African (and Indian) entrepreneurs to penetrate'.[4] In fact the Uganda Government was conscious that its measures would 'adversely affect Indian interests, and will cause hardship to the large number of petty Asiatic traders who earn a precarious livelihood by combining the purchase of native produce with the retail selling of trade goods'.[5] But it felt at the same time that the legislation was necessary to ensure the

[1] Colonial no. 57 (1931), op. cit., p. 103. The Ismaili community in particular did not fully associate with the political campaign of the Central Council of Indian Associations in Uganda.

[2] Entebbe Archives, file no. 5426, Part II, minute by the Ag. Chief Secretary, 22 Aug. 1927. As elsewhere in East Africa, so in Uganda, this legislation marked a logical conclusion of the European distrust and criticism of the Indian traders, which had gained currency since the early years of the century. See, for example, *Report of the Commission of Enquiry into the Cotton Industry of Uganda* (Entebbe, 1929), p. 24.

[3] *Report by K. P. S. Menon on Marketing Legislation in Tanganyika, Uganda and Kenya*, 1935; *E.A.S.*, 20 Jan. 1934, for representations by a Uganda Indian delegation to Sir Philip Cunliffe-Lister; and India Archives, Emigration—1934, file 169–8/34, L and O, 'Memorandum on the Indians in Uganda', traces generally the Indian position in Uganda.

[4] C. Ehrlich, 'Some Social and Economic Implications of Paternalism in Uganda', *Journal of African History*, iv, no. 2 (1963), 275–85.

[5] Uganda, *Proceedings of the Legislative Council*, 5 Dec. 1932, Appendix A. See also dispatch of the Uganda Govt., 11 May 1935, in India Archives, Emigration—1934, file 362/33, L and O.

competitiveness of Uganda produce in international markets, and to protect the African producers from the 'reckless competition' of a 'large number of middlemen buyers'. However, the Government assured the Indian traders that the system of exclusive licences would not be allowed to operate so as to create monopolies.[1]

Similarly in Tanganyika, the Indian Association, Dar es Salaam, the parent body of Indian political associations in that territory, reacted to European demands for constitutional progress and Closer Union in much the same way as the E.A. Indian National Congress. In a series of representations at the time, the Association opposed the scheme for Closer Union of the East African territories and complained of inadequate representation as well as of racial discrimination against the community, and asked for the introduction of a common roll.[2] But the Indian Question in Tanganyika, as in Uganda, tended to be dominated more by economic grievances arising out of the Government's regulation and control of trade. In 1923 the passage of legislation introducing rigid licensing regulations, the compulsory rendering of accounts in English or Swahili written in Roman script, and providing for a profits tax, aroused strong Indian protests, which found practical expression in a six-week closure of Indian shops.[3] This was largely due to the hardship such regulations would cause to the large number of semi-literate, petty Indian traders;

---

[1] *Report by K. P. S. Menon on Marketing Legislation . . .*, 1935; *Gazette of India Extraordinary*, 24 June 1935; and Uganda, *Proceedings of the Legislative Council*, 5 Dec. 1932, Appendix A.

[2] In fact the resolution of the Tanganyika Indians best expressed the Indian opposition to Closer Union: 'In whatever form the Closer Union is introduced in East Africa, it is bound to prejudicially affect the status of Indians in Tanganyika, in as much as a step under the conditions prevailing in East Africa will eventually develop into the Kenyanization of all these countries.' Cmd. 3378 (1929), op. cit., Appendix iii, pp. 19–20, 'Memorandum on the Hilton Young Commission Report on behalf of the Indian Association Dar es Salaam, with which are affiliated all other Indian Associations in Tanganyika'. Also quoted in Govt. of India dispatch of 24 Nov. 1930 in *Papers Relating to the Question of Closer Union . . .*, Colonial no. 57 (1931), p. 126. See also Sidney Webb (Lord Passfield) Papers, vol. iv, file E, item 108 (d); India Archives, Emigration—Dec. 1930, Pros. 123–4, part B, copy of Indian Association, Dar es Salaam, to League of Nations, 20 Oct. 1930;—Mar. 1931, Pros. 108–9, part B, Indian Association, Dar es Salaam, to Govt. of India, 10 Jan. 1931, contains resolutions of the Indian conference held in Dec. 1930 and refers to the boycott of the Joint Select Committee by the Indians in Tanganyika as a protest against unequal treatment. See also *Joint Select Committee on Closer Union*, vol. iii, *Appendices*, Appendix 30, pp. 226–7, memo. of the Indian Association, Dar es Salaam.

[3] *Report on Tanganyika Territory for 1923*, p. 13; *Dar es Salaam Times*, 17 Nov. 1923; and Dar es Salaam Archives, file no. 7092, vol. i.

and accordingly the Indians made direct representations against the legislation to the Imperial Government in 1924. Later, the whole issue was laid before an advisory committee appointed by the Government, and its recommendations provided for a number of concessions to the Indians. While their language, Gujerati, was not accepted for the purposes of keeping accounts, the application of the language requirements was postponed for three years. Further, the Government agreed to issue licences as a matter of course and to exempt the smaller traders from the profits tax.[1] The smaller Indian traders, engaged in trade based on country produce, were, however, to come under greater pressure following the introduction in 1932 of marketing and allied legislation. This owed its origin in part to the Government's hostility towards the 'trading system which had arisen and which was peculiarly Indian in framework'; while the arguments and counter-arguments later used elsewhere in East Africa were rehearsed in Tanganyika—the Indian leader there, Yusufali Jivanjee, later playing an important role in the activities of the Federation of the Indian Chambers of Commerce and Industry.[2]

Indian political agitation against such restrictive legislation seemed to reach a climax in Zanzibar during 1934–8, following the promulgation of a series of decrees in 1934 which sought, *inter alia*, to institute government control of the clove industry by establishing a Clove Growers' Association and restricted the transfer of land between the African and Arab agriculturists and Indian mortgagors. The legislation was based on the views expressed by a number of commissions concerning the growing indebtedness of the agricultural classes to Indian money-lenders and middlemen[3]—who like their

[1] India Archives, Emigration—Sept. 1925, Pros. 1–92, part A, memo. on Indians in East Africa by Mr. Ewbank, and Emigration—1934, file 169–8/34, L and O, departmental memo. on Indians in Tanganyika. See also Dar es Salaam Archives, files no. 7092, vol. ii (Licensing Ordinance of 1923) and no. 7596 (question of abolition of profits tax).

[2] *Report by K. P. S. Menon on Marketing Legislation . . .*, 1935; Proceedings of the Federation of Indian Chambers of Commerce and Industry, in Kenya Archives, file no. ARC(GH)—141 I; India Archives, Emigration—1933, file 344/33, L and O, copy of address by Y. Jivanjee to Indian merchants' meeting, Dar es Salaam, Oct. 1933, and Emigration—1934, file 362/33, L and O, dispatch of the Govt. of Tanganyika, 2 Apr. 1935.

[3] Zanzibar, *Report of the Commission on Agriculture* (Zanzibar, 1923); C. A. Bartlett and J. S. Last, *Report on the Indebtedness of the Agricultural Classes, 1933* (Zanzibar, 1934); *Report of the Commission on Agricultural Indebtedness* (Zanzibar Sessional Paper No. 5 of 1935); and B. H. Binder, *Report on the Zanzibar Clove Industry* (Zanzibar, 1936).

counterpart in the interior had long been the target of European criticism and hostility. And, as elsewhere in East Africa, it was justified mainly for the protection it afforded to the primary producers—as the Zanzibar Government pointed out: 'Reduced to essentials the issue is whether or not middlemen should be left free to exploit the industry for their own profit or whether the government is justified in regulating the operation of middlemen so as to secure for producers a fair and assured return for their produce.'[1] But the legislation also had the essential character, as similar measures elsewhere in East Africa, that if implemented in its original form it would have virtually sounded the death-knell of much of the Indian economic enterprise in East Africa. The Indian National Association in Zanzibar, led by Tyabali Karimjee, protested against the 'Clove Decrees' of 1934, pointing out that the Indian money-lender, who should more appropriately be described as an investor, and the middleman were being used as a 'scapegoat' for the depressed condition of the agriculturists, which owed much to government policy over development and taxation. Further, the commission that had reported on agricultural indebtedness in 1934 had taken a partisan attitude against the Indians by failing to consult members of that community. Above all the Indians felt that 'the real effect, if not the object' of the decrees would be to squeeze them out of the country economically.[2] The Indian position was broadly supported by the Government of India, following the report of K. P. S. Menon, who was deputed to Zanzibar in 1935, and had recommended that the racial ban on Indian landholding should be based on a 'more rational distinction' as between agriculturists and non-agriculturists, and that the whole question of indebtedness be re-examined.[3] Eventually, the Zanzibar Government undertook to employ public funds to pay off the Indian creditors in order to liquidate agricultural indebtedness;[4] while in 1937, following another report on the clove industry, an amended 'Clove Decree' was promulgated providing for the setting up of the Clove Growers' Association to deal with the

---

[1] Zanzibar, *Proceedings of the Legislative Council*, 30 Sept. 1937, address by the British Resident.

[2] 'Memorandum by the Indian National Association (Zanzibar), 25 February 1935', C.O. pamphlet no. E.A. 270. See also *Annual Report on Zanzibar for 1934*, p. 35.

[3] Report by K. P. S. Menon, dated 10 Sept. 1935, in Zanzibar Sessional Paper no. 5 of 1935.

[4] Zanzibar, *Proceedings of the Legislative Council*, 10 Dec. 1936.

purchase and export of the clove crop.[1] This, however, led to renewed Indian protests against the government monopoly of the industry in which the community had played a historic role; and appeals were made to the Bombay importers, who took about forty per cent of the crop, to boycott Zanzibar cloves. The policy of non-co-operation caused the Zanzibar government an estimated loss of £36,000 in revenue; while further negotiations between the Government and the Indian National Association during 1937–8 ended in agreement which provided for Indian representation on the Clove Growers' Association and their participation in the purchase and export of cloves under the general supervision of that body.[2] Much of the restrictive marketing legislation introduced in the East African countries during the 1930s, apart from its immediate effects on Indian enterprise, in the long run prevented the rise of an African commercial class, and had in fact aroused considerable African opposition also, although the main justification for it, paradoxically enough, was the need to protect African interests.[3]

Much of the political controversy in Kenya and East Africa generally during this period represented in essence a continuation of the Indian Question that had bedevilled Kenya politics since the beginning of the century. As before 1923, so also after that date, Indian political activity in the territories continued largely to be inspired by the nationalist movement in India—and was aimed in the main to obtain redress of the various racial disabilities imposed upon the community. It represented also their reactions to the continuing pressures from the Europeans—arising out of the political ambitions of that community. The growing political disaffection of the Indians in East Africa raised questions of Imperial significance directly affecting the position of India within the Empire. This was of crucial importance—for while the Indian political campaign was largely ineffective and many of the issues that formed the Indian Question were settled to the satisfaction of the Europeans, Indian political agitation and the support extended to their demands by the Government

---

[1] Zanzibar Sessional Papers nos. 13 and 14 of 1937; and B. H. Binder, *Report on the Zanzibar Clove Industry* (1936).

[2] Zanzibar, *Proceedings of the Legislative Council*, 2 Dec. 1937; Sessional Paper no. 6 of 1938; and *A Memorandum Concerning Certain Proposals to Modify the Clove (Purchase and Exportation) Decree, 1937* (Govt. Printer, Zanzibar, 1938). See also N. V. Rajkumar, *Indians Outside India*, p. 21.

[3] See C. Ehrlich, 'Some Social and Economic Implications of Paternalism in Uganda', *Journal of African History*, iv, no. 2 (1963), 275–85; and *E.A. Royal Commission 1953–55 Report*, Cmd. 9475 (1955), pp. 65, 69, 71.

of India had far-reaching significance, both for the initial declaration in favour of African paramountcy in 1923 and its subsequent reiteration in 1930. Similarly, their political disaffection in East Africa was of crucial importance in initiating Indian attempts to associate politically with the Africans—in so far as this was made possible by the under privileged status of the two communities *vis-à-vis* the Europeans. In a sense much of the Indian opposition to the political demands and aspirations of the Europeans—with the exception of immigration restrictions—coincided with African views[1] and facilitated political co-operation between the two communities.

Nowhere did political collaboration between Indians and the Africans during this period become so noticeable as in Kenya. The origins of such collaboration can be traced to the initial attempts by the various Indian leaders to support the political campaign of Harry Thuku. Later in the 1920s, some of the Indian leaders sought more direct collaboration with the Africans or actively supported their political activity. This was true, for example, of Indian assistance in printing the newspaper *Muigwithania*, which was edited by Johnstone (later Jomo) Kenyatta on behalf of the Young Kikuyu Association. The activities of the Young Kikuyu Association and later the Kikuyu Central Association also received the support of the Indian leaders, particularly the leading radicals, Isher Dass and U. K. Oza—the former accompanying Kenyatta to London in 1929.[2] Similarly, Shamsud–Deen later spoke in the Legislative Council in 1937 in support of the demands of Mulama, the younger brother of Mumia, to be installed as the paramount chief of the Abaluhya people; while A. B. Patel secured the participation of the Africans in the activities of the Kenya Highlands League.[3] But more

---

[1] Notice, for example, the resolutions passed by the E.A.I.N.C. in 1930—welcoming the reaffirmation of the principle of African Paramountcy and Imperial Trusteeship by the White Papers issued in that year; and asking for various restrictive measures relating to the policies over land and labour—as well as legislation involving racial discrimination—to be abolished. Copy of the resolutions and connected proceedings in India Archives, Emigration—Jan. 1931, Pros. 41–3, part B.

[2] *Joint Select Committee on Closer Union*, vol. ii, *Minutes of Evidence*, p. 421; F. D. Corfield, *The Origins and Growth of Mau Mau* (Nairobi, 1960), p. 266; and oral information, or see P. U. Oza to the editor, *E.A.S.*, 17 Mar. 1966.

[3] Kenya, *Legislative Council Debates*, 21 Apr. 1939, pp. 255–71, and 9 Mar. 1937, cols. 179–82; and Kenya Archives file no. Mombasa 2/283, 'Kenya Highlands League'. I am grateful to my colleague Dr. G. S. Were for the following information concerning the paramountcy of the North Kavirondo District (Western Kenya) in the 1930s. The question of Mulama succeeding Mumia

important were the activities of Isher Dass and Makhan Singh, the two Indian leaders with communist leanings. Makhan Singh organized the Labour Trade Union of East Africa in 1936 and has some claim to be regarded as the founder of African trade unionism in the area. Later, in 1939, his organization, together with the Young Kikuyu Association, was responsible for the first major African strike in Kenya—that of the dock workers in Mombasa.[1] Deported to India during the war, Makhan Singh returned later to revive the activities of his African trade union in association with Fred Kubai—and their arrest in 1950 for anti-government activity was to provoke a short-lived general strike by the Africans in Nairobi.[2] Meanwhile, Isher Dass, as a member of the Legislative Council from 1933 to 1942, made frequent representations on behalf of the Africans—especially in respect of their demands for more land, political representation, and the removal of restrictions on the growing of economic crops. In his evidence to the Carter Land Commission, Isher Dass, as well as the other Indian representatives, B. S. Varma and U. K. Oza, opposed the further alienation of land to the non-Africans and pointed to the growing dissatisfaction and resentment among African workers on European farms.[3] Later, Dass was apparently closely associated with the activities of the Kikuyu Central Association and its leader, Jesse Karuiki, whom he accompanied on a political mission to north Nyanza in 1938; and made frequent claims to speak on behalf of the Africans—especially in repeated demands that they should be given direct representation on the Legislative Council.[4] In August 1938, Isher Dass read into the record of the Legislative Council the memorandum submitted by the Kikuyu Central Association to the Imperial Government

arose because the latter had retired from the paramountcy, while continuing as the Nabongo (king) of the Wanga kingdom. Mulama had strong public support but his candidacy was opposed by the Administration.

[1] Kenya Archives, file no. Mombasa 106/58, Evidence: Mombasa Labour Commission of Enquiry, p. 3, where the Principal Labour Officer reported 'I believe that the Mombasa strike was organised by the East African Labour Trade Union assisted by the Young Kikuyu Association . . .'; *Report of the Commission Appointed to Examine the Labour Conditions in Mombasa* (Nairobi, 1939), and oral information.

[2] Bennett, *Kenya, A Political History*, pp. 125–6, and oral information.

[3] Kenya, *Land Commission, Evidence* (Nairobi, 1934), iii. 2887–8.

[4] Kenya, *Legislative Council Debates*, 25 Apr. 1934, p. 97; 28 June 1935, pp. 69, 73; 1 July 1935, pp. 110–11; 12 Nov. 1936, pp. 548, 559; and 17 Nov. 1937, p. 406. See also Kenya Archives, file no. N.P. ADM, 12/3/4, North Nyanza Monthly Intelligence Report, Sept. 1938.

complaining that the doctrine of African paramountcy was not being implemented, and protesting against the recommendations of the Carter Land Commission. Dass then appealed that the 'just demands of the Africans' should not be ignored, for the 'Africans, who in the not very distant future will be a nation . . . will one day judge us . . . for every act done'. Similarly in April 1939, speaking again of the increasing discontent and resentment among the Africans, Isher Dass read, amidst protests by the European non-official members, the more important memorandum submitted jointly by the Kikuyu Central Association and the Kavirondo Taxpayers Welfare Association to the Imperial Government. Amidst appeals that the memorandum should not be ignored, Dass warned, rather prophetically, that 'there will come a time when they [the Africans] . . . will realize that constitutional agitation is not the method and they will prefer some better method . . . in obtaining a successful reversal of [the present] policy'.[1] Meanwhile, in August 1938, Dass had also read into the record of the Legislative Council the memorandum submitted by the Kamba tribe in protest against the Government's de-stocking policy. In fact Isher Dass was closely involved in the Kamba protest march on Nairobi in July 1938 and assisted their leader, Samuel Mwindi Mbingu, in making representations to the Government. These were largely unsuccessful, and Dass was later accused of instigating the riot that followed the arrest of Mwindi Mbingu—rather in the fashion that Indian leaders were accused of complicity in the African riot in Nairobi in 1922—and this led to counter-accusations by him that the Government's lack of sympathy had turned a peaceful march into a violent disturbance.[2] Later, Indian leaders were to press for the release of the Kamba leader,[3] rather in the manner that similar demands were raised by them during the Mau Mau Emergency for the release of the detained African leaders. But such collaboration notwithstanding, political relations between the Africans and Indians tended on the whole to remain lukewarm, as one African leader later pointed out:

[1] Kenya, *Legislative Council Debates*, 9 Aug. 1938, pp. 67–72, 10 Aug. 1938, pp. 113–23, and 21 Apr. 1939, pp. 284–9.
[2] Ibid., 17 Aug. 1938, pp. 226–41.
[3] See E.A.I.N.C. records: Presidential Address by S. G. Amin, Sept. 1946. Amin, a lawyer in Nairobi, was involved in preparing the defence of Mwindi Mbingu. Also oral information from Amin. See also Kenya, *Legislative Council Debates*, 21 Apr. 1939, p. 322, petition by Isher Dass for the release of Mwindi Mbingu, who had been deported to Lamu in Oct. 1938.

I never thought I would ever side with the Indian community as I now do, but I am forced by circumstances and cannot help it. I must therefore say that in this [Legislative] Council the Indian members are more helpful to the African community than the Europeans because they think of what the African community desire.[1]

In the final analysis, however, the prolonged political controversy between the European and Indian communities was neutralized only by African intervention—the first of their political representatives having made his appearance in the Legislative Council at the end of this period. The political chess game between the two immigrant communities in which the Europeans had held a commanding position needed only an African checkmate to end it—and the arguments and the counter-arguments which the Europeans and Indians had used against each other were to provide the Africans with a ready-made political weapon against both of them. Indeed, the Europeans and Indians were conscious of this—but only to the extent of blaming each other for adverse propaganda. In 1930, for example, Sir Edward Grigg had pointed out that

Indian propaganda is always active amongst the more educated natives in ways that tend more and more to take the native out of his customary tribal life. Litigation is encouraged; grievances are fostered; the mind of the young native is turned towards political agitation. . . . If once a common electoral roll is established, the whole class of politically minded natives, small at present but certain in those circumstances to grow rapidly, will be concentrated on securing their own admission to the roll. It is also inevitable that Indian propaganda should speed them on that course.[2]

Similarly, the Indian leader Shamsud-Deen commented in 1944:

I really see very gloomy prospects for those who choose to remain in a foreign land inhabited by millions of Africans, who although not originally and naturally hostile to Indians, will not for long remain unaffected by the propaganda which has been persistently carried on by Europeans to make the Natives believe that the presence of Indians in these Regions is inimical to their progress and conflicting with their interests. . . .[3]

[1] Kenya, *Legislative Council Debates*, 4 July 1946, pp. 59–60, remarks of F. W. Odede.
[2] Grigg to Passfield, 11 Sept. 1930, in *Papers Relating to the Question of the Closer Union . . .*, Colonial no. 57 (1931), p. 12.
[3] E.A.I.N.C. records: Presidential Address by Shamsud-Deen, Apr. 1944.

CHAPTER VI

Epilogue: The Road to a Dilemma

BY the end of the Second World War the characteristics of the modern Asian population of East Africa had to a large extent been determined by the economic, social, and political developments of the preceding decades. But East Africa in 1945 stood at the threshold of a new era of accelerated change—during which many of the developments of the earlier years seemed to reach their logical conclusion, while others, overtaken by the events of the period, seemed to lose their previous importance. The former was true of the economic and social position of the Indian community in East Africa, the latter of its political role in the territories. But the economic progress made by the community—which strengthened its socio-economic position as a middle group within the three-tier system—coupled as it was with their increasing political vulnerability, helped seriously to compromise the position of the Asians in East Africa. On the eve of the independence of the East African countries, the Asian population was faced with a major dilemma about its future prospects in the territories.

The social and economic advancement of the Asians in the post-war period was accelerated by the gradual dilution of the rigid racial barriers of the early colonial period under the impact of new concepts of 'partnership' and 'multi-racialism'. But more important perhaps was the relative rapidity of economic development in the post-war period and the resulting increase in economic opportunity and rate of earnings—which enabled the Asians to continue to play an important role in the development of modern East Africa, largely within the limitations of the three-tier system.

Further improvements in the educational system contributed significantly to the greater social and economic mobility of the Asian population. The post-war period witnessed major improvements in the standards of education in the Indian schools as well as the establishment of greater facilities for secondary education. A series of development plans were instituted in the East African territories to meet the shortage of schools and staff arising out of a rapid increase in pupil enrolment.[1] These laid particular emphasis on secondary education and the establishment of Teacher Training Colleges to provide trained staff for Asian schools. Government capital expenditure on Asian education was increased on the basis of a fifty per cent (£ for £) grant-in-aid to schools. Further funds were raised by increases in fees and the Indian education tax. Such developments reflected, in part, the keen Indian interest in education. In fact, from the earliest times the lack of equal consideration in the social services provided by government—and especially the wide difference between government expenditure on European and Asian education, and the resulting poor standards of the Asian schools—had been a major political grievance of the Asians in East Africa.[2] The situation in this respect did not materially change in the post-war period: as the Kenya Education Department reported in 1958: 'it would seem that in the last fifteen years Government expenditure on Asian schools has not sufficed to prevent them from losing ground to European and to African schools'.[3] However, the development plans launched after the war contributed to an improvement of the standards of education and to the introduction of Higher School syllabuses in a number of secondary schools. These developments were of crucial importance in preparing an increasing number of students to proceed overseas for higher education—especially to England. Indeed a large proportion of the Asians who entered the liberal professions in East Africa during this period were able to do so because of the training they received in England. This, of course, involved them or their families in considerable financial sacrifice. But the willingness of the Asians, generally, to invest in education was revealed also by the substantial financial contributions made by the community towards the establishment of institutions of higher learning in East Africa. The most notable achievement in this

---

[1] See, inter alia, Tanganyika, Education Department, Triennial Survey 1955–57, pp. 30–3; Kenya, Educational Department, Triennial Survey 1958–60, p. 4; Report on Asian and European Education in Kenya 1958, pp. 2–4; and Uganda, Annual Report of the Education Department 1960, pp. 6, 69. The number of pupils in Asian schools doubled between 1948 and 1960—reaching a figure of 52,000 pupils in Kenya, 22,000 in Uganda, and 25,000 in Tanganyika.

[2] See, for example, Kenya, Report of the Select Committee on Indian Education (1949), note by A. B. Patel, p. 27; Report of Committee on Educational Expenditure (European and Asian) (Nairobi, 1948), p. 28, minority report by Chanan Singh; and Kenya, Legislative Council Debates, 19, 20, and 27 Nov. 1953.

[3] Kenya, Report on Asian and European Education in Kenya 1958, pp. 3, 23.

respect was the formation of the Gandhi Memorial Academy, which is now incorporated in University College, Nairobi.

The Asian economic role in East Africa underwent certain subtle changes during this period. On the one hand there was a marked increase in the number of Asians engaged in large-scale business operations or in the various liberal professions; while on the other hand the racial disabilities of the community continued to restrict its role to the traditional occupations—as shopkeepers, artisans, and subordinate employees. Moreover, their role in this respect was increasingly challenged by the growth of African competition and of hostility towards Asian predominance on the middle rungs of the economic ladder. This had the additional effect of accelerating the diversification of Asian enterprises into new fields of secondary manufacturing industries, or where possible, as in Uganda and Tanganyika, into agriculture. The steady accumulation of capital and the acquisition of technical and professional skills enabled a growing number of Asians to avail themselves of new opportunities for economic advancement. But the overall picture of the Asian economic role in East Africa did not change significantly during this period. A majority of their working population continued to engage in commerce and to fill the subordinate ranks in private and public employment. Their middle position within the three-tier system was also reflected by the rate of Asian earnings as compared to European and African incomes—although these represented a marked improvement from the earlier years. During the 1950s, the majority of the working Asians in Kenya earned between £180 and £550 per annum; while the average Asian incomes in Uganda in 1957 stood at between £400 and £500 per annum. By the beginning of the 1960s the position had improved further: figures available for Kenya reveal that a quarter of the Asians earned between £540 and £719, while nearly another quarter earned over £720 in 1961.[1] These figures can be taken as providing the general picture of the Asian economic condition in East Africa. The rise in incomes enabled a larger number of Asians to invest their capital in East Africa, so that both the Asian capital investment in the territories and their activities in a wide variety of capacities greatly increased during this period. By the eve of independence, the Asians of East Africa represented a major economic asset in the territories—providing crucial services as

[1] Sources: Kenya, Statistical Abstracts for 1955 and 1962; and Uganda, *Statistical Abstract*, 1958.

builders and contractors, wholesalers and retailers, manufacturers and industrialists, mechanics and technicians, administrative and professional staff, etc.

The social conditions of the community also underwent significant changes during this period and by the end of the colonial period the Asians presented, to some extent, the picture of a society transformed. The new generation born and brought up in East Africa had developed a greater consciousness of their countries of adoption and in the process had lost much of the sympathy of their parents for the places of their origin in India and Pakistan. Moreover, the younger generation of Asians, exposed to a highly urbanized East African environment, a system of education modelled on the western pattern, and higher standards of living, developed marked changes in food habits, mode of dress, and language—the last being influenced by their greater fluency in both English and Swahili. The impact of western institutions generally tended, however, to vary among the different Asian communities and was more marked among the Ismailia and Goan communities, whose receptiveness to such change was inspired, in the former, by the late Aga Khan and, in the latter, by its religious affinity. The process of social change among the Asians was, however, largely held in check by their growing isolation in East Africa. This was a historical legacy, for the Asian community had from the earliest times occupied a rather anomalous position. Its enterprise contributed to the development of the countries into modern states at a relatively rapid rate, while the community was also frequently used as the principal 'scapegoat' for the many ills of East Africa. Such circumstances were hardly conducive to social mobility in the community and have tended to reinforce the sectional and communal isolation of the Asians among themselves.

The political vulnerability of the Asians in East Africa, which also contributed to their isolation as a racial minority, was intensified by developments in the post-war period. The growth of African nationalism during this period led to the decline of the racial politics that had characterized much of the political activity during the colonial period—and led in the process to an end of the Asian role as a political pressure group in East Africa. This was also partly the result of the Partition of India in 1947, which precipitated a similar split among the Asians in East Africa, between the Muslims and non-Muslims. The decline of the Asian political role was also signified by the abandonment by the E.A. Indian National Congress of its inter-territorial role in 1952 and subsequently of its political role in 1962. Moreover, Indian political activity after the war was marked by its increasing subservience to African nationalism—for much of the political disaffection that had inspired Indian agitation in East Africa seemed to provide a basis for a common cause with African nationalism.

The principal impetus for a closer political collaboration between the African and the Indian leaders was provided by developments in India and the policies adopted by the Government of India after independence in 1947. The first Indian commissioner, Apa Pant, who arrived in Nairobi in 1948, actively supported African nationalist demands and encouraged attempts by local Indian leaders to collaborate with the African leaders. In 1949, Apa Pant arranged for an official visit to India by Mbiu Koinange and subsequently the Indian Government instituted scholarships for African students at Indian universities. During the Emergency in Kenya, such Indian support for the African demands became more noticeable. In fact, the Indians generally regarded Mau Mau as 'an orthodox nationalist struggle on the lines of India', and sympathized with its aims, if not its methods. The activities of Apa Pant at this time, together with those of Dewan Chamanlal—a leading Indian lawyer who, together with local Indian lawyers, participated in the defence of Jomo Kenyatta at the Kapenguria trial—were strongly objected to by the Kenya Government.[1] Meanwhile, at the local level, the immediate post-war years witnessed a series of joint meetings between the Indian Congress and the Kenya African Union—culminating in joint protests by the two bodies during 1950–1 against European constitutional demands, and in joint demands for the introduction of a common franchise.[2] Moreover, the local Asian newspapers sought to act as spokesmen for African opinion or directly sponsored the publication of the African vernacular newspapers.[3] As one contemporary observer commented on the political scene in Kenya in 1951:

African newspapers are printed on terms of easy credit on Indian presses; Indians give money to such bodies as K.A.U.; African political leaders are made welcome in Indian houses; one of the K.A.U. officials

[1] F. D. Corfield, *The origins and growth of Mau Mau*, p. 223; M. Blundell, *So Rough a Wind* (London, 1964), pp. 95, 112–13; and M. Slater, *The Trial of Jomo Kenyatta* (London, 1956).
[2] See p. 153, above; Corfield, op. cit., p. 56; and *Kenya Weekly News*, 19 and 26 May 1950.
[3] Corfield, op. cit., pp. 191–5.

(James Beauttah) is now touring India as a guest. The latest move, which has aroused great African enthusiasm, is the award of five scholarships to take Kenya Africans to Indian Universities.[1]

Such initial political co-operation between the Indians and Africans was, however, soon overshadowed by the rising intensity of African nationalism during the 1950s and the growing resentment among the Africans of the Asian position in the territories. The political initiative rapidly passed into the hands of the Africans, and Indian political activity faded into the background. The Indians continued, however, largely as an act of faith, to support the demands of African nationalism. At the time of the Lancaster House Conference in London in 1960, for example, the Kenya Indian Congress and the Kenya Muslim League issued a joint statement urging the grant of independence on the basis of a common electoral roll— although at the Conference itself, it was the Muslim leader, I. E. Nathoo, who stole the march on the relatively hesitant Congress members, by declaring full support for the African demands.[2] Once again, as in earlier years, it was left to the radical or liberal Indian leaders to seek more actively to make common cause with the Africans. The activities of the Indian trade unionist, Makhan Singh, in this respect had a considerable impact, although they were short-lived, for Makhan Singh was to spend over ten years in jail after his arrest in 1950. Similarly, P. G. Pinto, who became Secretary of the Kenya Indian Congress in 1951, took an active, pro-African stand during the Emergency, which led to his imprisonment for five years in 1954. Other liberal Indian leaders meanwhile continued a campaign for the release of Jomo Kenyatta and the other restricted African leaders. Subsequently, new Asian political organizations were formed in an attempt to seek a closer identity with the African nationalist movement. The Uganda Action Group formed by the Indians in 1959 was pledged to support the Uganda Peoples Congress led by Milton Obote, the Kenya Freedom Party formed in 1960 supported KANU as against KADU, while the Asian Association, Dar es Salaam, pledged its support to TANU. But the unwillingness of the Africans to accept Asians on equal terms within their nationalist movement became increasingly evident at this time. In 1959, for

---

[1] E. Huxley, *The Sorcerer's Apprentice* (London, 1951), pp. 57–8.
[2] See *E.A.S.*, 11 Jan. 1960; and Congress records, Nairobi: Presidential Addresses by S. C. Gautama, 1960, and S. G. Amin, 1958, and Statement of Policy, Mar. 1955.

example, at the Pafmecsa Conference at Moshi, representatives of the Uganda Action Group and of the Tanganyika Asians were accepted after some debate, not as full members of the Conference but merely as 'fraternal delegates'.[1] Similarly, none of the leaders of the pronationalist Asian organizations reaped any of the 'fruits of Uhuru'— only Amir Jamal in Tanzania rose to an important ministerial position in the independent African government. The activities of the more liberal Asian leaders were, however, merely a more concrete manifestation of the larger and overwhelming Asian support for African nationalism. As T. J. Mboya points out: 'The overwhelming majority of the Indian community in Kenya supported the African stand and wanted to adhere to standards set by Nehru and Gandhi, as friends and allies in the struggle for freedom and democracy.'[2]

In the final analysis, however, it was the attitude of African nationalism towards the Asians in East Africa that had the greater significance. For the mounting African criticism of the Asian socioeconomic position in the countries far outweighed the importance of Asian political collaboration with the Africans. On the eve of independence, it was apparent that the disintegration of the three-tier system, the reorganization of the East African countries under a policy of African paramountcy, and the redistribution of wealth under the concept of African Socialism would be a major target of the independent governments. The resulting pressures of Africanization in public and private employment, the problem of choosing between an East African citizenship or an expatriate status, and the recurrent danger of their being used as a 'scapegoat' posed a major dilemma for the Asians in East Africa. It seemed that their future in East Africa would be as difficult as their past.

[1] R. Cox, *Pan-Africanism in Practice* (London, 1964), p. 29.
[2] T. J. Mboya, *Freedom and After* (London, 1963), pp. 112–13.

SELECT BIBLIOGRAPHY

MATERIAL under this section has been arranged as follows:

I. PRIMARY SOURCES (A *to* E)

A. OFFICIAL ARCHIVES

A 1. India Office Records, London, and the Indian National Archives, New Delhi
   (*a*) Proceedings of the Emigration Department of the Government of India
   (*b*) Proceedings of the Foreign Department of the Government of India

A 2. Foreign Office Records, London
   (*a*) Dispatches
   (*b*) Foreign Office Confidential Prints

A 3. Colonial Office Archives, London
   (*a*) Dispatches
   (*b*) Colonial Office Confidential Prints

A 4. Records of the Bombay Government, Bombay

A 5. National Archives of Tanzania
   (*a*) Zanzibar
   (*b*) Dar es Salaam

A 6. Kenya National Archives, Nairobi
   (*a*), (*b*) Lands Department, Nairobi
   (*c*) Mombasa Provincial Archives

A 7. Uganda National Archives, Entebbe (referred to as Entebbe Archives in the text)

B. NON-OFFICIAL ARCHIVES

B 1. Records of the East African Indian National Congress, Nairobi

B 2. Sidney Webb (Lord Passfield) Papers, London

B 3. International Missionary Council, London: Papers of Dr. J. H. Oldham

B 4. Lord Francis Scott Papers, Nairobi

B 5. Minutes of the Uganda Chamber of Commerce, Makerere

C. OFFICIAL PUBLICATIONS

C 1. Parliamentary Papers

C 2. Official Reports and other publications

C 3. Proceedings of the Legislative Councils:
   (*a*) Proceedings of the Kenya Legislative Council
   (*b*) Proceedings of the Uganda Legislative Council
   (*c*) Proceedings of the Zanzibar Legislative Council

I. PRIMARY SOURCES

Each reference to the sources listed below is accompanied by a brief note indicating the subject-matter.

A. OFFICIAL ARCHIVES

A 1. INDIA OFFICE RECORDS, LONDON, AND THE INDIAN NATIONAL ARCHIVES, NEW DELHI

(a) *Proceedings of the Emigration Department of the Government of India*
These Proceedings have a common reference in both the above Archives, but for the period after 1922 only the material in the Indian National Archives has been seen.

June 1895—Proceedings no. 7, file 38, part B: Recruitment of Indian labour for German East Africa.

August 1895—Pros. 1, 3–4, file 38, part A: Indian labour for G.E.A.

December 1895—Pros. 11–12, file 64 of 1890, part A: Emigration to E.A.

January 1896—Pros. 7–8, file 63 of 1895 and 8 of 1896, part A: Emigration to Zanzibar.

July 1896—Pros. 9–17, file 38 of 1895, part A: Emigration for Uganda Railway.

July 1896—Pros. 18–55, file 2, part A: Emigration for Uganda Railway.

September 1896—Pros. 2–4, file 66, part A: Emigration to Africa.

September 1896—Pros. 12–23, file 2, part A: Emigration for U. Railway.

October 1896—Pros. 1, file 8, part A: Emigration to Zanzibar.

October 1896—Pros. 15–16, file 66, part A: Increased emigration to E.A.

January 1897—Pros. 3–4, file 18 of 1896, part A: Emigration to Zanzibar.

January 1897—Pros. 13–14, file 79 of 1896, part A: Indians in G.E.A.

February 1897—Pros. 8–14, file 5, part A: Indian labour for E.A.

March 1897—Pros. 1–6, file 5, part A: Indian labour for E.A.

March 1897—Pros. 7–11, file 10, part A: Form of agreement for Emigrants.

April 1897—Pros. 5–8, file 10, part A: Form of agreement for Emigrants.

May 1897—Pros. 10–39, file 10, part A: Emigration to E.A.

July 1897—Pros. 35-7, file 10, part A: Emigration to E.A.

August 1897—Pros. 4-6, file 37, part A: 'Free' Emigration to E.A.

September 1897—Pros. 1-2, file 5, part C: Emigration from Bombay.

September 1897—Pros. 8-14, file 10, part A: Emigration to U. Railway.

October 1897—Pros. 6-9, file 10, part A: Railway Agency at Karachi.

October 1897—Pros. 8-10, file 37, part B: Emigration from Bombay.

December 1897—Pros. 4-7, file 37, part B: 'Free' Emigration to E.A.

January 1898—Pros. 5, file 5, part B: Emigration to Zanzibar.

January 1898—Pros. 39-43, file 10, part A: Coolie emigration from Karachi.

February 1898—Pros. 7, file 21, part A: Coolie emigration.

April 1898—Pros. 6-11, file 21, part B: Coolie emigration.

June 1898—Pros. 7-8, file 7, part B: Openings for Indian artisans in E.A.

July 1898—Pros. 5-12, file 21, part A: Coolie emigration.

April 1899—Pros. 3-8, file 24, part A: Emigration to E.A.

April 1899—Pros. 9-14, file 27, part A: Emigration Agent in India for E.A.

July 1899—Pros. 17-21, file 27, part A: Emigration Agents in India for E.A.

November 1899—Pros. 3-8, file 54, part A: Clerks and artisans for E.A.

March 1900—Pros. 13-18, file 7, part A: Legalizing of emigration to E.A.

May 1900—Pros. 1-2, file 7, part A: Legalizing of emigration to E.A.

June 1900—Pros. 9-10, file 47, part B: Indian agricultural scheme for G.E.A.

October 1900—Pros. 2-3, file 71, part B: Emigration Agents in India for E.A.

February 1901—Pros. 3-7, file 7 of 1900, part A: Legalizing emigration.

March 1901—Pros. 1-9, file 20, part A: Legalizing of emigration to E.A.

March 1901—Pros. 16-17, file 19, part A: Emigration to G.E.A.

May 1901—Pros. 12, file 41, part A: Indian agricultural settlement in E.A.

May 1901—Pros. 1, file 39, part B: Immigration restriction in Zanzibar.

September 1901—Pros. 5-6, file 20, part A: Legalizing of emigration.

September 1901—Pros. 12, file 41, part A: Indian agricultural settlement.

January 1902—Pros. 16, file 11, part B: Indian agricultural settlement.

April 1902—Pros. 5-8, file 19 of 1901, part A: Emigration to G.E.A.

September 1902—Pros. 2, file 93, part B: Emigration to G.E.A.

November 1902—Pros. 15-17, file 103, part A: Coolie emigration.

February 1903—Pros. 4, file 8, part A: Coolie emigration.

February 1904—Pros. 11, file 19, part A: Indian agricultural settlement.

April 1904—Pros. 1, file 19, part B: Indian settlement at Kibos.

December 1905—Pros. 5-6, file 99, part B: Emigration of artisans.

February 1906—Pros. 4-5, 15-16, file 5, part A: Immigration into Zanzibar.

May 1906—Pros. 9, file 5, part A: Immigration regulation in Zanzibar.

August 1906—Pros. 13–16, file 73, part A: Indian settlement in E.A.

November 1906—Pros. 12–18, file 73, part A: Indian settlement in E.A.

April 1907—Pros. 2–4, file 44, part A: Administration of coolie affairs at Karachi.

July 1908—Pros. 23–4, file 70, part B: U. Railway agents at Bombay.

September 1908—Pros. 1, file 79, part C: Position of Indians in E.A.

September 1908—Pros. 5–6, file 79, part A: Indian representation.

December 1908—Pros. 23–5, file 110, part A: Voluntary emigration to E.A.

February 1910—Pros. 11–17, file 10, part B: Representations on behalf of Indians in East Africa.

March 1910—Pros. 1–2, file 20, part A: Recruitment of Indian artisans.

May 1910—Pros. 19–26, file 10, part B: Indian representations.

June 1910—Pros. 6–8, file 52, part A: Memorial of Indians in Zanzibar.

August 1910—Pros. 43, file 84, part B: Indian representation on Legco.

January 1911—Pros. 1–2, file 95, part A: Indian immigration to Zanzibar.

January 1911—Pros. 19, file 126, part B: Indian representation.

February 1911—Pros. 6–7, file 52, part A: Indian grievances in Zanzibar.

March 1911—Pros. 1–3, file 14, part A: Immigration to Zanzibar.

May 1911—Pros. 1–2, file 48, part A: Petition on behalf of Indians in E.A.

August 1911—Pros. 1, file 76, part A: Indian grievances in Zanzibar.

June 1912—Pros. 25, file 77, part B: Indians in G.E.A.

October 1912—Pros. 11–13, file 111, part A: Memorial on behalf of Indians in E.A.

May 1913—Pros. 2, file 60, part A: Uganda Licensing Ordinance, 1912.

June 1913—Pros. 13–15, file 45, part A: Representation on behalf of Indians in E.A.

February 1914—Pros. 34, filed: Position of Indians in E.A.

August 1914—Pros. 22, file 34, part A: Position of Indians in E.A.

April 1918—Pros. 11, filed: Position of Indians in E.A.

January 1919—Pros. 1, part B: Indian settlement in G.E.A.

April 1919—Pros. 32, filed: Future of G.E.A.

May 1919—Pros. 15, filed: Future of G.E.A.

June 1919—Pros. 35–40, part A: Indian representations re Uganda Cotton Rules.

October 1919—Pros. 1–8, part A: Indian Question.

August 1920—Pros. 7–35, part A: Uganda Cotton Rules, 1918.

October 1920—Pros. 4–5, filed: Resolutions of Kampala Indian Assoc.

November 1920—Pros. 1–116, part A: Indian Question.

February 1921—Pros. 4, file 36, part A: Indian Question.

March 1921—Pros. 3, 16–47, part A: Indian Question.

March 1921—Pros. 48–51, part A: Indian Question.

July 1921—Pros. 1–8, part A: Indian Question.

August 1921—Pros. 10–28, part A: Indian Question.

August 1921—Pros. 1–2, part B: Indian Question.

September 1921—Pros. 30–41, 43–64, 73–4, filed: Indian Question in Tanganyika.

October 1921—Pros. 16–19, filed: Indian Question in Zanzibar.

November 1921—Pros. 19–20, 39, 49, filed: Indian Question.

December 1921—Pros. 10, 14, 17–17A, 42, filed: Indian Question.

January 1922—Pros. 1, 11, filed: Indian Question.

June 1922—Pros. 20–6, 28–32, part B: Indian Question.

July 1922—Pros. 53, part B: Indian Question.

September 1922—Pros. 16–45, part A: Indian Question.

October 1922—Pros. 1–55, part A: Indian Question.

March 1923—Pros. 14–17, 29–33, part B: Indian Question.

June 1923—Pros. 26–73, part A: Indian Question.

June 1923—Pros. 21, 42, part B: Indian Question.

July 1923—Pros. 18, dep.: Indian Question.

November 1923—Pros. 73–157, part B: Indian Question.

July 1924—Pros. 1–65, part A: Position of Indians in E.A.

February 1925—Pros. 184–9, part B: Indians in Kenya.

September 1925—Pros. 1–92, part A: Departmental memo. on Indians in E.A.

May 1926—Pros. 23–6, part B: Indians in Tanganyika.

July 1927—Pros. 13–17, part A: Indians in Kenya.

February 1929—Pros. 1–31, part A: Position of Indians in E.A.

October 1929—Pros. 1–12, part A: Position of Indians in E.A.

December 1930—Pros. 123–4, part B: Indians in Tanganyika.

January 1931—Pros. 41–3, part B: Position of Indians in E.A.

March 1931—Pros. 108–9, part B: Indians in Tanganyika.

October 1931—Pros. 1–11, part A: The E.A.I.N.C. split.

1932—file 289/32, L and O: Position of Indians in E.A.

1933—file 214/33, L and O: Position of Indians in E.A.

1933—file 344/33, L and O: Controversy re Marketing legislation in E.A.

1934—file 78/34, L and O: Indians in Zanzibar.

1934—file 130/34, L and O: Position of Indians in E.A.

1934—file 169–8134, 169–9/34, L and O: Marketing legislation.

1934—file 362/33, L and O: Controversy re Marketing legislation in E.A.

1934—file 370/34, L and O: E.A. Indian representation to Government of India.

1935—file 62–44/35, L and O: Position of Indians in E.A.

(b) *Proceedings of the Foreign Department of the Government of India*

November 1866—Pros. 45–7, Pol. A: Slavery in Zanzibar.

May 1867—Pros. 141–3, Pol. A: Slavery in Zanzibar.

April 1868—Pros. 144–6, Pol. A: Slavery in Zanzibar.

June 1868—Pros. 54–7, Pol. A: Slavery in Zanzibar.

December 1868—Pros. 45–51, Pol. A: Slavery in Zanzibar.

1870—Pros. 57, 214, S.I: Control of Zanzibar Agency by Government of India.

January 1873—Pros. 226–31, Sec.: Control of Zanzibar Agency.

February 1873—Pros. 119–21, Sec.: Frere Mission to Zanzibar.

February 1873—Pros. 338–44, Pol. A: Zanzibar Slave Market.

June 1873—Pros. 334–5, Sec.: Memorandum by Frere.

July 1873—Pros. 23, Sec.: Proclamation by Rao of Kutch re Slave Trade.

July 1873—Pros. 235–6, Pol. A: Payment of Muscat subsidy by India.

August 1873—Pros. 116–116A, Pol. A: Control of Zanzibar Agency by India.

October 1873—Pros. 225, Pol. A: Closing of Zanzibar Slave Market.

October 1874—Pros. 48–9, Pol. A: Indians and Slave Trade.

December 1874—Pros. 61–4, Pol. A: Status of Indians at Zanzibar.

January 1877—Pros. 2–3, Genl. A: Status of Indians.

September 1880—Pros. 207, Pol. A: Zanzibar Customs.

July 1882—Pros. 532–54, Pol. A: Control of Zanzibar Agency by H.M.G

May 1883—Pros. 70–5, A Genl. E: H.M.G. to control Zanzibar Agency.

February 1883—Pros. 264, A Pol. E: Status of Indians at Zanzibar.

September 1883—Pros. 349–50, A Pol. E: Indian traders at Mombasa.

April 1884—Pros. 26–8, B Genl. E: Zanzibar trade reports.

May 1884—Pros. 29–71, A Pol. E: H.M.G. to control Zanzibar Agency.

July 1884—Pros. 161–2, A Pol. E: Indian Post Office at Zanzibar.

November 1884—Pros. 520–5, Extl. A: Indian Post Office.

October 1886—Pros. 25–33, Extl. A: Endowments in Zanzibar by Topan.

February 1889—Pros. 100–1, Extl. A: Recruitment of Indian labour by the I.B.E.A. Company.

October 1889—Pros. 10–15, Extl. A: Indian labour for I.B.E.A.

September 1890—Pros. 18, Extl. B: I.B.E.A. Company report.

November 1890—Pros. 94–5, Extl. A: Indian School at Zanzibar.

April 1891—Pros. 33–4, Extl. A: Indian school.

July 1895—Pros. 119, 159–70, Extl. A: Indians in G.E.A.

June 1900—Pros. 196, Extl. B: Indians in G.E.A.

See also: India Office, Political Department, Political and Secret Letters Received, Zanzibar and Aden: Letters from Zanzibar, 1875–83, vol. i.

A 2. FOREIGN OFFICE RECORDS, PUBLIC RECORD OFFICE, LONDON

(a) *Dispatches*

F.O. 84/425, Hamerton to Aberdeen, 21 May 1842 (Trade in Zanzibar).

F.O. 84/540, Hamerton to Aberdeen, 2 January 1844 (Indians in Zanzibar).

F.O. 84/1357, Kirk to Bombay, 24 August 1871 (Jairam Sewji).

F.O. 84/1344, Kirk to Granville, 28 September 1871 (Firm of Jairam Sewji).

F.O. 84/1357, Livingstone to Kirk, 30 October and 17 November 1871 (Activities of Indian traders).

F.O. 84/1344, Kirk to Bombay, 24 November 1871 (Jairam Sewji).

F.O. 84/1357, Kirk to Granville, 25 and 27 January 1872 (Jairam Sewji).

F.O. 84/1357, Kirk to Bombay, 10 April and 17 December 1872 (Indian traders in Zanzibar).

F.O. 84/1357, Kirk to Granville, 22 May and 6 August 1872 (Indian traders in E.A.).

F.O. 84/1357, Kirk to Bombay, 13 September 1872 (Rebuts Livingstone's allegations).

F.O. 84/1391, Frere to Granville, 2 May 1873, enclosed 'Memorandum on the subject of the Muscat subsidy'.

F.O. 84/1391, Frere to Granville, 7 May 1873, enclosed 'Memorandum on Banians or natives of India in East Africa', and 'Memorandum on the position and authority of the Sultan of Zanzibar'.

F.O. 84/1391, Frere to Granville, 10 May 1873, enclosed 'Memorandum on instructions and suggestions'.

F.O. 84/1391, Frere to Granville, 29 May 1873 (Indians in Zanzibar).

F.O. 84/1773, Kirk to Salisbury, 11 March 1886 (Indian traders).

F.O. 84/1773, Kirk to Salisbury, 1 May 1886 (Tarya Topan).

F.O. 84/1773, Kirk to Salisbury, 10 May 1886 (Indian currency).

F.O. 84/1774, Kirk to Salisbury, 4 June 1886 (Indians in German sphere).

F.O. 84/1774, Kirk to Salisbury, 5 June 1886 (Indians in German sphere).

F.O. 84/1774, Holmwood to Salisbury, 25 July 1886 (Customs).

F.O. 84/1775, Holmwood to Salisbury, 23 September 1886 (Customs).

F.O. 84/1910, Euan Smith to Salisbury, 22 October 1888 (Peera Devji).

F.O. 84/2084, India Office to Foreign Office, 14 June 1890 (Indian Post Office at Zanzibar).

F.O. 84/2062, Euan Smith to Salisbury, 30 July 1890 (Indian School at Zanzibar).

F.O. 2/117, Employment of Indian troops in the Protectorates, 1889–96.

F.O. 2/143, Employment of Indian troops in the Protectorates, 1897.

F.O. 2/170, Employment of Indian troops in the Protectorates, January to August 1898.

F.O. 2/171, Employment of Indian troops in the Protectorates, September to December 1898.

F.O. 2/204, Johnston to Salisbury, 11 and 13 October 1899 (Indians and the Uganda Railway).

F.O. 2/256, Employment of Indian troops in the Protectorates, January to June 1899.

F.O. 2/257, Employment of Indian troops in the Protectorates, July to December 1899.

F.O. 2/297, Johnston to Salisbury, 18 February 1900 (Indian precedents for E.A.).

F.O. 2/299, Johnston to Salisbury, 5 May 1900 (Indian contingent in Uganda).

F.O. 2/428, Employment of Indian troops in the Protectorates, January to July 1900.

F.O. 2/429, Employment of Indian troops in the Protectorates, August to December 1900.

F.O. 2/431, Agency in India for African Protectorates, 1896–1900.

F.O. 2/443, Lansdowne to Eliot, 3 and 27 August 1902 (Indian settlement in E.A.).

F.O. 2/550, Employment of Indian troops in the Protectorates, January to May 1901.

F.O. 2/552, Agency in India for African Protectorates, 1901.

F.O. 2/569, Eliot to Lansdowne, 5 January 1902, enclosures, and minute by Hill, 25 February 1902 (Indian settlement).

F.O. 2/571, Eliot to Lansdowne, 25 April and 8 May 1902 (Indian settlement).

F.O. 2/576, Whitehouse to O'Callaghan, 13 February 1902, enclosures (Indians and the Uganda Railway).

F.O. 2/576, Eliot to Lansdowne, 31 March 1902 (European Settlers' opposition to the Indians).

F.O. 2/671, Coolie Emigration from India to African Protectorates, 1895–1902.

F.O. 2/788, Employment of Indian troops in the Protectorates, 1902–3.

F.O. 2/791, Agency in India for African Protectorates, 1902–3.

F.O. 2/795, Nairobi buildings, 1900–3.

F.O. 2/805, Eliot to Lansdowne, 21 January 1902, enclosed petition of the European colonists dated 4 January 1902, and comments thereon.

F.O. 2/894, Agency in India for African Protectorates, 1904.

F.O. 2/914, Stewart to Lansdowne, 16 January 1905, enclosed report on cotton growing in the E.A.P.

F.O. 2/916, Stewart to Lansdowne, 7 March 1905, enclosed report on Ukamba Province by Ainsworth.

F.O. 2/956, Coinage and currency in E.A. and Uganda, 1900–5.

(b) *Foreign Office Confidential Prints*

F.O.C.P. no. 2314 (Slave-dealing and slave-holding by Kutchees in Zanzibar, 1819–70).

F.O.C.P. no. 1936, pp. 17–22 (Report on Zanzibar, 1870–1, by Kirk).

F.O.C.P. no. 4637, p. 59 (Zanzibar Customs, 1880).

F.O.C.P. no. 6454, pp. 201, 207 (Sewa Hajee).

F.O.C.P. no. 7040, pp. 10–12 (Indian labour for Uganda Railway, 1897).

F.O.C.P. no. 7212, p. 227 (Indian traders along the Railway, 1898).

F.O.C.P. no. 7400, pp. 108–12 (Indian troops).

F.O.C.P. no. 7400, p. 269 (Influx of Indians into Ukamba, 1899).

F.O.C.P. no. 7402, p. 40 (Role of Indian troops in Uganda, 1899).

F.O.C.P. no. 7403, pp. 54–5 (Report on G.E.A. by the Aga Khan, 1899).

F.O.C.P. no. 7422, pp. 116–19 (Indian traders along the Railway, 1899).

F.O.C.P. no. 7422, pp. 245–7, 268–9 (Importation of coolies for the Railway, 1899).

F.O.C.P. no. 7675, p. 32 (Report on G.E.A., 1900).

F.O.C.P. no. 7690, pp. 16–17 (Johnston's support for Indian settlement, 1901).

F.O.C.P. no. 7690, pp. 65–87 (Report on G.E.A., 1901, by Hollis).

F.O.C.P. no. 7732, pp. 253–6, 440 (Affairs of A. M. Jeevanjee, 1901).

F.O.C.P. no. 7732, pp. 312, 369 B and C (Support for Indian settlement in E.A.).

F.O.C.P. no. 7823, pp. 161–2 (Indian caravan traders, 1901).

F.O.C.P. no. 7823, p. 174 (Report by D. O. Rabai, 1901).

F.O.C.P. no. 7823, p. 198 (Johnston on Indian traders and the circulation of currency in Uganda, 1901).

F.O.C.P. no. 7867, pp. 7–15 (Eliot's report on the E.A.P., June 1901).

F.O.C.P. no. 7922, p. 200 (Chief Engineer's report on Uganda Railway, June 1902).

F.O.C.P. no. 7946, pp. 28, 197 (Allidina Visram, 1902).

F.O.C.P. no. 7946, pp. 96–9 (Scheme for Indian settlement, 1902).

F.O.C.P. no. 7946, pp. 133, 156–7 (Memorandum by European settlers and official views thereon, 1902).

F.O.C.P. no. 7953, p. 108 (Indians in G.E.A., 1902).

F.O.C.P. no. 7953, pp. 187–8 (Scheme to settle Indian soldiers in East Africa, 1902).

F.O.C.P. no. 8438, pp. 121–2 (Report regarding Indian settlement, 1905).

F.O.C.P. no. 8438, pp. 255–71 (Ainsworth's report on Ukamba Province, 1905).

F.O.C.P. no. 8691, pp. 30–3 (Decline of Zanzibar as a commercial entrepôt, 1905).

A 3. COLONIAL OFFICE ARCHIVES, PUBLIC RECORD OFFICE, LONDON

(a) *Dispatches*

C.O. 533/1, Stewart to Lansdowne, 14 March 1905, enclosed report on the financial position and trade of the E.A.P. by Bowring and Marsden.

C.O. 533/2, Stewart to Lyttelton, 6 July 1905, enclosed report on the Uganda Railway for 1904–5 by H. A. F. Currie.

C.O. 533/3, Stewart to Lyttelton, 9 August 1905, enclosed memorandum on prospects for traders by Ainsworth and Marsden.

C.O. 533/3, Stewart to Lyttelton, 14 August 1905 (Opposes settlement of Indians in the Highlands).

C.O. 533/3, Jackson to Lyttelton, 26 August 1905, enclosed report of the Treasurer, E.A.P.

C.O. 533/4, Jackson to Lyttelton, 7 October 1905 (British Indian methods of Government).

C.O. 533/4, Jackson to Lyttelton, Telegram, 12 October 1905 (Indian Immigration, attached minute paper gives details of the Kibos scheme).

C.O. 533/4, Jackson to Lyttelton, 18 October 1905, enclosed petition of the European Colonists' Association, 23 August 1905.

C.O. 533/4, Lyttelton to Jackson, 25 October 1905 (Indian Immigration).

C.O. 533/5, Jackson to Lyttelton, 11 November 1905, enclosed minutes by Hobley, Ainsworth, and Jackson on the European Petition.

C.O. 533/6, I.O. to C.O., 8 July 1905, and enclosure (Administration of the affairs of Uganda Railway Coolies by Protector of Emigrants, Karachi).

C.O. 533/7, Bombay Agent Simson to C.O., 3 August 1905, and enclosures (Recruitment of Indian postal clerks for E.A.).

C.O. 533/19, Sadler to Elgin, 5 December 1906, enclosed report on Indian immigration.

C.O. 533/19, Jackson to Elgin, 20 and 22 December 1906, and enclosures (Subordinate Indian staff).

C.O. 533/59, Sadler to Crewe, Telegram, 12 April 1909 (Sanderson Committee).

C.O. 533/59, Jackson to Crewe, 20 May 1909 (Appointment of Jeevanjee to Legco).

C.O. 533/59, Jackson to Crewe, 21 May 1909 (Indian immigration).

C.O. 533/62, Girouard to Crewe, Telegram, 23 September 1909 (Opposes Indian agricultural settlement and Jeevanjee's appointment).

C.O. 533/63, Girouard to Crewe, 13 November 1909 (Interim report on the E.A.P.).

C.O. 533/102, Girouard to Harcourt, 19 February 1912 (Replacement of Jeevanjee).

C.O. 533/160, I.O. to C.O., 13 January 1915, 8 June 1915, C.O. to I.O., 21 January 1915, and minute of 10 June 1915 (Importation of Indian labour for Kilindini Harbour works).

C.O. 533/160, W.O. to C.O., 24 January 1915 (Indian Expeditionary Force for East Africa).

C.O. 536/74, Jeevanjee to C.O., Telegram, 14 January 1914 (Protest regarding Uganda Cotton Rules).

C.O. 536/79, Confidential report on Uganda Cotton Industry by S. Simpson, 31 July 1912, and memorandum thereon.

C.O. 537/402, Belfield to Harcourt, 27 August 1914 (Strike of Indian subordinate staff).

(b) *Colonial Office Confidential Prints*

C.O.C.P. 879/87/771, pp. 88–114 (Details regarding European Colonists' Petition, 1905).

C.O.C.P. 879/87/772, p. 165 (Memorandum on Traders in East Africa).

C.O.C.P. 879/87/772, p. 188 (Buildings leased by Government from Jeevanjee).

C.O.C.P. 879/92/844, p. 169 (Indian role in E.A.P., 1906).

C.O.C.P. 879/105/954, pp. 57–140, 146–53 (Girouard's Reports on the E.A.P., 1910).

A 4. RECORDS OF THE BOMBAY GOVERNMENT, MAHARASHTRA STATE ARCHIVES, BOMBAY

Bombay Government Archives, Political Department (hereafter referred to as P.D.), vol. no. 316, Muscat 1841/2, Compilation no. 101 (Establishment of British Agency in Zanzibar).

P.D. vol. Muscat 1842, Compilation nos. 59 and 145 (Establishment of British Agency in Zanzibar).

P.D. vol. 43 of 1842, Compilation no. 350 (Establishment of British Agency in Zanzibar).

P.D. vol. 59 of 1844, Compilation no. 289 (Firm of Jairam Sewji).

P.D. vol. 33 of 1861, Compilation no. 15 (Muscat–Zanzibar dispute).

P.D. vol. 135 of 1868, Compilation no. 478 (Emancipation of slaves in Zanzibar).

P.D. vol. 144 of 1870, Compilation no. 1198 (Firm of Jairam Sewji).

P.D. vol. 143 of 1871, Compilation no. 1659 (Zanzibar Customs).

P.D. vol. 145 of 1871 (Unfriendly attitude of Bhargash).

P.D. vol. 230 of 1873, Compilation no. 88 (Zanzibar Slave Market).

P.D. vol. 280 of 1874, Compilation no. 1963 (Status of Indians in Zanzibar).

P.D. vol. 185 of 1887, Compilation no. 453 (Torya Topan).

P.D. vol. 281 of 1877, Compilation no. 62 (Indian School in Zanzibar) and Compilation no. 309 (Status of Indians at Zanzibar).

P.D. vol. 220 A of 1889, Compilation no. 873 (Peera Dewji).

P.D. vol. 174 of 1891, Compilation nos. 279 and 1063 (Indian School in Zanzibar).

P.D. vol. 134 of 1895, Compilation nos. 107 and 356 (Recruitment of Indians for service in G.E.A. and Congo).

Bombay Government Judicial Department, vol. 96 of 1896, Compilation no. 1170 (Emigration of artisans to E.A.).

Bombay Government, General Department (hereafter referred to as G.D.), vol. 119 C of 1896, Compilation no. 671, Part I (Coolie emigration to E.A.).

G.D. vol. 120 C of 1896, Compilation no. 671, Part II (Coolie emigration).

P.D. vol. 137 of 1896, Compilation no. 795 (Emigration Agents at Bombay for the Uganda Railway).

P.D. vol. 143 of 1896, Compilation nos. 307 and 902 (Coolie Emigration to E.A.).

G.D. vol. 142 C of 1897, Compilation no. 671, Part I (Coolie emigration).

G.D. vol. 143 C of 1897, Compilation no. 671, Part III (Coolie emigration).

G.D. vol. 178 C of 1898, Compilation no. 671 (Coolie emigration).

G.D. vol. 179 C of 1898, Compilation no. 671, Parts II and III (Coolie emigration).

P.D. vol. 23 of 1899, Compilation no. 1140 (Agent in Bombay for the African Protectorates).

P.D. vol. 63 of 1900, Compilation no. 1097 (Indian artisans for G.E.A.).

G.D. vol. 245 C of 1900, Compilation nos. 94, 103, 120 (Coolie emigration).

G.D. vol. 277 C of 1901, Compilation no. 40 (Legalizing emigration to E.A.).

G.D. vol. 278 C of 1901, Compilation nos. 91, 106, 120 (Emigration to E.A.).

G.D. vol. 279 C of 1901, Compilation nos. 141, 159 (Emigration to E.A.).

G.D. vol. 280 C of 1901, Compilation no. 181 (Emigration to E.A.).

G.D. vol. 323 C of 1902, Compilation no. 54 (Emigration to E.A.).

G.D. vol. 340 C of 1903, Compilation no. 82 (Emigration to E.A.).

Judicial Department, vol. 88 of 1904, Compilation no. 49 (Emigration to E.A.).

G.D. vol. 394 C of 1906, Compilation no. 55 (Indian settlement in E.A.).

G.D. vol. 5 C of 1907, Compilation no. 64 (Illegal emigration to E.A.).

G.D. vol. 8 C of 1909, Compilation no. 9 (Voluntary emigration to E.A.).

G.D. vol. 59 of 1910, Compilation no. 417 (Illegal emigration to E.A.).

G.D. vol. 71 of 1911, Compilation no. 1199 (Emigration to E.A.).

P.D. vol. 122 of 1912, Compilation no. 1541 (Memorial to Government of India on behalf of Indians in E.A.).

P.D. vol. 113 of 1913, Compilation 1282 (Memorial to Government of India on behalf of Indians in E.A.).

P.D. 1914, Compilation no. 1335 (Emigration to G.E.A.).

A 5. NATIONAL ARCHIVES OF TANZANIA

These were consulted before the National Archives were established. References to relevant material in the records in Zanzibar and Dar es Salaam are therefore provided separately.

(*a*) *Zanzibar*

Serial no. E 11, Hamerton to Bombay, Outward Letters no. 13 of 1848 and no. 12 of 1849 (Firm of Jairam Sewji).

Serial no. E. 19, Hamerton to Bombay, Outward Letters no. 9 and 13 of 1854 (British Indians in Zanzibar).

Serial no. E. 26, Rigby to Bombay, Outward Letter no. 23 of 1858 (Trade between Zanzibar and Bombay).

Serial no. E. 26, Rigby to Bombay, Outward Letter no. 46 of 1859 (Report on Zanzibar).

Serial no. E. 28, Rigby to Bombay, Outward Letter no. 3 of 1860 (Report on Zanzibar).

Serial no. E. 41, Churchill to Bombay, Outward Letter no. 50/193 of 1868 (Jairam Sewji).

(*b*) *Dar es Salaam*

File no. 3150 (1920) (Segregation of Races).

File no. 3033/3 (1920-2) (Sale of ex-enemy property).

File no. 7235 (1923) (Indian Question).

File no. 7596 (1924-5) (Controversy re the Profits Tax).

File no. 7092, vol. i (1922) and vol. ii (1926) (Trading Licensing Ordinance, 1923).

File no. 7017 (1925) (Indian education).

File no. 7652 (1925) (Sewa Hajee).

A 6. KENYA NATIONAL ARCHIVES, NAIROBI

The Mombasa Provincial records are quoted separately as a part of them were consulted in Mombasa before they were moved to the National Archives in Nairobi.

(*a*)

PC/CP. 1/1/2: Machakos District Political Record Book, 1889-1912.

PC/NZA. 3/22, 1/1 to 1/16 and 3/22/1, 3: Indian settlement at Kibos.

PC/NZA. 1/2: Nyanza Province Annual Reports, 1905-45.

MKS/1: Machakos District Annual Reports, 1909-16.

PC/CP. 9/3/1: Land Settlement, 1909.

MKS/57: Machakos District Political Record Book, vol. ii, 1910-11.

KBU/2, 3, 4: Kiambu District Annual Reports, 1910, 1911, and 1912.

TTA/5: Political Record Book, Taita District, vol. i, 1913-25.

PC/RVP. 2/8/2–21: Uasin Gishu District Annual Reports, 1913–45.

PC/CP. 1/3/4: Machakos District Political Record Book, 1914–21.

NFD. 11: Annual Reports, Samburu District, 1914–28.

ELGM/10: Elgeyo–Marakwet District Misc. Correspondence, 1914–30.

DC/KAJ. 9/1/1: Political Record Book, Kajiado District.

PC/CP. 4/3/1: Central Province Annual Reports, 1934–8.

PC/CP. 15/1/2: Political Record Book, Central Province, 1921–9.

PC/CP. 4/2/3: Ukamba Province Annual Reports, 1925–32.

ARC/(GH)—103: Indian Education, 1929–48.

ARC(GH)—141 I: Federation of Indian Chambers of Commerce and Industry of Eastern Africa.

PC/CP. 4/1/2: Kikuyu Province Annual Reports, 1920–32.

ARC(GH)—77: A. M. Jeevanjee.

(b) *Lands Department, Nairobi*

File no. 15993: General Question of Policy re Indians in E.A.P.

(c) *Mombasa Provincial Archives*

(i) Material seen at Mombasa:

Shelf 65, file 6: 'Uganda Railway, Outward, 1898–1900.'

Shelf 66, file 10: 'Inward Uganda Administration 1896–99.'

Shelf 66, file 11: 'Uganda Railway, Inward, 1898–1900.'

Shelf 76, file 50: 'Ukamba Outward 1899.'

Shelf 88, file 138: 'Inward H.M. Commissioner 1906.'

Shelf 64, file 260 of 1912: Annual Reports 1911–12 from Districts.

Shelf 1, file 37 of 1912: Quarterly Reports 1911 from Districts.

Shelf 8, file 177: Correspondence with Agents in India.

Shelf 12, file 204: Legal Status of Indians in E.A., 1914.

Shelf 30, file 404: Indian School, Mombasa, 1915–21.

Shelf 50, file 1215: Indian Association in E.A., 1916–21.

(ii) Material seen at Nairobi:

Mombasa file no. 103/7: Allidina Visram Soap Factory, 1907.

Mombasa file no. 2/126: Township property in Mombasa.

Mombasa file no. 3/286: Abolition of Bombay Agency.

Mombasa file no. 38/605: Visram's goods at Kisumu, 1915–16.

Mombasa file no. 37/576: Permits to open shops, 1915–16.

Mombasa file no. 42/797: Indian mills on alienated lands, 1917.

Mombasa file no. 43/902: Segregation of races, 1918.

Mombasa file no. 64/10: Political unrest, 1923.

Mombasa file no. 2/253: Closer Union Commission, 1927–31.

Mombasa file no. 2/1/2: Municipal Government Mombasa, 1930–2.

Mombasa file no. 2/241: Financial Inquiry, Lord Moyne, 1932.

Mombasa file no. 2/283: Kenya Highlands League, 1938–9.

Mombasa file no. 106/58: Evidence, Mombasa Labour Commission of Inquiry, 1939.

A 7. UGANDA NATIONAL ARCHIVES, ENTEBBE

Class A29, item 1: Correspondence with Government of India, 1900–6.

Class A27, item 4: Indian surveyors for Uganda, 1901–5.

File no. 1703/1909: Artisans from India.

File no. 386 of 1909: Emigration from India to Crown Colonies.

Secretariat Minute Papers, nos. 1608, 2115, 2974: Indian Contingent in Uganda.

File no. 1827/1909: Report on Cotton by H. Bell.

File no. 1323/1909: Ivory trading in Karamoja.

File no. 409/1906: Busoga trade prospects.

File no. 5426, Part I and II: Policy of Concentration in petty townships and trading centres.

File no. 661: Regulation of cotton buying in Eastern Province.

File no. 8629: Federation of Indian Chambers of Commerce and Industry.

File no. 5387: Cotton Ginners Association.

File no. C. 585: Visit of Revd. C. F. Andrews.

File no. 5550: Indian Association, Kampala.

File no. 539, Part I and II: Indian education in Uganda.

File no. 7401: Sugar mill at Lugazi.

File no. 141: Residence by Non-European on Land.

File no. 6024: Report on the E.A.I.N.C. for 1919.

File no. 4092: Indian newspapers in E.A., 1920.

File no. 1138: Buganda Province Annual Reports from 1909.

File no. 2135: Northern Province Annual Reports from 1909.

File no. 703: Eastern Province Annual Reports from 1909.

File no. 925: Eastern Province Annual Reports from 1908–9.

File no. 1972 C: Buganda Province Monthly Reports, 1914.

File no. 4832: Allidina Visram (contains comprehensive information).

File no. 1330: Allidina Visram's agents in Eastern Province and Abyssinia.

File no. 1145/1909: Allidina Visram and the Oil Industry in Bukedi.

File no. 831/1907: Allidina Visram and Toro Produce.

File no. 6520: Miscellaneous: Allidina Visram.

File nos. 57 and 72: Allidina Visram's Agents in Congo, 1908-9.

File no. 4303: Allidina Visram and trade in hoes.

File nos. 553, 756, and 4699: Allidina Visram and porters.

File no. 5677: Allidina Visram and war with Germany.

File no. 1207: Allidina Visram and Agent at Mbale, 1907.

File nos. 46, 87, 262, 579, 671, 990, 1016, 1322, and 5075: Allidina Visram's land.

File no. 806: Allidina Visram, Leather Tannery, Entebbe, 1907.

File no. 131: Allidina Visram, Erection of ginnery and oil factory at Entebbe, 1910.

File no. 1208: Allidina Visram and coffee, 1907.

File no. 569: Allidina Visram and timber industry, 1908.

File nos. 146, 409, 483: Allidina Visram and timber industry, 1909.

B. NON-OFFICIAL ARCHIVES

B I. RECORDS OF THE EAST AFRICAN INDIAN NATIONAL CONGRESS

(now the Kenya Indian Congress) Nairobi

Files marked:

'Correspondence and Proceedings of the Indian Association Nairobi, 1917–1922.'
'Correspondence 1918.'
'East Africa Indian Deputation to London 1920.'
'Outward 1920–23.'
'Indian Association Nairobi: Report for the Year 1921.'
'Correspondence 1922.'
'Correspondence with Kenya and Uganda Governments 1921.'
'Correspondence with Indians Overseas Association.'
no. 43: 'Correspondence with Kenya Government re Poll Tax 1924.'
no. 26: 'Correspondence 1925–27.'
'Resolutions 1931 Congress.'
'Miscellaneous Correspondence 1931–33.'
'Outward 1933.'
'Secretary's Report 1933–34.'
'Correspondence 1935.'
'Secretary's Report 1938.'
'1939 Correspondence.'
'Inter-territorial Conference 1946.'

In addition, the following printed material in the Congress records provides valuable information (some of this material can now also be found in the History Department Archives, University College, Nairobi):

(i) *Presidential Addresses* (including Resolutions of Sessions), by T. M. Jeevanjee (1914), Sarojini Naidu (1924), Tyeb Ali (1927), H. N. Kunzru (1929), A. D. Sheth (1932), J. B. Pandya (1934), A. H. Kaderbhoy (1935), A. B. Patel (1938, 1942, and 1945), S. G. Amin (1946), Shamsud-Deen (1944), D. D. Puri (1948), and S. Gautama (1960).

(ii) 'Memorandum on the Federation of British East African Territories and Constitutional Changes in Kenya submitted by the E.A.I.N.C. to the Hilton Young Commission.'

(iii) 'Supplement to the Memorandum submitted by the E.A.I.N.C. to the Hilton Young Commission.'

(iv) 'Memorandum submitted by the Executive Committee of the E.A.I.N.C. to the Secretary of State for the Colonies on the "Reservation of Highlands of Kenya for Europeans", 7 October 1938.'

(v) 'Petition of the E.A.I.N.C. to the King to Disallow Religious Separate Electorates, 10 January 1952.'

B 2. SIDNEY WEBB (LORD PASSFIELD) PAPERS, London School of Economics

Vol. iv, file E, item 108 (d): Boycott of the Joint Select Committee by the Tanganyika Indians.

Vol. v, file F, item 123, 128, and 134 (i): E.A.I.N.C. Split 1931.

B 3. INTERNATIONAL MISSIONARY COUNCIL, Edinburgh House, London, *Papers of Dr. J. H. Oldham*

Box marked: 'Kenya Indians.'

File marked: 'Kenya Indians: Colonial Office.'

File: 'Kenya Indians: General Correspondence.'

File: 'Kenya Indians: Indian Delegation and Correspondence with India.'

File: 'India, C. F. Andrews.'

File: 'East Africa: Indians in East Africa.'

File: 'Kenya Indians: Archbishop of Canterbury.'

File: 'Native Unrest (1922): Harry Thuku.'

B 4. LORD FRANCIS SCOTT PAPERS, University College, Nairobi

File no. D/37: Resolutions passed at Conference on Constitutional Advance, July 1933.

File no. E/25–6: Resolutions passed by the Convention of Associations, September 1935.

File no. E/10: Statement of the Settlers' Case 1935.

B 5. MINUTES OF THE UGANDA CHAMBER OF COMMERCE, Makerere University College Library, Kampala

These minutes, especially for the decade after 1905, provide useful information about the early Indian traders in Uganda.

C. OFFICIAL PUBLICATIONS

C I. PARLIAMENTARY PAPERS

Report by Sir A. Hardinge on the condition and progress of the East African Protectorate from its establishment to the 20th July 1897, C. 8683 (1897).

Report by Sir A. Hardinge on the British East Africa Protectorate for the year 1897–98, C. 9125 (1899).

Report on the Uganda Railway by Sir G. Molesworth, C. 9331 (1899).

Despatch from H.M. Special Commissioner in Uganda relating to travellers in the Protectorate, Cd. 590 (1901).

Report by H.M. Special Commissioner on the Protectorate of Uganda, Cd. 671 (1901).

Final Report of the Uganda Railway Committee, Cd. 2164 (1904).

Reports relating to the administration of the East African Protectorate, Cd. 2740 (1905).

Correspondence relating to affairs in the E.A.P., Cd. 4122 (1908).

Correspondence relating to the tenure of land in the E.A.P., Cd. 4117 (1908).

Report of the Committee on Emigration from India to the Crown Colonies and Protectorates, Part I, Cd. 5192 (1910).

Ibid., Part II, *Minutes of Evidence*, Cd. 5193 (1910).

Ibid., Part III, *Papers laid before the Committee*, Cd. 5194 (1910).

Correspondence regarding the position of Indians in East Africa, Cmd. 1311 (1921).

Report by Sir Benjamin Robertson, dated 4 August 1920 regarding the proposed settlement of Indian agriculturists in Tanganyika Territory . . ., Cmd. 1312 (1921).

Indians in Kenya, Cmd. 1922 (1923).

Report of the East Africa Commission, Cmd. 2387 (1925).

Future policy in regard to Eastern Africa, Cmd. 2904 (1927).

Report of the Commission on Closer Union of the Dependencies in Eastern and Central Africa, Cmd. 3234 (1929).

Report of Sir Samuel Wilson on his visit to East Africa, Cmd. 3378 (1929).

Memorandum on native policy in East Africa, Cmd. 3573 (1930).

Statement of the conclusions of H.M.'s Government in the U.K. as regards Closer Union in East Africa, Cmd. 3574 (1930).

Report by the Financial Commissioner (Lord Moyne) on certain questions in Kenya, Cmd. 4093 (1932).

East Africa Royal Commission 1953–1955 report, Cmd. 9475 (1955).

C 2. OFFICIAL REPORTS

C. P. Rigby, *Report on the Zanzibar Dominions* (Bombay, 1861).

Handbook for East Africa, Uganda and Zanzibar (Mombasa, 1904).

E.A.P., *Report of the Land Committee* (Nairobi, 1905).

W. J. Simpson, *Report on sanitary matters in the E.A.P., Uganda and Zanzibar* (Colonial Office, 1915).

E.A.P., *Economic Commission report* (Nairobi, 1919).

T. Sleith, *Report on trade conditions in British East Africa Uganda and Zanzibar* (Cape Town, 1919).

Uganda, *Report of the Uganda Development Commission* (Entebbe, 1920).

Proceedings of the Standing Joint Committee on Indian affairs (London, 1921).

Zanzibar, *Report of the Commission on Agriculture* (Zanzibar, 1923).

Kenya, *Report of the Local Government Commission* (Nairobi, 1927).

Uganda, *Report of the Commission of Enquiry into the cotton industry of Uganda* (Entebbe, 1929).

Uganda, *Report of the Local Government Committee* (Entebbe, 1930).

Report by the Rt. Hon. V. S. S. Sastri, regarding his Mission to East Africa (Delhi, 1930).

Joint Select Committee on Closer Union in East Africa, vol. i, *Report* (London, 1931).

Ibid., vol. ii, *Minutes of Evidence.*

Ibid., vol. iii, *Appendices.*

Papers relating to the question of Closer Union of Kenya, Uganda and Tanganyika Territory, Colonial no. 57 (1931).

C. A. Bartlett and J. S. Last, *Report on the indebtedness of the Agricultural Classes, 1933* (Zanzibar, 1934).

Kenya, *Land Commission, Evidence*, vol. iii (Nairobi, 1934).

Report by K. P. S. Menon on marketing legislation in Tanganyika, Uganda and Kenya, 1935, C.O. Pamphlet no. 274.

Zanzibar, *Report of a sub-committee of Zanzibar Advisory Council on Education, on grants-in-aid and on the reorganization of Indian education* (Zanzibar, 1935).

Report of the Commission appointed to enquire into and report on the financial position and system of taxation of Kenya, Colonial no. 116 (1936).

B. H. Binder, *Report on the Zanzibar clove industry* (Zanzibar, 1936).

A. A. Kazimi, *An Enquiry into Indian education in East Africa* (Nairobi, 1948).

Report of the Commission on the Civil Services of Kenya, Tanganyika, Uganda and Zanzibar (London, 1948).

Kenya, *Report of the Committee on Educational Expenditure (European and Asian)* (Nairobi, 1948).

Kenya, *Report of the Select Committee on Indian education* (Nairobi, 1949).

Tanganyika, *Department of Education: Triennial Survey 1955–57* (Dar es Salaam, 1958).

Kenya, *Report on Asian and European education in Kenya* (Nairobi, 1958).

Uganda, *Annual Report of the Education Department 1960* (Entebbe, 1960).

India, *Gazette of India Extraordinary*, 24 June 1935, refers to the marketing legislation in East Africa.

Kenya, *Official Gazette* (see especially the issue of 18 August 1920 and 17 August 1923).

Zanzibar, *Official Gazette* (the various issues during the 1890s are particularly useful).

Census Reports for Kenya, Uganda, Tanganyika, and Zanzibar and *Annual Reports* for Kenya, Uganda, Tanganyika, and Zanzibar.

C 3. PROCEEDINGS OF THE LEGISLATIVE COUNCILS

(*a*) *Proceedings of the Kenya Legislative Council*

31 October 1910: Jeevanjee's allegations in London.

18 January 1915, pp. 11–12: Objects of the Crown Lands Ordinance.

19 June 1917, pp. 19, 21: Indian demands for elective representation.

9 December 1918, pp. 44–8: Indian Question.

24 February 1919, p. 3: Northey's views on the Indian Question.

29 November 1920, p. 6: The Milner 'solution'.

10 February 1921, pp. 85–6: Segregation.

8 March 1927, p. 27: Indian elections.

30 August 1927, pp. 300–1: Grigg's views on the Indian Question.

25 April 1934, p. 97: I. Dass.

9 May 1934, pp. 185–210: Separate European and Asian Civil Service.

28 June 1935, pp. 69, 73: I. Dass.

1 July 1935, pp. 110–11: I. Dass.

3 July 1935, pp. 188–231: J. B. Pandya's opposition to marketing legislation.

5 November 1936, pp. 392–406: J. B. Pandya.

12 November 1936, pp. 545–59: Indian representation on municipal councils.

16 November 1936, pp. 610–11: Indian representation on municipal councils.

10 November 1937, p. 189: Opposition to Transport Licensing Bill.

12 November 1937, p. 261: Opposition to Transport Licensing Bill.

17 November 1937, pp. 387–8, 406: I. Dass.

9 August 1938, pp. 67–72: I. Dass speaks on behalf of Kikuyu Central Association.

10 August 1938, pp. 116–23: I. Dass on behalf of K.C.A.

17 August 1938, pp. 226–41: I. Dass speaks on behalf of the Kamba Protest Movement.

9 November 1938, p. 205: Indian representation on municipal councils.

21 April 1939, pp. 255–71: A. B. Patel's motion against the Highlands Order-in-Council.

21 April 1939, pp. 284–9: I. Dass reads African petition regarding Highlands.

14 December 1939, p. 361: Shamsud-Deen on racial discrimination in Civil Service.

14 December 1939, p. 389: I. Dass.

26 November 1946, p. 371: Indian views on Government expenditure.

29 November 1946, pp. 479–91: A. B. Patel.

23 October 1953, pp. 107–8: E. Mathu's views on Asians.

(b) *Proceedings of the Uganda Legislative Council*

3 March 1921, Appendix B: Indian Question.

10 June 1921, Appendix A and p. 15: Indian Question.

20 August 1921, Appendix A and p. 15: Indian Question.

28 May 1926, Appendix B: Indians in Uganda.

5 December 1932: Marketing legislation.

(c) *Proceedings of the Zanzibar Legislative Council*

10 December 1936: Address by the British Resident re the clove controversy.

30 September 1937: Address by the British Resident re the clove controversy.

2 December 1937: Address by the British Resident re the clove controversy.

Sessional Paper no. 5 of 1935: Report of the Commission on Agricultural Indebtedness.

Sessional Paper no. 10 of 1935: Indian education.

Sessional Paper no. 13 of 1937: Regulation of the clove industry.

Sessional Paper no. 14 of 1937: Regulation of the clove industry.

Sessional Paper no. 6 of 1938: Regulation of the clove industry.

D. NON-OFFICIAL PUBLICATIONS

D I. NEWSPAPERS

(i) East African Standard (*Nairobi*)

6 January and 22 December 1906: Sadler's relations with the Indians.

13 January 1906: Indian traders supplying 'rebels' at Kilwa.

17 February 1906: Indian traders supplying 'rebels' at Kilwa.

7 April 1906: Indian mass meeting at Mombasa.

15 December 1906: Indian delegation to London.

25 January, 3 May, and 21 June 1919: Indian Question.

18 and 20 August and 11 December 1920: Indian Question.

17 July 1926: Obituary on M. A. Desai.

20 January, 21 and 28 April, and 5 May 1934: Political controversy in Kenya and Uganda.

11 January 1960: Joint statement by Indian Congress and Muslim League.

13 December 1962, 25 April 1963, 1 October 1964, and 18 March 1966: Information about four leading Asian businessmen.

16 November 1962, 31 December 1965, and 1 January 1966: A. M. Jeevanjee as founder of the *Standard*.

(ii) The Leader of B.E.A. (*Nairobi*)

27 June 1908: Indian petition for representation.

2 April, 7 and 21 May, 3 and 17 September and particularly 1 October 1910, and 17 April 1915: for information about Jeevanjee.

8 and 15 July 1916: for information about Allidina Visram.

9 December 1918, and 25 February, 4, 11, 18, and 25 March 1922: Indian Question.

1 and 8 April 1922: Harry Thuku and the Indians.

See also: *The Leader Annual and Gazetteer of British East Africa 1914.*

D 2. CONTEMPORARY PUBLICATIONS: BOOKS, PAMPHLETS AND ARTICLES

Under this category only those works are mentioned which have pro-vided valuable Primary information. Other contemporary publications have been listed as secondary sources. The list is arranged chronologically:

J. H. SPEKE, *Journal of the discovery of the source of the Nile* (London, 1863).

—— *What led to the discovery of the source of the Nile* (London, 1864).

R. F. BURTON, *Zanzibar, city, island and coast*, 2 vols. (London, 1872).

The Last Journals of David Livingstone, 2 vols. (London, 1874).

J. CHRISTIE, *Cholera epidemics in East Africa* (London, 1876).

V. L. CAMERON, *Across Africa*, 2 vols. (London, 1877).

H. M. STANLEY, *Through the Dark Continent*, 2 vols. (London, 1878).

J. F. ELTON, *Travels and researches among the lakes and mountains of East and Central Africa* (London, 1879).

P. L. MCDERMOTT, *British East Africa or IBEA* (London, 1893).

F. D. LUGARD, *The rise of our East African Empire*, 2 vols. (London, 1893).

J. R. J. MACDONALD, *Soldiering and surveying in B.E.A., 1891–94* (London, 1897).

J. AINSWORTH, 'A description of the Ukamba Province, E.A.P. 1900', C.O. Pamphlet no. 6.

F. L. O'CALLAGHAN, 'Uganda Railway', *Professional papers of the Corps of Royal Engineers 1900*, xxvi, Paper viii, C.O. Pamphlet no. 7.

H. SAMUEL, 'The Uganda of today', *Journal of the Society of Arts*, ii, no. 2626 (20 March 1903), C.O. Pamphlet no. 15.

H. H. JOHNSTON, *The Uganda Protectorate*, 2 vols. (London, 1902).

R. N. Lyne, *Zanzibar in contemporary times* (London, 1905).

J. H. Patterson, *The man-eaters of Tsavo* (London, 1907).

W. S. Churchill, *My African journey* (London, 1908).

A. M. Jeevanjee, *An appeal on behalf of Indians in East Africa* (Bombay, 1912).

Koloniale Monatsblatter, Berlin (1913).

A. M. Jeevanjee, *Sanitation in Nairobi* (Bombay, 1915), C.O. Pamphlet no. 214.

Deutsches Koloniale Lexicon, vol. ii (Berlin, 1920).

C. F. Andrews, *The Indian Question in East Africa* (Nairobi, 1921), C.O. Pamphlet no. 61.

Lord Delamere and C. K. Archer, *Memorandum on the case against the claims of Indians in Kenya* (Nairobi, 1921).

East African Standard, The Indian problem in Kenya, April–October 1921 (Nairobi, 1922).

Indians Abroad: *Kenya* (Bulletin of the Imperial Indian Citizenship Association, Bombay, 1923).

W. M. Ross, *Kenya from within* (London, 1927).

A. H. Hardinge, *A diplomatist in the East* (London, 1928).

Indians abroad: *East Africa: Royal Commission on the Union of East Africa* (Bulletin of the Imperial Indian Citizenship Association, Bombay, 1928).

C. W. Hobley, *Kenya from chartered company to Crown Colony* (London, 1929).

Speeches by H.E. Sir Edward Grigg, 1925–30 (Nairobi, 1930).

F. J. Jackson, *Early days in East Africa* (London, 1930).

P. D. Master, *Segregation of Indians in Kenya* (Mombasa, 1931).

Memorandum by the Indian National Association, Zanzibar, 25 February 1935, C.O. Pamphlet no. 270.

T. J. Mboya, *Freedom and after* (London, 1963).

M. Blundell, *So rough a wind* (London, 1964).

E. ORAL INFORMATION

This was derived from interviews with a number of people in East Africa—the more important among them being:

S. G. Amin (Nairobi); Chanan Singh (Nairobi); J. F. Dastur (Kampala); Mohammed Sheriff Dewji (Zanzibar); Fetehali Dhalla (Mombasa); S. S. Dhillon (Mombasa); A. Jamal (Dar es Salaam); Sir Yusufali Jivanjee and Karimjee Jivanjee family (Dar es Salaam); C. B. Madan (Nairobi); Muljibhai Madhvani family (Jinja); A. N. Maini family (Kampala); Makhan Singh (Nairobi); Nanji Kalidas Mehta family (Jinja); H. E. Nathoo (Nairobi); J. M. Nazareth (Nairobi); A. J. Pandya (Mombasa);

A. B. Patel (ex-Mombasa); Dr. M. M. Patel (Kampala); N. M. Patel (Dar es Salaam); V. S. Patel (Zanzibar); K. K. Radia (Kampala); M. A. Rattansey (Dar es Salaam); K. M. Shah (Mombasa); R. G. Vedd (Jinja); and H. A. Visram (Kampala).

II. SECONDARY MATERIAL

I. BOOKS

G. BENNETT and C. ROSBERG, *The Kenyatta election: Kenya 1960–61* (London, 1961).

G. BENNETT, *Kenya: A political history* (London, 1963).

N. R. BENNETT, *Studies in East African history* (Boston, 1963).

H. BRODE, *Tippoo Tib* (London, 1907).

—— *British and German East Africa* (London, 1911).

R. L. BUELL, *The native problem in Africa*, 2 vols. (New York, 1928).

CHANAN SINGH, *The Indian case against the Immigration Bill* (Nairobi, 1947).

F. D. CORFIELD, *The origins and growth of Mau Mau: an historical survey* (Nairobi, 1960).

R. COUPLAND, *East Africa and its invaders* (Oxford, 1938).

—— *The exploitation of East Africa, 1856–1890* (London, 1939).

LORD CRANWORTH, *Kenya Chronicles* (London, 1939).

I. M. CUMPSTON, *Indians overseas in British territories, 1834–54* (Oxford, 1953).

G. DELF, *Asians in East Africa* (London, 1963).

M. R. DILLEY, *British policy in Kenya Colony* (New York, 1937).

Y. S. A. DRUMKEY, *Drumkey's Year Book of East Africa* (Bombay, 1908).

C. ELIOT, *The East Africa Protectorate* (London, 1905).

G. S. P. FREEMAN-GRENVILLE, *The medieval history of the coast of Tanganyika* (London, 1962).

N. GANGULEE, *Indians in the Empire overseas* (London, 1947).

D. GHAI (ed.), *Portrait of a minority: Asians in East Africa* (Nairobi, 1965).

J. GRAY, *History of Zanzibar* (London, 1962).

R. G. GREGORY, *Sidney Webb and East Africa* (Berkeley, 1962).

LORD HAILEY, *An African survey* (London, rev. ed. 1957).

W. K. HANCOCK, *Survey of British Commonwealth affairs*, 2 vols. (London, 1938).

V. HARLOW and MRS. E. M. CHILVER (eds.), *History of East Africa*, vol. ii (Oxford, 1965).

M. F. HILL, *Permanent way*, vol. i (Nairobi, 1949).

L. W. HOLLINGSWORTH, *The Asians of East Africa* (London, 1960).

C. HORDEN, *Military operations in East Africa*, vol. i (London, 1941).

G. Hunter, *The New societies of tropical Africa* (London, 1962).

E. Huxley, *The sorcerer's apprentice* (London, 1951).

K. Ingham, *The making of Modern Uganda* (London, 1958).

—— *A history of East Africa* (London, 1962).

W. Junker, *Travels in Africa*, Tr. A. H. Keane (London, 1892).

Kenya Indian Congress, *A spotlight on the Asians of Kenya* (Nairobi, 1963).

C. Kondapi, *Indians overseas, 1839–49* (New Delhi, 1951).

C. Legum, *Must we lose Africa* (London, 1954).

N. Leys, *Kenya* (London, 1924).

W. R. Louis, *Ruanda-Urundi 1884–1919* (Oxford, 1963).

D. A. Low and R. C. Pratt, *Buganda and British overrule* (London, 1960).

F. D. Lugard, *The dual mandate in British Tropical Africa* (London, 1922).

P. Mitchell, *African afterthoughts* (London, 1954).

H. Moyse-Bartlett, *The King's African Rifles* (Aldershot, 1956).

G. H. Mungeam, *British Rule in Kenya, 1886–1912* (Oxford, 1966).

R. Oliver, *The missionary factor in East Africa* (London, 1952).

—— *Sir Harry Johnston and the scramble for Africa* (London, 1959).

—— and G. Mathew (eds.), *History of East Africa*, vol. i (Oxford, 1963).

S. Pandit, *Asians in East Africa: who's who* (Nairobi, 1963).

H. R. A. Philp, *A new day in Kenya* (London, 1936).

S. Playne and F. H. Gale, *East Africa (British)* (London, 1908–9).

J. B. Purvis, *Through Uganda to Mount Elgon* (London, 1909).

N. V. Rajkumar, *Indians outside India* (New Delhi, 1951).

K. Robinson and F. Madden, *Essays in Imperial Government presented to Margery Perham* (Oxford, 1963).

R. Robinson and J. Gallagher, *Africa and the Victorians* (London, 1961).

J. Roscoe, *The soul of Central Africa* (London, 1922).

C. E. B. Russell, *General Rigby, Zanzibar and the slave trade* (London, 1935).

Saben's Commercial Directory and Handbook of Uganda 1947–48 (Kampala, 1948).

G. F. Sayers, *The handbook of Tanganyika* (London, 1930).

J. Strandes, *The Portuguese period in East Africa*, tr. Jean F. Wallwork (Nairobi, 1961).

H. M. Stanley, *In darkest Africa*, 2 vols. (London, 1890).

S. Wood, *Kenya: The tensions of progress* (London, 1960).

2. ARTICLES

G. BENNETT, 'The development of political organization in Kenya', *Political studies*, v, no. 2 (June 1957), 113–30.

N. R. BENNETT, 'Americans in Zanzibar 1825–45', *Tanganyika notes and records*, no. 56 (March 1961), 101–6.

—— 'Americans in Zanzibar 1845–65', *Tanganyika notes and records*, no. 57 (September 1961), 121–31.

E. EHRLICH, 'Some social and economic implications of paternalism in Uganda', *Journal of African history*, iv, no. 2 (1963), 275–85.

J. GRAY, 'Early connections between the U.S. and East Africa', *Tanganyika notes and records*, no. 22 (December 1946), 55–86.

H. S. MORRIS, 'Indians in East Africa: a study in a plural society', *British journal of sociology*, vii, no. 3 (1956).

D. F. POCOCK, '"Difference" in East Africa: A study of caste and religion in modern Indian society', *Southwestern journal of anthropology*, 13, no. 4 (Winter 1957), 289–300.

G. C. WHITEHOUSE, 'The building of the Kenya and Uganda Railway', *Uganda journal*, 12, no. 1 (March 1948), 1–15.

3. UNPUBLISHED THESES

C. EHRLICH, 'The marketing of cotton in Uganda 1900–1950' (London Ph.D., 1958).

J. ILIFFE, 'The German administration in Tanganyika 1906–1911' (Cambridge Ph.D., 1965).

H. S. MORRIS, 'Immigrant Indian communities in Uganda' (London Ph.D., 1963).

D. F. POCOCK, 'Indians in East Africa, with special reference to their social and economic situation and relationship' (Oxford D.Phil., 1955).

C. SOFER, 'Some aspects of race relations in an East African town' (London Ph.D., 1953).

INDEX

Abaluhya, 168.
Achariar, S., 119 n., 120 n.
Addis Ababa, 78.
Aden, 83 n.
Afghanistan, 39 n.
Africa: scramble for, 25; South, 64, 100, 101, 101 n., 103, 104, 107, 160; southern, 123, 124, 127.
African: Africanization, 178; cultivation and crops, 68, 80, 165, 169; and Indian traders, 65, 65 n.; and Legislative Councils, 150, 162 n., 171; nationalism, 175, 176, 177, 178; paramountcy, 126–7, 132, 146, 149, 150, 168, 168 n., 170, 178; political activity, 124, 125, 153 n., 168, 169, 170, 176, 177; press, 176; produce, 86, 88, 94, 96, 146, 157, 158, 163, 164, 167; small traders, 136, 136 n., 163; Socialism, 178; *Standard*, 55; trade unions, 169, 169 n.; trusteeship, 106, 107, 112, 116 n., 117 n., 123, 146.
Afro-Asian, 1 2.
Aga Khan, 13 n., 175.
agriculture: Director of in Kenya, 68; Indian, 29, 30, 30 n., 31, 31 n., 64, 65, 65 n., 66, 67, 67 n., 68, 68 n., 69, 69 n., 70, 97, 107, 129, 132, 166, 174; *see also* crops.
Ainsworth, John, 54, 56, 56 n., 60–1, 61 n.; on Indian economic role, 57, 58, 82, 87; on racial conflict in Kenya, 100, 101 n.
Ajmer, 31.
Ali, Tyeb, 147.
All India Muslim League, 105, 108.
Amani, 47.
America, 63, 63 n., 78; Consul from at Zanzibar, 4, 16; traders from at Zanzibar, xiii, xiii n., xiv, 11.
'americani', 56, 56 n.
Amin, C. J., 118 n., 119, 161.
Amin, S. G., xii n., 170 n., 177 n., 201.
Andrews, Revd. Charles F.: criticizes Simpson Report 1915, 110 n.; and Morrison's views on future of

German East Africa, 117 n.; on regional political differences among Indians, 119 n.; supports Kenya Indians 1920, 121 n.; visits East Africa, 123–4; as a member of delegation from India to London 1923, 127 n.
Ankole, 91.
Arabia, 1–2.
Arabs, 30, 123, 165.
Archbishop of Canterbury, 127, 127 n.
Army, Indian, 40; *see also* troops.
Asians, vii n., xv; *see also* Indians.
Asian Association, Dar es Salaam, 177.
Associations: African political, 124, 168, 169, 169 n., 170; European political, 100, 101, 101 n., 103, 109, 116, 116 n. 124; Indian economic, 165, 166, 167; Indian political, xii, xiii, 96, 103, 104, 112, 113–14, 117, 118, 119, 124, 125, 127, 128, 129, 130, 148, 153 n., 154 n., 161, 162, 162 n., 163, 163 n., 164, 166, 167, 177; *see also* individual titles.
Australia, 53.

Bagamoyo, 9, 25, 49, 51, 52, 53, 58, 58 n., 77.
Baluchis, 13.
Baluchistan, 39.
Balulu, 80, 91.
Banyan, 8 n., 9, 12, 12 n., 13 n., 14 n., 15 n.
Baringo, 86.
bazaars, 84, 85, 86, 87, 88, 90, 91, 94, 99, 100, 106 n., 110, 112.
Beauttah, James, 177.
Belfield, Sir Henry, 109, 109 n.
Bell, Sir Hesketh, 69, 69 n., 77.
Bengal, 36.
Berlin, 46; Act of 1885, 111.
Bhanjee, Waljee, 83.
Bhargash, Seyyid, 17, 21.
Bhattias, 12, 12 n., 13, 14, 14 n., 141.
Bhima, Wat, 3, 4 n., 15, 17.
Bombay, 12, 33, 36, 57, 60, 63, 71, 72, 77, 82, 93, 108, 139; Government, x, 3, 4, 5, 16, 16 n., 18 n., 25, 31, 34;

PRINTED IN GREAT BRITAIN
AT THE UNIVERSITY PRESS, OXFORD
BY VIVIAN RIDLER
PRINTER TO THE UNIVERSITY